ADVANCES IN HEALTH PSYCHOLOGY

D0415375

Also by Christine Horrocks

INTERVIEWS IN QUALITATIVE RESEARCH (*with N. King*)

Advances in Health Psychology

Critical Approaches

Edited by

Christine Horrocks

and

Sally Johnson

palgrave
macmillan

Selection, editorial matter and Introduction © Christine Horrocks and
Sally Johnson 2012
Individual chapters © Individual Contributors 2012

All rights reserved. No reproduction, copy or transmission of this
publication may be made without written permission.

No portion of this publication may be reproduced, copied or transmitted
save with written permission or in accordance with the provisions of the
Copyright, Designs and Patents Act 1988, or under the terms of any licence
permitting limited copying issued by the Copyright Licensing Agency,
Saffron House, 6–10 Kirby Street, London EC1N 8TS.

Any person who does any unauthorized act in relation to this publication
may be liable to criminal prosecution and civil claims for damages.

The authors have asserted their rights to be identified as the authors of this work
in accordance with the Copyright, Designs and Patents Act 1988.

First published 2012 by
PALGRAVE MACMILLAN

Palgrave Macmillan in the UK is an imprint of Macmillan Publishers Limited,
registered in England, company number 785998, of Houndmills, Basingstoke,
Hampshire RG21 6XS.

Palgrave Macmillan in the US is a division of St Martin's Press LLC,
175 Fifth Avenue, New York, NY 10010.

Palgrave Macmillan is the global academic imprint of the above companies
and has companies and representatives throughout the world.

Palgrave® and Macmillan® are registered trademarks in the United States,
the United Kingdom, Europe and other countries.

ISBN: 978–0–230–27538–6

This book is printed on paper suitable for recycling and made from fully
managed and sustained forest sources. Logging, pulping and manufacturing
processes are expected to conform to the environmental regulations of the
country of origin.

A catalogue record for this book is available from the British Library.

A catalog record for this book is available from the Library of Congress.

10 9 8 7 6 5 4 3 2 1
21 20 19 18 17 16 15 14 13 12

Printed and bound in Great Britain by
CPI Antony Rowe, Chippenham and Eastbourne

Contents

Contributors

Katy Day is Senior Lecturer in Psychology at Leeds Metropolitan University where she is a founding member of the Feminism and Health Research Group. Her research interests are in the areas of Critical Health and Social Psychology. She has conducted and published research on media discourse around femininity and alcohol consumption, women's constructions of gender, class and alcohol consumption and discourses around femininity, food, eating and the body on pro-eating-disorder websites and within pro-eating-disorder web-based communities. She is particularly interested in the links between identities and 'risky' health practices, especially those that are 'gendered' and 'classed'.

Rebekah Fox is Research Fellow at the Institute of Leadership and Management in Health at Kingston University. Her background is in Cultural Geography, and she previously worked in the Department of Health and Social Care at Royal Holloway, University of London. Her research interests include human–companion animal relations, pregnancy, food, health and the body, and leadership in healthcare settings.

Christine Horrocks is Professor of Applied Social Psychology and Head of Department at Manchester Metropolitan University. Previously she had been Director of the Centre for Applied Psychological Research at the University of Huddersfield. Completing a range of National Health Service (NHS)-funded projects her research has focussed primarily on community-based interventions and health promotion. She is interested in developing innovative and inclusive participatory methods, and she co-authored 'Interviews in Qualitative Research' (with Nigel King, 2010).

Sally Johnson is Lecturer at the University of Bradford and a health psychologist. She currently leads the Applied Health and Social Psychology Group based in the Division of Psychology. She is co-editor of the *Psychology of Women Section Review*. Her research and publications focus on the implications of the social construction of the female body for health and well-being in relation to particular biological and social markers encountered across the lifespan. This includes women's reproductive health, specifically breastfeeding, menstruation and bodily changes as a result of pregnancy, the female body and ageing, and motherhood. She utilises qualitative research methods, particularly feminist approaches.

Carolyn Kagan is Professor of Community Psychology at Manchester Metropolitan University in the Department of Psychology and directs the Research Institute for Health and Social Change. She works on participative community projects in partnership with local people, finding creative ways to evaluate community projects and to facilitate change in human services. She works on projects in the community, with disabled people and their families and services, and with people living in poverty. Much of the work is action oriented, with projects extending over several years, and involving the establishment of new forms of community organisation.

Nigel King is Professor of Applied Psychology and Director of the Centre for Applied Psychological Research, University of Huddersfield. He has a long-standing interest in the use of qualitative methods in 'real world' research, especially in health and organisational contexts. His main area of empirical research in recent years has been collaborative working in community supportive and palliative care. Other current topics include the psychology of gardening, patient and lay-carer experiences of back pain and ethical aspects of reality television. His theoretical interests are mainly in phenomenology and Personal Construct Psychology (PCP), and his methodological writing has focused on thematic analysis (especially the 'template' style) and the practice of interviewing. He is the co-author of *Interviews in Qualitative Research* (with Christine Horrocks, 2010).

Bregje de Kok is Lecturer at the Institute for International Health and Development at Queen Margaret University, Edinburgh. Bregje obtained a PhD (Psychology) from the University of Edinburgh, and worked there as an Economic and Social Research Council/Medical Research Council (ESRC/MRC) postdoctoral research fellow in Sociology. Her research interests concern professionals' and lay people's interpretations and moral judgements of sexual and reproductive health problems, and how such interpretations affect care sought and provided. In her PhD, she used discursive psychology to examine how people in Malawi construct infertility, its causes, consequences and solutions, and how they thereby manage normative expectations and moral judgements (e.g. blame).

Victoria Lavis is Lecturer in Psychology at the University of Bradford. Her research is influenced by her interest in qualitative and multi-method research. Her co-authored chapter in this book relates to her PhD research which aimed to critically consider the ways in which health services respond to women experiencing domestic violence. Her more recent research relates to her previous experience working within forensic psychology in the UK male prison estate, exploring the utility of appreciative inquiry methods in assessing the Prison Service response to the growing diversity of its population in terms of age, disability, sexuality, faith and ethnicity.

Rebecca Lawthom is Reader in Community Practice at Manchester Metropolitan University. Based in the Department of Psychology and the Research Institute for Health and Social Change (RIHSC). Rebecca's research interests cohere around processes and impacts of marginalisation. She is a feminist and community psychologist who researches, collaborates and participates with groups in arenas of marginalisation. Currently these include disability, refugee and asylum seeker health, arts and health. She uses collaborative processes and qualitative methods to access experience and facilitate social change. She co-authors work directing it into spaces such as disability studies, feminism, community psychology and qualitative methods.

Paula Lokman is involved in Public Health teaching and research at the University of Liverpool Laureate Online Education and European Health Management Association (EHMA). Her main research interests are in the field of sociology of the body, gender and health. Recently, she has been conducting studies in leadership and patient care in the NHS and hospital accreditation systems in Europe.

Catriona Macleod is Professor in the Psychology Department at Rhodes University, South Africa. Her research interests are 'teenage pregnancy', abortion, sex education, and sexual and reproductive healthcare systems. She is principal investigator for a multi-institutional and multi-disciplinary Critical Sexual and Reproductive Health Studies programme. She is author of *'Adolescence', Pregnancy and Abortion: Constructing a Threat of Degeneration*.

Kate Milnes is Senior Lecturer in Psychology at Leeds Metropolitan University and is a member of the University's Feminism and Health Research Group. She is a committee member and Honorary Treasurer of the British Psychological Society's (BPS) Psychology of Women Section (POWS). Her research interests include qualitative and feminist methodologies, narrative psychology and media representations of gender, sexuality, sexual relationships and sexual health. She is also interested in constructions of third-wave feminism, the notion of subcultures and online communities as sites of resistance, and young people and alcohol use.

Michael Murray is Professor of Applied Social and Health Psychology and Head of the School of Psychology at Keele University. He has published widely on psychological aspects of health, illness and ageing and on critical and qualitative approaches to health psychology including the edited collections *Critical Health Psychology* (2004) and *Qualitative Health Psychology: Theories and Methods* (with Kerry Chamberlain, 1999). He is Associate Editor of the *Journal of Health Psychology* and of *Psychology & Health* and sits on the editorial boards of various other journals.

Paula Nicolson is Visiting Honorary Professor with the Applied Health and Social Psychology Group at Bradford University. She joined Royal Holloway University of London in September 2005 and was Head of the Department of Health and Social Care for the next three years. She was Principal Investigator on the National Institute of Health Research study of leadership in the NHS, which inspired her current contribution and is author of several books including two related ones – *Gender, Power and Organisation: A Psychological Perspective* (1996) and *Having It All* (2002).

Michael Richards is a PhD student in Community Psychology and Critical Disability Studies. He currently facilitates a group of men labelled with 'learning difficulties' in activities relating to film, photography, art and drama. The aim is for them to become critically aware of themselves and to improve their health. In addition, he has worked on many community projects relating to health and group work on issues such as relationships, domestic abuse, sexuality, masculinity and identity. He also leads a men's group at a drug intervention project and works at a young person's residential care home.

Bridgette Rickett is an active committee member of the British Psychology Society, Psychology of Women Section and founder member of Feminism and Health Research Group at Leeds Metropolitan University. Having worked at the University for ten years, she is currently Senior Lecturer whose main research interests are critical social psychological explanations of health, in particular, feminist perspectives on health, including talk around femininity, risk and violence in the workplace and organisationally situated sexual harassment, harassment and bullying. She also has an interest in equality, diversity and organisational identities and more generally debates and issues around gender, identity and space.

Emma Rowland is Research Fellow in the Faculty of Health Science at the University of Southampton. Her background is in social and cultural geography and is currently conducting her PhD at Royal Holloway, University of London. Her research interests include the role of emotion and affect in the delivery of patient care, leadership, gender and professional boundaries in healthcare settings, social inequalities of health and pre-hospital emergency care.

Judith Sixsmith is Professor of Adult Social Care at Manchester Metropolitan University. Based in the Department of Social Work and the Research Institute for Health and Social Change, her research interests revolve around the social inclusion, participation and empowerment of people who are marginalised within health and social care systems. Often taking a gendered perspective and using qualitative methods, she specialises in working with older people and is currently directing research projects concerning care-related in-home technologies and investigating processes of community participation.

Wendy Stainton Rogers is Chair in Health Psychology at the Open University, Visiting Professor of Gender and Health at Leeds Metropolitan University and Chair of the International Society for Critical Health Psychology. Ever a troublemaker, Wendy's career has mainly been spent improving on how we do child care and putting the 'justice' back into youth justice. Her best-known book is *Explaining Health and Illness* (1991), and she has co-edited *The Sage Handbook of Qualitative Research in Psychology* (with Carla Willig, 2009). Her latest book, *Social Psychology*, was published in 2011, and it is dedicated, as she is, to her growing brood of grandchildren.

Ryan Woolrych is Research Associate, working for the Research Institute for Health and Social Change who has been actively involved in a number of projects working within an area of deprivation in the North-West. He has worked with local residents, community organisations and an urban regeneration company to develop active dialogue and shared learning around understandings of health, well-being and place. To this end, he has developed a participatory approach to his research, engaging in visual and creative methods where local residents are engaged in the collection, analysis and dissemination phases of research. He is currently writing up a PhD thesis in the area and disseminating research.

How Can We Advance Health Psychology?

CHRISTINE HORROCKS AND SALLY JOHNSON

Health psychology and the development of critical action

The first part of this book aims to locate heath psychology in its contemporary context. This is in terms of the development of health psychology in general, and critical health psychology in particular. The three chapters in Part I explore this context in relation to the development of language-based approaches, community health psychology and critical approaches to health psychology in general. Furthermore, Part I, as well as the book as a whole, aims to develop the critique of mainstream health psychology by specifically focusing on contexts which impinge upon health and illness leading to inequalities in health. In doing so, our contributors engage in recent developments in critical health psychology, offering insights into potential courses of action with the aim of improving health.

Health psychology is a relatively young sub-discipline of psychology. In order to develop its credibility within the broader scientific community it adopted the main standards and methods of psychology at the time of its inception (Murray & Chamberlain, 1999) and these continue to dominate. Adopting these standards and methods also enabled it to gain credibility within medical science as it spoke in the familiar language of 'prediction and control' (Murray & Chamberlain, 1999, p. 5). This acceptance has been advanced through its accommodation of psychological and social dimensions within the biopsychosocial model. The main way in which this framework is put into practice is through the testing and elaborating of theoretical models such as the Theory of Planned Behaviour and the Health Belief Model, and the investigation of mechanisms such as psychoneuroimmunology. Approaches such as the Theory of Planned Behaviour aim to investigate a combination of hypothetical constructs which represent 'biological', 'psychological' and 'social' variables (Crossley, 2008). However, it has been argued that these approaches only pay lip service to social and contextual aspects of health and illness. This is because they invariably investigate social cognitions such as attitudes and control beliefs (Mielewczyk & Willig, 2007) which are, by their very nature, individual perceptions of social phenomenon. The linkage of certain attitudes and beliefs to a range of health behaviours has achieved a degree of success. However, the multifaceted and complex nature of health behaviour is underexplored in these approaches (see Mielewczyk & Willig, 2007 for an extended critique of the Theory of Planned Behaviour).

Such critiques of traditional approaches to health psychology have increasingly emerged to the extent that critical health psychology is now a distinct movement. The developing critique of psychology as a discipline over the past 20 years (see for example, Fox & Prilleltensky, 2009) provided the conditions for a similar critique of health psychology. This was in conjunction with insights from earlier anthropological, sociological and psychological work on health and illness (see, for example, Herzlich, 1973; Blaxter, 1983) which emphasised, for instance, the importance of social representations and culture in understanding health behaviour. At the forefront of the development of critical health psychology were publications such as *Material Discourses of Health and Illness*, edited by Lucy Yardley, in 1997; *Qualitative Health Psychology: Theories and Methods*, edited by Michael Murray and Kerry Chamberlain, in 1999; and *Rethinking Health Psychology*, by Michelle Crossley, in 2000. These publications coincided with the *First International Conference on Critical and Qualitative Approaches to Health Psychology*, which led to the formation of the *International Society of Critical Health Psychology* which now holds biennial conferences. This organisation, together with a growing body of work, shares a common dissatisfaction with the positivist nature of mainstream health psychology and, in particular, its focus on the individual and lack of serious consideration of the broader context.

Those engaging in critical health psychology take a variety of different theoretical (including social constructionism, post structuralism, feminism, Marxism) and methodological (including discourse analysis, participatory action research, narrative analysis) approaches. A key aim is 'to (re)conceptualize "health behaviour" in such a way as to invite meaning and context into any analysis of health-related phenomena' (Mielewczyk & Willig, 2007, p. 825). This reformulation involves investigating health-related activities (rather than behaviours) which can be understood only through their relationship with wider social practices and hence context is *all* important. In particular this includes contextual aspects such as the social, political and cultural dimensions of health and illness. Critical health psychology's initial focus was on critiquing mainstream health psychology; however, recent debates have moved on to consider how such a reformulation of health psychology might take place (see the collection of papers in *The Journal of Health Psychology* volume 11, part 3, 2006 and Crossley (2008) for an extended discussion of recent debates). In particular, these debates have centred on how this movement can contribute to *social change* and *action*, and the potential for action is the overarching theme of this book.

In Chapter 1 Sally Johnson elaborates on the recent debate between critique and action which centres on differences of opinion about how, and to what extent, action is, or should be, the goal of critical health psychology. This involves a 'call for action' on the one hand versus a focus on critique on the other. However, she avoids engaging in a polarised debate about the merits or shortcomings of each and explores how a number of language-based approaches might simultaneously focus on working to achieve improvements in health while retaining a strong sense of critique. In particular she explores how feminist post structuralist theorists' emphasis on the negotiation of gender-related discourse and/or practice can be both limiting and potentially detrimental to health and well-being whilst also offering opportunities for empowerment and change. This is illustrated by drawing on her analysis in two different studies which explored women's accounts of negotiating the embodied experiences of both pregnancy and breastfeeding. Through this kind of analysis, she argues, it is possible to reflect upon constraining discourses, which once identified can then be worked upon. She discusses various ways in which this could be achieved, for example, through further participatory action research, but argues that this needs to be done simultaneously through health psychologists' engagement as scholar–activists facilitating 'receptive social environments' (Campbell et al., 2010).

The potential of the scholar–activist in critical health psychology is developed further by Michael Murray in Chapter 2. Murray discusses the historical development of the scholar–activist tradition. This arose as a reaction against the 'scientific–practitioner' approach which dominated clinical psychology, situated as it was within a biomedical framework in the United States in the 1960s. The model of community psychology which arose in the 1970s was based upon an activist model of engagement and an identification of the need to work at a community level in order to challenge social injustice and inequality. He also explicates the Christian aims and revolutionary history of a more radical approach to community action which arose in South America in the 1950s and 60s and led to the development of participatory action research. Though psychology has not always appropriated these early ambitions, certain versions of community psychology have more recently reclaimed them. Murray argues that because of the way in which health psychology developed, with its narrow focus on the individual, it is only recently that the value of connections between health and community psychology, with the aim of promoting health, have been made. Community health psychology has evolved, as has community psychology, with a more or less accommodating approach to critical engagement. The more critical approaches advocate the connection of intra-community processes with the broader socio-political context. Murray further argues that, this evolving movement fosters connections with developments in critical social and health psychology as well as in community psychology. He goes on to outline a number of ways in which community health psychology can be developed, in particular, through the involvement of the critical scholar–activist, documenting challenges this presents.

Wendy Stainton Rogers contextualises her chapter (Chapter 3) with a summary critique of mainstream psychology's continuing preoccupation with social cognition to explain health-related behaviour change. She then elaborates on what critical health psychology can offer in terms of serious consideration of context. She juxtaposes traditional health psychology's focus on the individual and health behaviours against recent recommendations made by NICE (National Institute for Health and Clinical Excellence – the British Government-sponsored body which, at the time of writing, provided guidance on the best ways to promote health and prevent and treat illness) on behaviour change interventions at individual, community and population levels. Stainton Rogers was part of the group who developed the guidelines, along with more traditional health psychologists, and academics and lay members from a diverse range of disciplines and interest groups. What is interesting to note, she argues, is that social cognition hardly gets a mention in the guidance. The importance of the 'socioeconomic and cultural context' in which behaviour change takes place, and, especially, the need to 'identify and attempt to remove social, financial and environmental barriers that prevent people from making positive changes' are much more to the fore. She argues that given the make-up of the group this is not surprising, but more fundamentally they show a sense of unease with the underpinnings of mainstream health psychology and its individualistic approach to health. She advocates that to make a difference we need to tell better stories in health psychology and that critical health psychology is contributing to this.

Social identities, intersectionality and advancing health psychology

Psychologists are increasingly concerned with the effects of categories such as gender, social class, race/ethnicity and sexuality on health and well-being (Cole, 2009). Attempts to understand the effects of social categories and related identities have taken various forms. Typically in traditional approaches to health psychology, categories such as gender and socio-economic status are conceptualised as one of a number of variables within a larger conceptual model and are therefore underexplored. Another approach is to identify the psychological characteristics associated with particular social groups as mediators of health behaviour (see for example, Lee et al., 2008; Zimmerman & Sieverding, 2010), but, as discussed earlier, these kinds of studies are based on individual perceptions of social phenomenon with scant regard to the social context. In critical approaches to health psychology social identities move centre stage. They are seen as one of the key contexts in which health-related activities are played out. It is the meanings and performances related to social identities which are the focus of analysis. In Part II contributors elucidate on meanings derived from our social positionings, concomitant identities and the implications of these for health and action. The notion of intersectionality was developed by feminists and critical race theorists to conceptualise analytic approaches to considering the meaning and consequences of occupying a range of different social categories simultaneously (see for example Cole, 2009). Though it is not our intention to develop specific frameworks around intersectionality, authors of the chapters in this part discuss intersectional aspect of social identity, such as gender, social class, age and sexuality, in their consideration of this particular context of health-related activities.

In Chapter 4 Katy Day focuses on social class, arguing that this should be a central concern to health psychologists because of health inequalities which have been linked to class. In this chapter Day critically reviews recent mainstream psychological literature on socioeconomic status and health-risk behaviours. She also considers recent representations of class in the British media. She argues that both psychology and media representations promote images of working class people as feckless and simply not exercising agency in order to reduce risk-related behaviours. She then considers what critical psychological perspectives offer to an understanding of social class. She argues that these perspectives invariably regard our actions and experiences as inseparable from the social context. She then goes on to explore contemporary critical research on working-class identities, drinking and diet. In doing so Day highlights how social class and gender intersect. She argues that research on class and health needs to move away from a narrow focus on considering socioeconomic status alone, as class encompasses much more than this, including social identity, values and discourse. Not only this, but research needs to consider the intersection of class with other social identities such as gender, race, regionalism and sexuality. In addition, such research should be undertaken across the range of classes, not just with the working class. By identifying problems with the class system and its implications for health, Day argues that critical health psychologists will be in a better position to act as agents of change in taking this critical agenda to wider audiences such as policy makers.

In exploring another key social category, gender, Christine Horrocks' chapter (Chapter 5) discusses the mounting interest in men's health in developed countries. She outlines a range of health inequalities and growing concern regarding men's health. However, she argues that these inequalities are not monolithic, and a range of other factors such as socioeconomic status and ethnicity intersect to produce inequalities between men as well as between men and women. Horrocks explores explanations for men's propensity towards health-damaging behaviours. She considers the 'life style choice' explanation but critiques this by drawing on the concept of hegemonic masculinity which many theorists now use to explain men's health 'choices'. She argues that this dominant version of masculinity creates a sense of reality for many men and that this formulation places gender as a situated social and interactional accomplishment. Horrocks also critically discusses the 'gender mainstreaming' approach in which a gender-sensitive approach to health policy, research and services development is promoted. Drawing on the work of Bakhtin she situates men's health-related behaviour as arising out of human action which is situated, relational and participatory rather than an individual choice. She criticises aspects of the gender-sensitive approach which are based on the accommodation of hegemonic masculinity by arguing that in Bakhtinian terms these are 'monologisms' which function to shut down dialogue as to why men are not using normative routes into services. She outlines how Bakhtin's notion of the 'carnivalesque' (which aims to reveal, undermine and even eradicate the hegemony of an ideology) could be used to challenge hegemonic masculinity and more substantially tackle male-related health inequalities than has been the case thus far.

A consideration of gender is further elaborated in Bridgette Rickett's chapter (Chapter 6) on women and occupational risk. In reviewing the literature on occupational health, Rickett notes the absence of data for women in statistics on occupational accidents, injuries and illness as well as in psychological theorising and research which has mainly emanated from studies with male populations. In addition, she shows how dominant psychological approaches to occupational health do not substantially consider the political, historical and social world workers inhabit. She argues that there has been recent recognition of these omissions, and there is now a growing awareness of including gender sensitivity in policy. This is in conjunction with a body of research which aims specifically to explore women and occupational risk more substantially. In particular, she discusses the potential of research which focuses on discourse, gender identity and occupational risk. She draws on an illustration from her own research with female door supervisors (bouncers) which explores the intersection of gender, social class and heteronormative sexuality.

In this, and her other research on women's occupations in work spaces considered dangerous, Rickett concludes that women's attempts to avoid harm and damage are often compromised by organisationally shared understandings of women and their capabilities. Importantly, her research indicates that by striving to challenge unfair gendered expectations and ideologies that hinder being successful and respected in their jobs, women are often forced to compromise their health and safety at work.

In Chapter 7 Kate Milnes reviews and critically evaluates the dominant social cognition to the study of sexual health and its promotion. She argues that because of its individual focus on attitudes and related sexual health intentions, this approach is often disempowering and neglects the material, cultural and ideological context of people's sexual lives. As a result, she suggests that interventions based upon this model have limited potential for bringing about change or creating possibilities for action. Through an analysis of sexual health promotion materials available on the internet, Milnes considers how sexual health 'choices' are shaped by dominant constructions of youth, gender, class and sexuality. She therefore argues that taking a critical approach to sexual health promotion involves conceptualising sex and sexual relationships as 'situated practices' rather than as individual behaviours. This reconceptualisation creates possibilities for action while still acknowledging the constraints that cultural, structural and material contexts place on people's sexual lives. By providing opportunities to deconstruct and critique dominant discourses around gender, sex and sexuality and providing spaces and resources to explore alternative discourses, she believes that critical approaches to sexual health promotion have the potential to engage people in an active process of negotiation with regard to their sexual health and well-being.

Modernisation and democratisation in healthcare

Accepting the need to incorporate wider political contexts and agendas into our appreciation of health psychology means it is crucial to identify how the current global economic and political climate is placing healthcare services and their delivery under pressure. Governments are looking for ways to limit and reduce healthcare spending while at the same time engaging in a dialogue that offers assurances around maintaining levels of service. There is growing interest in the delivery of 'lean healthcare' (see Waring & Bishop, 2010) and ongoing debates regarding proposed reforms and restructuring, with claims that managerialism has replaced professionalism in the social organisation of healthcare (Kitchener, 2000). Indeed, Martin et al. (2009) argue that healthcare and other public services are under pressure as governments globally view them as ill-suited to contemporary economic and social requirements. Efforts to reform health service organisation and delivery include introducing markets, endeavouring to improve collaboration between providers and workforce reconfiguration.

In their chapter (Chapter 8) Paula Nicolson and colleagues explore the organisational configuration of National Health Service Trusts in the UK. Interestingly they identify that organisational configuration, specifically in relation to leadership, is seldom written about within 'health psychology'. This is indeed interesting in light of the centrality of psychological thinking within the leadership research literature and the concomitant emphasis in critical health psychology on exploring power relationships. Their work reveals a complex picture which both challenges and identifies ongoing hierarchical power and gender-based struggles with differences in leadership styles having the potential to impact on healthcare delivery and patient-care. Moreover, in their analysis individualistic accounts of leadership are usurped, being overtaken with a more fluid and discursively located performance that embraces the critical agenda. Yet this chapter also comfortably engages with a more intra-psychic interpretation of experience which describes how organisations infiltrate our consciousness. Hence we experience and hold an intellectual/cognitive and emotional sense of an organisation; this then raises questions about how organisational healthcare cultures, particularly in such turbulent times, are influenced and reproduced. Arguably, the rhetoric of healthcare 'modernisation' in the UK, and similar policies elsewhere, are legitimatory discourses that become adopted or resisted impacting on the success or failure of efforts to reconfigure professional boundaries and healthcare more generally.

Foucault's philosophical analyses exposed the unacknowledged assumptions and regulatory practices in healthcare. Interrelationships between power, knowledge and the body are exemplified in the power of medicine and notions of the 'clinical gaze' where the body is an object of inquiry and the individual a 'case' needing to be worked upon (Henderson, 1994). Concerns around the distribution of knowledge in healthcare and what this tells us about the nature of relationships and interaction has been extensively commented upon. However, with 'modernisation' come new modes of governance in healthcare and ever changing relationships that warrant scrutiny. These more recent moves towards modernisation link into shifting boundaries around professional expertise and increasing confidence in systems and auditable rules and procedures exemplified in, for example 'care pathways' which are care management technologies that chronologically map out activities in the healthcare process (see for example Pinder et al., 2006). Another modernising move is the notion of the 'expert patient' which, under the guise of democratisation, has emerged in UK health policy (Department of Health,

2001; Fox et al., 2005). Work to transform the healthcare professional/doctor–patient relationship from a professional-led interaction to one that is more of a healthcare professional–patient partnership in which 'expert patients' are able to articulate their individual needs and thus receive appropriate treatments seems unassailable as a definitive goal. Of course there is sound reasoning for developing patient expertise: with the growth of web-based health-related information, interactive forums and consumer websites people have been transformed into 'reflexive consumers' of healthcare (Henwood et al., 2003).

In Chapter 9, Victoria Lavis and Christine Horrocks present research looking at the healthcare professional–patient interaction, critically assessing entrenched professional power and structural constraints that might define, and to an extent determine, engagement with an ideology that places patients as experts who have insights into their specific healthcare needs. Their work looks beyond a somewhat consumerist view of the expert patient to one that embraces a respect for the person in their situational milieu. Indeed their work suggests that professionals may cling to their power to control patients and information, not listening to or even dismissing the patients' efforts to theorise or explain their health issues. Interestingly, Tang and Anderson (1999) suggest that professionals need to recognise the relationship between their power and knowledge before they can share expertise with patients. This was evident in Lavis and Horrocks' research where training was pivotal in bringing about a change in the construction of the patient. There was a shift from 'directive' practices, where patients were expected to comply with the healthcare professional's prescribed course of action, to ones that had a far more 'participatory' focus where the patient was able to identify pathways and take control.

Taking up the critique agenda of this book such apparent success should not blind us to the recognition that, as Fox et al. (2005) suggest, 'if the "expert patient" is to be understood as a reflexive project of self-governance, then it is indeed a "technology of the self", a disciplining of the body in relation to systems of thought' (p. 1308). Within these observations is embedded the usual individualising with people positioned as responsible for self-management of health and well-being. Notions of empowerment, sharing of power and user-led healthcare do offer avenues for action and change by resisting the imposition of power, but it is important to also envisage other implications. Significantly, without doubt all patients may not wish, or be able, to lay claim to the material and/or technical competence necessary to take responsibility for their health.

Similarly, in Chapter 10, the notion of democratisation and complexities with unforeseen implications are taken up by Catriona Macleod, who focuses on the rhetoric of 'choice' and the issue of advocacy in relation to women and abortion in South Africa. She convincingly outlines how an ideology of choice obscures the stigma associated with abortion and the social conditions where women live their lives. She points to the 'psychologisation' of abortion and the emergence of 'post-abortion syndrome' whereby instead of women being portrayed as autonomous decision makers with regard to their health and well-being they are positioned as inadvertently being subjected to psychological harm as a consequence of abortion. Out of this concern materialises a route for anti-abortion activists to claim a somewhat moral standpoint in terms of denying women access to abortion – women are being saved from ensuing guilt and remorse. However, modification is needed to appreciate that the landscape is complex, with Macleod arguing for a 'reproductive justice' approach which foregrounds the contextual nature of women's lives situating abortion within wider social, political and cultural practices. Importantly her work makes the reader aware of the need to avoid simplistic and homogenising explanations which assume equal access to health resources with liberatory practices, and efforts with regard to democratisation, needing to be far more than rhetorical pronouncements.

Making a change: health inequalities and community well-being

In many respects the chapters in Part IV (the final section) of the book bring together and harness the change and action-oriented promise of critical health psychology to 'make a difference'. Elsewhere, Murray (2004) eloquently but succinctly explains that health psychology can adopt strategies that more effectively position it in ways that promote health through social rather than individual change. He argues that working with participants and communities, rather than attempting to impose a particular framework, opens up possibilities for a process of 'collaborative change'. Hence as has already been outlined he advocates a more action-oriented role for scholars and researchers that embraces their co-action in not only the process of knowledge construction but also in their potential to impact in the arena of people's lives and wider political contexts.

The first chapter in this part by Bregje de Kok (Chapter 11) begins with a clear exposition of critical health psychology's commitment to be positioned with the oppressed and disenfranchised and work in ways that address inequalities. Using her work in Malawi which she accurately describes as 'resource poor' country de Kok explains how such non-western contexts have been largely ignored by critical, discursive approaches. In this chapter the resultant problematic of discursive approaches with regard to the explanation and inclusion of more structural and material factors is bravely tackled. The micro approach taken in much discursive work is situated as accountable but also hugely effective in bringing about change when deployed to this end. She uses her own work exploring the constructions of infertility in Malawi to showcase the action potential of discursive psychology. Consequently, in de Kok's work discursive psychology bestows insights into interpersonal issues with various social actors using discursive devices in response to infertility. However, she does not leave it there – de Kok goes on to suggest ways that her work can be used to develop health promotion strategies and inform and improve communications between professionals and the professionals and their clients. Highlighted is the need for 'actionable understandings' (Murray & Campbell, 2004) which echo sentiments which underscore the need to challenge and subvert social injustices through our scholarly work and activism.

Nigel King's chapter (Chapter 12) offers an uplifting and skilfully drawn account of connections between the natural world and our engagement with its potential to enhance our lives. Situating his work within wider environmental, evolutionary and psychological thinking offers a convincing analysis that points towards the beneficial properties of community located 'green exercise' projects. Working with communities in deprived areas in the North of England he presents an analysis that reveals the prospective benefits for health and well-being inherent in community allotment projects. Evident is the way that people's environments shape the nature of their existence with participation in allotment gardening providing openings for new ways of being. His work makes visible the importance and value of collectives with the sharing of knowledge, produce and experience adding to the recuperative value of 'being outdoors' and in contact with the natural world. King highlights the macro level linkages of his work and the way that participation in 'green exercise' connects to wider environmental campaigns. Stressed also is the more localised impact, with the protection and extension of urban green space essential and critical to health and well-being.

We end the book with a chapter by Rebecca Lawthom and colleagues (Chapter 13) who carefully outline the nature of participative methodologies in critical community psychology. Taking up the ongoing critique of individual approaches to health and well-being that pervade this book and other work in the domain of critical health psychology, Lawthom et al. advocate a 'values-based approach' where social justice, collaboration and social and community processes are the focus, embracing a public health and 'wellness' approach. The way that community psychology views the prevention of ill health as residing in wider social context is convincingly made with issues and problems facing disadvantaged and oppressed people and communities having deep historical roots. As Prilleltensky and Nelson (2002, p. 12) explain oppression is 'a state of domination where the oppressed suffer the consequences of depravation, exclusion, discrimination, exploitation, control of culture, and sometimes even violence'. Lawthom et al.'s work demonstrates action that goes well beyond the mere political rhetoric of participation (Milewa et al., 1999), illustrating that taking joint action that ensures community participation is truly collaborative and meaningful. A series of projects which employed creative arts are presented within their community psychology framework. Health and well-being messages are shared and discussed in ways that focus on the social and relational aspects of community life thus avoiding problem-based individualising accounts. Their work convincingly demonstrates the value of building on the strengths of people and communities providing very useful examples that can serve as beacons for those of us who are unsure and/or inexperienced in this sphere.

Again we are able to see that health and well-being and community participation are more than rhetorical concepts used to fulfill a political ideology. Work is ongoing that advances our understandings and practical application of health psychology beyond critique into the domain of action to bring about change. Still, Cleaver (2002), when reflecting on participatory approaches distinguishes between efficiency arguments, where participation is a tool for achieving better outcomes, and equity and empowerment arguments whereby participation increases individuals' capacity to improve or change their lives. She encourages consideration of how the structures of participatory projects secure the interests of those experiencing inequalities asking what are the 'linkages' between participation and the 'furthering of their social and economic good' (p. 54). Throughout this book there is evidence of work that makes manifest such linkages; we should nonetheless heed the cautionary note in Cleaver's observations while at the same time taking encouragement from the examples in this collection and beyond that have infiltrated to some extent the bastions of more mainstream health psychology. Finally, we hope that the collection of chapters in this book will help in the (re)telling of health psychology and advance stories that will provide insights into how the adoption of theories, methods and practice informed by more critical approaches to health psychology can make a difference.

REFERENCES

Blaxter, M. (1983) 'The causes of disease: women talking'. *Social Science and Medicine*, 17(2), 59–69.

Campbell, C., Cornish, F., Gibbs, A. & Scott, K. (2010) 'Heed the push from below: how do social movements persuade the rich to listen to the poor?' *Journal of Health Psychology*, 15, 962–71.

Cleaver, F. (2002) 'Institutions, agency and the limitations of participatory approaches to development'. In B. Cooke and U. Kathari (eds) *Participation: The New Tyranny?* New York: Palgrave Macmillan.

Cole, E. R. (2009) 'Intersectionality and research in psychology'. *American Psychologist*, 64(3), 170–80.

Crossley, M. (2008) 'Critical health psychology: developing and refining the approach'. *Social and Personality Psychology Compass*, 2, 21–33.

Department of Health (2001) *The Expert Patient: A New Approach to Chronic Disease Management for the 21st Century*. London: Department of Health Publications.

Fox, D. & Prilleltensky, I. (eds) (2009) *Critical Psychology: An Introduction*. 2nd edn. London: Sage.

Fox, N. J., Ward, K. J. & O'Rourke, A. J. (2005) 'The "expert patient": empowerment or medical dominance? The case of weight loss, pharmaceutical drugs and the Internet'. *Social Science and Medicine*, 60(6), 1299–309.

Henderson, A. (1994) 'Power and knowledge in nursing practice: the contribution of Foucault'. *Journal of Advanced Nursing*, 20, 935–39.

Henwood, F., Wyatt, S., Hart, A. & Smith, J. (2003) '"Ignorance is bliss sometime": Constraints on the emergence of the "informed patient" in the changing landscapes of health information'. *Sociology of Health and Illness*, 25(6), 589–607.

Herzlich, C. (1973) *Health and Illness: A Social Psychological Analysis*, trans. D. Graham, London: Academic Press.

Kitchener, M. (2000) 'The bureaucratization of professional roles: the case of clinical directors in UK hospitals'. *Organization*, 7(1), 129–54.

Lee, J. E. C., Lemyre, L., Turner, M. C., Orpana, H. M. & Krewski, D. (2008) 'Health risk perceptions as mediators of socioeconomic differentials in health behaviour'. *Journal of Health Psychology*, 13(8), 1082–91.

Martin, G. P., Currie, G. & Finn, R. (2009) 'Reconfiguring or reproducing intra-professional boundaries? Specialist expertise, generalist knowledge and the "modernisation" of the medical workforce'. *Social Science and Medicine*, 68(7), 1191–98.

Mielewczyk, M. & Willig, C. (2007) 'Old clothes and an older look: the case for a radical makeover in health'. *Theory and Psychology*, 17, 811–37.

Milewa, T., Valentine, J., & Calnan, M. (1999) 'Community participation and citizenship in British health care planning: narratives of power and involvement in the changing welfare state'. *Sociology of Health and Illness*, 21(4), 445–65.

Murray, M. (ed.) (2004) *Critical Health Psychology*. London: Palgrave Macmillan.

Murray, M. & Campbell, C. (2004) 'Community health psychology: promoting analysis and action for social change'. *Journal of Health Psychology*, 9(2), 187–95.

Murray, M. & Chamberlain, K. (1999) *Qualitative Health Psychology: Theories and Methods*, London: Sage.

Pinder, R., Petchey, R., Shaw, S. & Carter, Y. (2006) 'What's in a care pathway? Towards a cultural cartography of the new NHS'. In D. Allen and A. Piljick (eds), *The Social Organisation of Healthcare Work*, Oxford: Blackwell Publishing.

Prilleltensky, I., & Nelson, G. (2002) *Doing Psychology Critically: Making a Difference in Diverse Settings*. Basingstoke: Palgrave Macmillan.

Tang, S. Y. S. & Anderson, J. M. (1999) 'Human agency and the process of healing: lessons learned from women living with chronic illness – re-writing the expert'. *Nursing Inquiry*, 6, 83–93.

Waring, J. J. & Bishop, S. (2010) 'Lean healthcare: rhetoric, ritual and resistance'. *Social Science and Medicine*, 71, 1332–40.

Zimmerman. F. & Sieverding, M. (2010) 'Young adults' social drinking as explained by an augmented theory of planned behaviour: the roles of prototypes, willingness, and gender'. *British Journal of Health Psychology*, 15(3), 561–81.

PART I

HEALTH PSYCHOLOGY AND THE DEVELOPMENT OF CRITICAL ACTION

Working with the Tensions between Critique and Action in Critical Health Psychology

SALLY JOHNSON

Introduction

In this chapter I will focus on critical health psychology's potential to contribute to social change and action in order to improve health. I will begin by outlining the debate between critique and action which centres on differences of opinion about how, and to what extent, action is, or should be, the goal of critical health psychology. This involves a 'call for action' on the one hand versus a focus on critique on the other (see Crossley, 2008; Hepworth, 2006). However, I will not be engaging in a polarised, and thus artificial debate as it has been acknowledged that these do not represent absolute positions (see Gergen & Zielke, 2006; Murray & Poland, 2006; Willig, 1999). To this end, I will explore how a number of approaches might simultaneously focus on working to achieve improvements in health whilst retaining a strong sense of critique. Firstly, I will explore how language-based approaches have brought into focus constraints upon action but also discuss their potential to inform change. I will then develop this by exploring specifically how feminist post-structuralist theorists have emphasised that the negotiation of gender-related discourse and/or practice can be both limiting and potentially detrimental to health and well-being whilst also offering opportunities for empowerment and change. I will illustrate this by drawing on my own analysis in two different studies which explored women's accounts of negotiating the embodied experiences of both pregnancy and breastfeeding. Finally, I will discuss how users of health advice and health professionals can be engaged in the planning and execution of poststructurally informed research, thus simultaneously undertaking critical analysis whilst also seeking to improve health and well-being.

The debate: critique versus action

Over the past decade critical health psychology has emerged as a distinct movement. While its initial focus was on critiquing mainstream health psychology a key recent debate has centred on how it can contribute to social change and action (see Crossley, 2008; Hepworth, 2006). Crossley (2008) identifies differences of opinion about how and to what extent, action is, or should be, the goal of critical health psychology, highlighting a 'call for action' on the one hand versus a focus on critique on the other.

The broadness and diversity which critical health psychology has fostered means that there is now a range of different approaches originating from disparate epistemological and ontological positions which have come under its umbrella. Consequently the ways in which both knowledge and being are viewed within each have implications for the possibilities of bringing about beneficial health-related change. Though there are a range of approaches, one distinction which has been made is between community public health and language/discourse approaches (McVittie, 2006). In a review of publications representing this distinction more generally, Davidson et al. (2006) found that while community psychology is more action orientated than critical scholarship (mainly equated with language/discourse approaches) it fails to challenge institutionalised power structures. This is supported by Nelson and Prilleltensky (2010) who argue, drawing on an ecological[1] metaphor, that community action tends to focus on micro and meso levels of change and has, to date, failed to substantially engage with macro level structures and interventions. They also argue that interventions have tended to be more ameliorative than transformative, in that they only improve health and well-being for those involved in initiatives. However, while they are not arguing that ameliorative interventions are unimportant, they state that greater emphasis needs to be placed on transformative ones which challenge social injustice and inequalities of power more broadly. Davidson et al.'s (2006) review also found that, though critical scholarship is more challenging of the status quo in *theory*, it does not produce actions which challenge and bring about change. These criticisms of both community psychology and critical scholarship are somewhat concerning given critical psychology's and critical health psychology's emphasis on emancipation and social justice.

These aims are reflected in the debate between critique and action. The call for action involves not only describing reality but seeking to change it in order to improve health. Within this moral project of social justice and transformation, critical health psychologists have been argued to be agents of change and defined as scholar–activists rather than as the traditional scientist–practitioner (see Campbell & Murray, 2004; Murray & Poland, 2006; Murray Chapter 3 in this book). Campbell and Murray (2004) argue that an activist community health psychologist's role is to encourage collective action through the involvement of the group of people whose health is affected by social injustice and inequality. A key method that is used to achieve this end is participatory action research. This is defined as a collaborative endeavour where researchers work with community members to identify an area of concern, generate knowledge about it and plan and carry out action aimed to address it (see Brydon-Miller, 2004). Lee (2006) even argues that critical health psychology should be an explicitly left-wing endeavour focusing on research and practice that benefits participants rather than getting engrossed in the subtleties of method or epistemology. Though there have been some successes in terms of action in community approaches, these have tended to be at micro and meso levels and ameliorative rather than transformative as suggested in Nelson and Prilleltensky's general criticisms of community psychology. However, Campbell et al. (2010) report on the development of three successful pro-poor social movements (situated in Brazil, India and South Africa respectively) which have begun to address, for example, better access to health services and anti-retroviral therapy nationally. Their success has been achieved not only through community psychologists' engagement in developing the 'voice' of the poor by promoting critical thinking about the roots of their poverty but, importantly, through the facilitation of 'receptive social environments' where their 'voice' has been heard and acted upon. Campbell et al. argue that the latter is what community health psychologists need to pay more attention to in order to bring about meaningful macro level change.

On the other hand, it has been argued that while action is central to some approaches in critical health psychology, others focus on critique. The dangers inherent in adopting overarching principles and linking these to action have been identified within certain language/discourse-based approaches by McVittie (2006). McVittie's reservations about critical health psychology's potential to bring about meaningful change come from approaches such as discursive psychology.

Discursive psychology, as developed by Mick Billig, Derek Edwards, Jonathan Potter and Margaret Wetherell in the late 1980s and through the 1990s, challenged the internalised or cognitivist focus of much of psychology. For instance, in social cognition, dominant in mainstream health psychology, the emphasis is on how individuals' cognitions such as attitudes and control beliefs combine to explain health-related behaviours (Mielewczyk & Willig, 2007). This has been challenged by discursive psychologists, who instead focus on how people use language and imagery at a *micro* level. The action orientation of discourse is emphasised in that it is used to accomplish certain ends in everyday interactions, such as the management of responsibility and blame. Language is therefore used variably and fluidly to achieve certain goals and does not represent underlying cognitive structures. Therefore targeting cognition in an effort to change health-related behaviour in the ways suggested in models widely used in health psychology, such as the Health Belief Model and the Theory of Planned Behaviour, will not be fruitful (see Chapters 2, 3, 4 & 7 for further discussion and critique of social cognition in relation to particular approaches and topic areas in health psychology). This kind of discursive analysis, and its critique of traditional approaches in health psychology, alerts us to the importance of the performative nature of language within specific social interactions and contexts. Therefore there are dangers and difficulties in developing general principles and guidelines for initiating and sustaining health-related change.

Scholars have also alerted us of the inherent values and biases always present in scientific evidence and theory which will inevitably lead to certain kinds of application, most notably, in mainstream psychology, a focus on individual responsibility for health. The alternative put forward by critical psychologists is to adopt approaches such as discourse analysis which is reflective on how knowledge is created (see Gergen & Zielke, 2006; Willig, 1999). However, Gergen and Zielke (2006) warn that focusing simply on critique can lead to certain problems. For instance, critique can simplify complex problems, and create resistance among the target group resulting in polarisation, which reduces the potential for meaningful dialogue. They therefore warn that the rhetoric of critique may not be particularly useful in instigating change.

Having outlined the positions identified in the debate between action and critique, it is important to stress that many scholars and activists acknowledge the positions identified are not absolute. For instance most involved in action-based approaches also encourage reflexivity and critique (see Campbell & Murray, 2004; Murray & Poland, 2006) and those seeking ways forward frequently advocate an amalgamation of the two (for example, see Gergen & Zielke, 2006; Willig, 1999). I also do not wish to engage in a polarised elaboration of this debate as it has been acknowledged that this may not be the best way forward. Therefore, the aim of this chapter is to find ways of working with both critique and action. However, the focus will be on an examination of how particular language/discourse-based approaches might be employed to simultaneously focus on working to reduce social inequalities in health whilst retaining a strong sense of critique.

A way forward: critique *and* action

Linking micro to macro contexts

As already argued, discursive psychology highlights the ways in which micro contexts can inhibit the potential for action. This has provided an important critique of mainstream psychology and health psychology, but many critical psychologists emphasise the importance of making links between micro accounts and broader contexts such as relationships between participants, their lives and roles, and the history and culture in which they are embedded (e.g. Wetherell, 1998). I will now outline some examples of how explorations of micro contexts in health-related discursive research have been linked to macro issues and consider their potential for action.

The accounting practices of individuals' within their immediate social context have been identified as important in a recent discursive analysis of accounts of explanations for not taking action to solve fertility problems in the developing country of Malawi (de Kok & Widdicombe, 2008). Accounting practices have been defined as being what people do with their talk, and it has been argued that these practices can limit or facilitate future action (Willig, 1999). de Kok and Widdicombe (2008) outline how scholars have argued that in developing countries not being able to bear children or not having enough children can have serious psychological and social consequences, in that the infertile are frequently ostracised, stigmatised and blamed (e.g. Dyer et al., 2002). Using a discursive psychological analysis, de Kok and Widdicombe illustrate that their participants' accounts of inaction to solve fertility problems contained a need to justify not taking action or stopping help seeking for infertility because becoming a parent is seen as such a normative expectation in this culture. In addition, their participants avoided blame by demonstrating previous prolonged commitment and effort in addressing their infertility. Thus their micro accounting practices, mobilised to avoid blame and justify action/inaction, are linked to broader macro cultural expectations. The potential for action derived from such an analysis, de Kok and Widdicombe argue, could be to promote the development of alternative accounting practices. These alternatives facilitate not taking action or discontinuing treatment at an earlier stage than is commonly the case in developing countries, and thus reduce some of the adverse physiological, financial, psychological and social consequences of infertility in these settings. With regard to action, the role, and importance of accounting practices could be emphasised to health practitioners and used to design interventions to promote the use of alternative linguistic resources (de Kok & Widdicombe, 2008). Also see de Kok (Chapter 11) for further discussion of discursive psychology's potential to address the call to action.

Similarly, Seymour-Smith (2008) combined micro and macro levels of analysis to explore differences in men's and women's engagement in cancer self-help groups. She argues that research suggests men participate less than women in cancer self-help groups (e.g. Cella & Yellan, 1992), despite potential health benefits (Fitch, 2000). Through her fine grained discursive analysis she illustrates men's resistance to being positioned as members of self-help groups. She identifies their orientation towards accounts of membership that centre on offering help, whereas women's participation was accounted for as receiving help. Seymour-Smith links this micro level of analysis to dominant representations of masculinity, in that masculinity is associated with strength rather than weakness. She argues that this kind of analysis has implications for health promotion in that the performative nature of identity negotiation needs to be taken into account when naming such groups, and arguably other health-related activities, aimed at men. In her analysis, the term 'self-help' is identified as problematic for men because of dominant constructions of masculinity. She and others (e.g. Gough & Conner, 2006) have also argued that health professionals should employ gender-specific and targeted interventions that appeal or conform to hegemonic masculinity. However, Horrocks (Chapter 5) somewhat critiques this approach to action with regard to men's health by arguing that it fails to challenge authoritative discourses of hegemonic masculinity.

Discourse-orientated approaches which work from micro to macro levels of analysis emphasise the value of interrogating the performative aspects of language in health-related contexts whilst also considering how self-presentation links to dominant macro constructions. There are therefore benefits of integrating this kind of critical analysis into more action-orientated approaches such as participatory action research in community health settings so that there is potential to change, not only the more immediate health constraining issues but also challenge broader detrimental discourses and practices. The next section will consider further how broader health-impeding discourses might be challenged.

Linking macro to micro contexts

Another key approach to analysing language places greater emphasis on the constraining nature of discourse at a more macro level, drawing on the work of Michel Foucault (1926–1984). However, it is acknowledged that, though some scholars have made a distinction between this and discursive psychology, others argue that this distinction is not always clear-cut (see Willig, 2004). The aim of a Foucauldian-informed discourse analysis is to question how a particular phenomenon has come to be as it is (Parker, 1997). This is achieved by identifying discourses within a text as well as exploring the positionings that these lead to and how they can reproduce particular power relations (Parker, 1999). Making certain discursive constructions and power relations visible, it is argued, means that they become a site for active resistance which in turn opens up possibilities for action and social change (Burman & Parker, 1993; Gergen & Zielke, 2006). This approach has offered valuable insights into the insidious ways in which power operates in relation to health (see, for example, Adams & Dell, 2008; Day et al., 2003; Gilbert, 2008; Pond et al., 2010).

Though it is hard to assess the impact these critiques have had on action, and the review by Davidson et al. (2006) discussed earlier suggests this is not substantial, they could be used to inform action. In addition, such approaches incorporate possibilities for agency and change which will be explored in this section. In addition, see Chapters 6, 8 and 9 for further examples of how Foucauldian discourse analysis can be used to inform action.

I will now develop my exploration of Foucauldian language-based approaches by examining specifically how feminist poststructuralists draw on this approach to conceptualise the potential for change in relation to gender and health and explore possible courses of action drawing upon this form of critique. The constraining and oppressive nature of constructions of femininity is a central theme within the feminist literature (see for example, Humm, 1992). However, feminist poststructuralists critique deterministic notions of femininity. They argue that women are active agents and are able to, some extent, take up a range of positions which allow them to resist or problematise particular constructions of femininity which open up possibilities for change. However, because processes of power restrict the alternatives available to women, the possibilities are not limitless (Weedon, 1997).

Using some illustrations drawn from my own analysis in two different studies, I will now explore how this form of critique has been used and its potential for change. The examples involve a feminist poststructuralist analysis of women's accounts of negotiating the embodied experiences of both pregnancy and breastfeeding.

The constraining nature of particular discursive constructions of femininity is demonstrated in various ways within these analyses. For example, in a study involving interviews with women in the latter stages of pregnancy, one way in which the pregnant body was constructed was as transgressing ideals for feminine beauty and thus seen in a negative way as being fat and less attractive (see Johnson et al., 2004). This supports gender ideologies around prescriptions that women's bodies should conform to specific ideals of feminine beauty (see, Bordo, 1993). In a study using audio diaries and interviews to explore women's early experiences of breastfeeding, an analysis of the practice of expressing breast milk revealed that this was largely carried out as a way of aligning subjectivity with cultural ideologies of motherhood (see Johnson et al., 2009; Johnson et al., in press). Faced with particular difficulties, including pain and discomfort, and uncertainties about their ability to breastfeed and the amount of milk their babies were receiving, expressing breast milk was constructed as a way of negotiating the moral imperative that 'breast is best', thereby ensuring 'good' mothering. This was because the women who engaged in this practice were still providing breast milk and therefore doing their best to ensure that health outcomes for their baby were being maximised.

However, also identified in these analyses is active resistance to, or empowering aspects of, these seemingly constraining discursive constructions which could lead to, or be promoted as, forms of action. For instance, the pregnancy as transgressing idealised feminine beauty construction was often countered by claims of it being acceptable to be 'fat' when pregnant (Johnson et al., 2004). By mobilising this construction, the women were able to engage in a relaxation of the usual standards applied in assessing feminine beauty. Being pregnant, to some extent, freed them from the objectifying male gaze because pregnancy and sexuality are not synonymous (Johnson et al., 2004; Johnson, 2010; Young, 1984). In our analysis of the practice of expressing breast milk and feeding it via a bottle we have highlighted how expressing was constructed as being empowering (see Johnson et al., 2009; Johnson et al., in press). It was described as a practice which could be used to manage the realities of modern motherhood such as shared parenting as it gave fathers an opportunity to be engaged in feeding and 'bond' with their baby, as well as the mothers the freedom to be able to feed in public uninhibited by concerns about exposing the breast and a way to prepare to return to work. It also allowed for some control over the unpredictable and demanding aspects of early breastfeeding.

With regard to the latter example, such an analysis suggests that one form of action that might arise is to support the expression of breast milk as an additional strategy for managing breastfeeding (see Johnson et al., in press). However, our engagement in a critical analysis also alerts us to the dangers of taking this at face value as it highlights the constraining nature of broader social and cultural factors in that expressing breast milk was also constructed as a way of negotiating cultural inhibitions and contradictory demands. This kind of analysis therefore suggests that action should also be channelled at challenging these constraining constructions (Johnson et al., in press).

Thus a poststructuralist critical lens not only identifies possibilities for action and empowerment, but it also provides opportunities to reflect upon discourses identified at a macro level. Once identified, these can then be worked upon, in order that they are transformed and reconstituted in less oppressive ways (Davies et al., 2006; Weedon, 1997). Though the application of discourse analytic work has been acknowledged as problematic (Willig, 1999), this could be achieved through, for example, providing spaces for pregnant and breastfeeding women, and those involved in their care, to discuss more empowering constructions which in turn could lead to challenges to problematic discursive constructions. This could be achieved through further participatory action research and the development of the 'voice' of women themselves as well as practitioners. However, to address critical health psychology's call for action at a more macro level would also involve health psychologists as scholar–activists facilitating 'receptive social environments' (Campbell et al., 2010). This would mean the promotion of, and lobbying for, such analyses to those who hold the power to bring about change. For example, this could include lobbying for the inclusion of such critical engagement in health professional education, promoting it to groups such as the National Childbirth Trust as well as in media aimed at new parents.

In another study that I and a colleague have been involved in, we have developed this action dimension further. The aims of the project are to explore processes by which mothers engage with parenting advice (specifically, immunisation) and trace the paths from scientific research, through professional services, key publications, websites, and informal sources and networks to the user. This project involves a poststructuralist analysis, in that it explores how individuals actively engage with, negotiate and implement decisions on the basis of the information they receive. It also considers the ways in which the interaction of expert advice and parenting are shaped by powerful representations of science and motherhood, which in turn are shaped within complex discursive constructions of power, knowledge, gender, class and 'race' (Burman, 2008). However, it has also sought to involve mothers as users of health advice and health professionals in its planning and execution in the form of an advisory panel of users. It is hoped that this will increase its relevance and usefulness both for participants and for service users more broadly. Therefore it aims to keep a strong focus on critique whilst incorporating the potential for action, both during, and as a result of the project. Thus while reflecting a critical participatory approach to research which is action orientated, the involvement of a range of key stakeholders may also improve the reception of its findings by those who hold the power to bring about broader change.

Working with critique *and* action

In this chapter, I have highlighted the main facets of the action/critique debate but argued that rather than seeing these as diametrically opposed positions, we should move towards working with the tensions between them to develop a truly critically informed action-orientated critical health psychology. Analyses of power and how it operates are essential if we are to work towards change and improvement of health, and these are necessary, I would argue, to inform action. With this in mind, I have focused on how language-based approaches which have the potential to undertake rich analyses of the operation of power might be usefully employed in more action-orientated approaches. This supports Cook's (2005) argument that discourse analysis can be productively used as part of critical ethnography and participatory action research approaches in health promotion. The combining of these approaches therefore is a potential way of not only describing reality and engaging with a critical analysis of it but seeking to change that reality in order to improve health and well-being. It is also a way of engaging in being an agent of change, rather than merely critiquing the status quo (Gergen & Zielke, 2006; Murray & Poland, 2006; Murray Chapter 2). However, critical health psychologists working within this kind of framework still need to consider how best to facilitate the creation of the reception of such analyses by those who hold the power to bring about change.

Key points

1. Polarised debates focusing on either critique or action may not be that useful in developing critical health psychology's aims of contributing to meaningful social change in order to improve health.
2. A useful way forward for critical health psychology is to simultaneously work towards achieving improvements in health whilst retaining a strong sense of critique.
3. Language-based approaches such as discursive psychology and Foucauldian discourse analysis can be used not only to critique but also to inform action.
4. Examples of how language-based approaches can contribute to both critique and action include identifying and working upon potentially constraining and detrimental discourses and practices with key stakeholders and seeking to influence those who hold the power to bring about change.

NOTE

1. The ecological metaphor is defined by Nelson and Prilleltensky (2010) as 'the relationship between individuals and the multiple social systems in which they are embedded' (p. 77). The interdependence of these is derived from Bronfenbrenner's (1977) ecological model which consists of three levels of analysis: the micro includes the most immediate i.e. family, friends, neighbourhood; the meso defined as relationships between different micro systems; and the macro defined as community, societal and cultural structures.

REFERENCES

Adams E. & Dell, P. (2008) 'Being a good mother: a discourse analysis of women's experiences of breast cancer and motherhood', *Psychology of Women Section Review*, 10(1), 3–12.
Bordo, S. (1993) *Unbearable Weight: Feminism, Western Culture and the Body* Berkeley, CA: University of California Press.

Bronfenbrenner, U. (1977) 'Towards an experimental ecology of human development', *American Psychologist*, 32, 513–31.

Brydon-Miller, M. (2004) 'Using participatory action research to address community health issues', in M. Murray (ed.) *Critical Health Psychology* Basingstoke and New York: Palgrave Macmillan.

Burman, E. (2008) *Deconstructing Developmental Psychology*, 2nd edn. (Hove: Routledge).

Burman, E. & Parker, I. (eds) (1993) *Discourse Analytic Research: Repertoires and Readings of Texts in Action* London: Routledge.

Campbell, C., Cornish, F., Gibbs, A. & Scott, K. (2010) 'Heed the push from below: how do social movements persuade the rich to listen to the poor?' *Journal of Health Psychology*, 15, 962–71.

Campbell, C. & Murray, M. (2004) 'Community health psychology: promoting analysis and action for social change', *Journal of Health Psychology*, 9, 187–95.

Cella, D. F. & Yellen, S. (1993) 'Cancer support groups: the state of the art', *Cancer Practice*, 1, 56–62.

Cook, K. E. (2005) 'Using critical ethnography to explore issues in health promotion', *Qualitative Health Research*, 15, 129–38.

Crossley, M. (2008) 'Critical health psychology: developing and refining the approach', *Social and Personality Psychology Compass*, 2, 21–33.

Davidson, H., Evans, S., Ganote, C., Henrickson, J., Jacobs-Priebe, L., Jones, D. L., Prilleltensky, I. & Riemer, M. (2006) 'Power and action in critical theory across disciplines: implications for critical community psychology', *American Journal of Community Psychology*, 38, 35–49.

Day, K., Gough, B. & McFadden, M. (2003) 'Women who drink and fight: a discourse analysis of working class women's Talk', *Feminism and Psychology*, 13, 141–58.

Davies, B., Browne, J, Gannon, S., Hopkins, L, McCann, H & Wihlborg, M. (2006) 'Constituting the feminist subject in poststructuralist discourse', *Feminism and Psychology*, 16, 87–103.

de Kok, B. C. de & Widdicombe, S. (2008) '"I really tried": management of normative issues in accounts of responses to infertility', *Social Science and Medicine*, 67, 1083–93.

Dyer, S. J., Abrahams, N., Hoffman, M. & van der Spuy, Z. M. (2002) 'Men leave me as I cannot have children: women's experiences with involuntary childlessness', *Human Reproduction*, 17, 1663–68.

Fitch, M. (2000) 'Supportive care for cancer patients', *Hospital Quarterly*, 3(4), 39–46.

Gergen, K. J. & Zielke, B. (2006) 'Theory in action', *Theory and Psychology*, 16, 229–309.

Gilbert, E. (2008) 'The art of governing smoking: discourse analysis of Australian anti-smoking campaigns', *Social Theory and Health*, 6, 97–116.

Gough, B. & Conner, M. T. (2006) 'Barriers to healthy eating amongst men: a qualitative analysis', *Social Science and Medicine*, 62, 387–95.

Hepworth, J. (2006) 'Strengthening critical health psychology: a critical action orientation', *Journal of Health Psychology*, 11, 401–8.

Humm, M. (1992) *Feminism: A Reader* London: Harvester Wheatsheaf.

Johnson, S., Burrows, A. & Williamson, I. (2004) 'Does my bump look big in this? The meaning of bodily changes for first time mothers-to-be', *Journal of Health Psychology*, 9, 361–74.

Johnson, S., Williamson, I., Lyttle, S. & Leeming, D. (2009) 'Expressing yourself: a feminist analysis of talk around expressing breast milk', *Social Science and Medicine*, 69, 900–7.

Johnson, S. (2010) 'Discursive constructions of the pregnant body: conforming to or resisting body ideals?' *Feminism and Psychology*, 20, 249–54.

Johnson, S., Leeming, D., Lyttle, S. & Williamson, I. (in press) 'Empowerment or regulation? exploring the implications of women's perspectives on expressing breast milk', in P. Hall Smith, B. L. Hausman & M. Labbok *Beyond Health, Beyond Choice: Breastfeeding Constraints and Realities* New Brunswick, NJ: Rutgers University Press.

Lee, C. (2006) 'Critical health psychology: who benefits?' *Journal of Health Psychology*, 11, 355–59.

McVittie, C. (2006) 'Critical health psychology, pluralism and dilemmas: the importance of being critical', *Journal of Health Psychology*, 11, 373–77.

Mielewczyk, F. & Willig, C. (2007) 'Old clothes and an older look: the case for a radical makeover in health behaviour research', *Theory and Psychology*, 17, 811–37.

Murray, M. & Poland, B. (2006) 'Health psychology and social action', *Journal of Health Psychology*, 11, 379–84.

Nelson, G. & Prilleltensky, I. (eds) (2010) *Community Psychology: In Pursuit of Liberation and Well-Being*, 2nd edn. Basingstoke: Palgrave Macmillan.

Parker, I. (1997) 'Discursive psychology', in D. Fox & I. Prilleltensky, (eds) *Critical Psychology: An Introduction* London: Sage.

Parker, I. & The Bolton Discourse Network (1999) *Critical Textwork: An Introduction to Varieties of Discourse and Analysis* Buckingham: Open University Press.

Pond, R., Stephens, C. & Alpass, F. (2010) 'Virtuously watching one's health: older adults' regulation of self in pursuit of health', *Journal of Health Psychology*, 15, 734–43.

Seymour-Smith, S. (2008) '"Men don't like that sort of thing": men's negotiation of a "troubled" self-help group identity', *Journal of Health Psychology*, 13, 785–97.

Weedon, C. (1997) *Feminist Practice and Poststructuralist Theory*, 2nd edn Oxford: Blackwell.

Wetherell, M. (1998) 'Positioning and interpretative repertoires: conversation analysis and post-structuralism in dialogue', *Discourse and Society*, 9(3), 387–412.

Willig, C. (ed.) (1999) *Applied Discourse Analysis: Social and Psychological Interventions*, Buckingham: Open University Press.

Willig, C. (2004) 'Discourse analysis and health psychology', in M. Murray (ed.) *Critical Health Psychology* Basingstoke: Palgrave Macmillan.

Young, I. M. (1984) 'Pregnant embodiment: subjectivity and alienation', *Journal of Medicine and Philosophy*, 9, 45–62.

CHAPTER 2

Critical Health Psychology and the Scholar–Activist Tradition

MICHAEL MURRAY

The current dominant approach within health psychology has been characterised as 'scientistic', individualistic and apolitical (e.g. Chamberlain, 2000; Marks, 2002; Murray & Campbell, 2003). There are alternatives to this approach which are informed by different epistemologies, values and practices. The aim of this chapter is to review the development of a more scholar–activist approach within health psychology and to consider the challenges it presents. The term scholar–activist has a long heritage within the social justice movement and refers to the tradition of exposing, subverting and challenging social injustices through a combination of various forms of scholarly work and activism (e.g. Murray & Poland, 2006). This chapter considers how this approach has interrupted the development of the more scientistic approach within psychology in general and more specifically health psychology.

Health psychology is in many ways a child of the '60s. At that time there was much debate and challenge within psychology and the social sciences as a whole not only in terms of theories and methods but also about their roles in the broader society. In 1970 George Albee was elected President of the American Psychological Association, committed to radicalising the discipline and profession. At that time, Albee (1969) wrote,

> We must realise that the terrible suffering that exists in our society among the disenfranchised, the poor, the havenots, can only be remedied by direct confrontation with the establishment, by the socialisation of our care-delivery systems, by the development of adequate tax-supported public facilities, staffed with competent BA-level interventionists using social models which can only

be developed as creative people find out about the real problems... The times are right for revolution! (p. 7)

Such a call energised many psychologists, especially those working in the field of mental health, to explore new ways of practising. They were dissatisfied with the individualist assumptions and 'scientist–practitioner' model favoured by clinical psychology that sought to emulate the power and methods of medicine. In the United States, this move led in the 1970s to the development of community psychology based on a more community-activist approach to health intervention. This turn to the community was premised upon an awareness of the social basis of mental health and the need to work collectively to challenge social oppression in its myriad forms.

Around the same time another influential psychologist, William Ryan, highlighted the role of ideological forces in disempowering social change movements. In his influential text 'Blaming the victim', Ryan (1971) described how both researchers and government placed responsibility for poverty not on structural injustices but rather on the behaviours of those who are poor. Ryan was also trained in clinical psychology but realised that its limitations flowed from an acceptance of a wider 'victim-blaming' ideology. In his introduction to the 1976 edition of the book, Ryan recalled that he wrote it after realising that the major political successes of the 1960s in introducing civil rights legislation and reducing social inequality were being threatened by new governmental initiatives that were often couched in superficially progressive language:

> It was out of fear that efforts would be made to halt that progress that I wrote this book. I saw – too narrowly and imperfectly I would think today – the specific ideology of Blaming the Victim as a major weapon being used to slow down progress toward equality... The generic formula of Blaming the Victim – justifying inequality by finding defects in the victims of inequality – has been retained, but in a much wider, more malevolent and dangerous form. (p. xii–xiii)

After its activist beginnings, the many radical ideas that underlay the establishment of community psychology in North America were followed by attempts to integrate it more into mainstream psychology by adopting many of the dominant positivist methods of research and paying lesser attention to socio-political issues. It became especially concerned with developing and evaluating community initiatives rather than challenging broader structural injustices. The past decade has seen various attempts to return to the original radical aims of its founders. This reassessment has included a turn to other traditions of social activism.

Latin America

While the community psychology that developed in North America often favoured accommodative local action, the community social psychology that developed in Latin America drew upon a much more radical tradition. From the outset in the 1960s this approach was infused with a greater political awareness and borrowed extensively from the writings of Catholic social justice activists such as Gustavo Gutierrez (1971/1988) and Camilo Torres (see Gerassi, 1971) as well as from the popular education ideas of Paulo Freire and the other social scientists/activists who were developing participatory action research.

The 1950s and 1960s was a period when a variety of dictatorial governments were entrenched in many South American countries. There was widespread poverty and social injustice and sustained military repression of any opposition movement. In this context an approach developed within the Catholic Church that publicly championed the interests of the poor and oppressed and which adopted what came to be known as 'liberation theology'. Gustavo Gutierrez, who coined this term, argued that the struggle against poverty and injustice flowed from Christian teachings. It was Gutierrez who developed the idea that Christians should adopt, what he termed, a 'preferential option for the poor' by which he meant that they have a moral responsibility to take the side of the poor and to work with them to create a better world (see http://liberationtheology.org/).

These ideas on the moral impetus for social action to challenge structural injustices were taken up by various psychologists and social scientists in Latin America. Ignacio Martin-Baro, who was a psychologist and priest from El Salvador, enthusiastically championed these ideas. He strongly criticised the 'scientistic mimicry' of North American psychology and its individualism. As he argued,

> The problem with individualism is rooted in its insistence on seeing as an individual characteristic that which oftentimes is not found except within the collectivity, or in attributing to individuality the things produced only in the dialectic of interpersonal relations. Through this, individualism ends up reinforcing the existing structures, because it ignores the reality of social structures and reduces all structural problems to personal problems. (Martin-Baro, 1994, p. 22)

Martin-Baro further argued that psychologists should also adopt the 'preferential option for the poor' and work with the marginalised and the oppressed to develop strategies of change and opposition to repression. As he stated,

> We have to redesign our theoretical and practical tools, but redesign them from the standpoint of the lives of our own people: from their sufferings, their aspirations, and their struggles. (p. 25)

He added, 'but to create a liberation psychology is not simply a theoretical task; first and fundamentally it is a practical task' (p. 25). These words and actions soon brought him to the attention of the military dictatorship in his country. On 16 November 1989 Martin-Baro and several of his colleagues were murdered by the Salvadoran Army. However, his ideas continue to infuse radical community social psychology throughout the world (see http://www.martinbarofund.org/).

The type of action favoured by those who championed liberation theology ranged from local community action to armed guerrilla struggle. An example of both these approaches was the work of Camilo Torres, a Columbian priest and sociologist, who helped to organise mass opposition to the repressive government in that country in the 1960s. Torres helped to establish the sociology department in the National University of Columbia but was soon removed from his academic position because of his work in organising students and workers. His university colleagues at that time included Orlando Fals Borda, one of the key founding figures of Participatory Action Research (see Fals et al., 1991). Being frustrated by the state and the church, in his efforts to mobilise mass opposition to government repression Torres decided that the only alternative was to join the armed guerrilla movement. He argued that it was necessary to engage in military action to overthrow the established government and to secure social justice. At the time he resigned his position as a priest to join the guerrilla army he issued a statement in which he wrote, 'I believe that the revolutionary struggle is appropriate for the Christian and the priest. Only by revolution, by changing the concrete conditions of our country, can we enable men [sic] to practise love for each other' (Gerassi, 1971, p. 334). Even more forcefully he argued, 'The Catholic who is not a revolutionary is living in mortal sin' (1971, p. 17). Shortly after he joined the guerrilla army he was killed in an ambush in 1966. However, his ideas still infuse contemporary debate in Latin America about forms of social change although they are strongly denounced by the church establishment. Within critical community psychology there remains discussion about the potential for initiating and sustaining local social change and the limitations imposed by larger socio-political institutions.

This debate is evident within participatory action research (PAR) which informs much of community psychology. This approach developed from the liberatory ideas of Fals Borda and others and the ideas of popular education developed by Paulo Freire, a Brazilian educator. Freire (1970) characterised the traditional approach to education as 'an act of depositing, in which the students are the depositories and the teacher is the depositor' (p. 53). In the more critical approach, the educator engages with the students in an active dialogical manner to encourage them to consider the broader social and structural restraints on their lives and how they can begin to challenge these restraints through collective action. He used the term *conscientisation* to describe this process of developing critical consciousness: 'Problem-posing education affirms men and women as beings in the process of becoming – as unfinished, uncompleted beings in and with a likewise unfinished reality' (p. 65).

Freire stressed that his work was 'rooted in concrete situations' working with poor peasants. He emphasised the collaborative nature of his work and described the radical as someone who 'does not become the prisoner of a "circle of certainty" within which reality is also imprisoned...This person does not consider himself or herself the proprietor of history or of all people, or the liberator of the oppressed; but he or she does commit himself or herself, within history, to fight at their side' (p. 21). While the ideas of PAR have now become mainstream within much community activism, when they were originally formulated in the 1960s they were strongly opposed by the military dictatorship in Brazil who imprisoned Freire. He subsequently fled the country but returned in the 1980s where he served for a period as provincial minister of education in Sao Paulo. Currently, a range of organisations have been established to promote and extend his ideas (e.g. http://www.freire.org/).

Developing a more critical community psychology

The development of these more radical ideas contributed to the revitalisation of community psychology in North America and elsewhere. An illustration is the work of Brinton Lykes and her colleagues (Lykes et al., 1996). Lykes enthusiastically followed in the footsteps of Martin-Baro and spent considerable periods working with members of the Mayan community in Central America who had been victims of sustained violence and social exclusion. In this context, she was not only informed by ideas from PAR and liberation psychology but she has added to this her understanding of feminist and narrative research. She noted that one reaction of the Mayan people to years of suffering was silence. 'The state thereby silences the population through terror, exploiting fear in a particular way' (Lykes, 1997, p. 727). As a means of combating this reaction, Lykes found that working with the women through narratives and storytelling was a key way of breaking through this silence and exploring new ways of living.

Lykes' approach was to develop an activist participatory research model that had as its inspiration the passionate scholarship championed by feminists such as DuBois (1983). She described this approach as 'a process through which the researcher accompanies the participant or subject over time, participating and observing while resourcing the participant and his or her community who, in turn, resource the researcher' (p. 728). By this process of active engagement the researcher becomes involved in a joint process of reflection and change. Lykes continued, 'The process reflects a willingness to risk entering another's life and allowing him or her to enter one's own. Understanding one's possibilities for continuing engagement are thus shaped by an experience of shared subjectivity. As importantly, one's self-understanding as researcher is reframed' (p. 729).

This is a dramatic turning away from the 'scientistic mimicry' decried by Martin-Baro. However, while radical at a local level its impact in the longer term will depend upon the extent of support from and engagement with larger societal institutions. There is not a simple solution to this tension. It depends upon the issues, the community, the time and the broader society. Critical community psychologists are involved in an ongoing process of engagement and reflection upon these processes to explore how they can sustain and expand support for social change beyond small groups and to locate their work within particular societies. Thus the character of their work is not fixed but is always looking for new opportunities to develop local capacity and to further expose and to challenge oppressive social arrangements.

Health psychology

In comparison with community psychology, from the outset health psychology adopted a very individualistic and accommodative approach to society. Joseph Matarazzo is often credited with drafting many of the formative documents of the new discipline. He urged this new discipline not to be cautious – but to 'aggressively investigate and deal with the role of individual behaviour and lifestyle' (Matarazzo, 1980). Health psychology turned away from connecting health and illness with the broader societal context as had been advocated by Albee (1969). Instead its concern was to 'deal with' those individual behaviours that supposedly caused ill-health.

Rather than developing social and collective strategies to 'deal with' structural inequalities health psychologists turned to the evolving social cognition models of individual attitude change. The theoretical approach developed by Fishbein and Ajzen (1975) became the dominant orientation within health psychology as the discipline sought professional recognition. The approach derived much of its legitimacy from the information-processing models that had become popular within mainstream cognitive psychology at that time. As Fishbein and Ajzen stated in their foundational text,

> Generally speaking, we view humans as rational animals who systematically utilize or process the information available to them. The theoretical structure or conceptual framework we have adopted assumes a causal chain linking

beliefs, formed on the basis of available information, to the person's attitudes, beliefs, and attitudes to intentions, and intentions to behaviour. (p. vi)

Although their formulation of the relationship between attitudes and behaviour included reference to social norms it was very much an individual change model that made limited connection with the broader social world. The following 30 years has witnessed various attempts by health psychologists to refine and extend this attitude model, but the basic assumptions are similar to the original formulation.

However, more recently there have been various attempts to reconnect health and community/social psychology and to explore new forms of social activism designed to promote health. The challenge to the social cognition was initially on methodological grounds. Health psychology researchers became frustrated at the quantitative methods of investigation (Murray & Chamberlain, 1999). The past 15 years have seen an explosion of interest in a wide variety of qualitative research methods. However, being concerned with enhancing the quality of lives health psychologists who started to use qualitative methods also began to query to what extent this approach contributed to this action. Writing earlier we argued, 'there is a danger that this sustained concern with language can divert attention from broader material issues' (Murray & Campbell, 2003, p. 233).

This debate about the relationship between the study of language and social change is one that continues. The recent exchanges between Corcoran (2009) and Potter (2010) illustrate the continuing debate. In his original critique of the limitations of mainstream discourse analysis, it is interesting that Corcoran (2009) turned to critical health psychology as providing a guide to developing a more activist alternative. This is not to say that scholars within the critical health psychology community have resolved this debate, but that rather, as is the case with this collection, they are more obviously engaged in the debate.

Some health psychologists have begun to reach out to more activist forms of social inquiry – ones that are not premised upon information processing and behaviour-controlling assumptions. In particular, they have turned to various forms of community-based participatory action research. As in community psychology, in general, there are different orientations within this approach. The more accommodationist orientation focuses on processes within the community, while the more critical orientation aim to connect intra-community processes with the broader socio-political context. A primary aim of the critical orientation is,

to promote analysis and action that challenges the restrictions imposed by exploitative economic and political relationships and dominant systems of knowledge production, often aligning themselves with broad democratic movements to challenge the social inequalities which flourish under global capitalism. (Campbell & Murray, 2004, p. 190).

This emergent approach has deliberately attempted to connect with other developments in critical social and health psychology and with developments in community psychology. In devising strategies for social and community change, critical health psychologists are aware of the need to understand and to respect the local knowledge held by communities. As Jovchelovitch (2007) has argued, a starting point for change must be 'a deep commitment to the belief that ordinary people have a contribution to make and know what they are talking about and an acceptance of the incompleteness and limitations of one's own knowledge' (p. 156).

An example is the CALL-ME project which was established to explore the character of social isolation among older residents of a disadvantaged urban neighbourhood and to investigate the potential of collaboratively developing community social activities (Murray & Crummett, 2010). One such activity was a community arts project. This is defined as the use of multiple forms of creative arts activities in a community setting. It requires the active involvement of local people in its development and an awareness of the broader socio-political context within which the action is located (Webster & Buglass, 1997). At the outset, the researchers invited a group of older residents to reflect upon their neighbourhood and to consider a plan of action to promote social interaction. When the idea of a community arts project was introduced some of the local residents were ambivalent but agreed to participate not least because it was something to do.

Over a period of two years a group of older residents met on a weekly basis to experiment with a range of art forms including painting, pottery and glass engraving. They met for two hours each week and were led by a local community arts worker. During this period they completed a number of arts projects. At the completion of each project the participants organised a community exhibition of their work. They invited not only local residents but also city officials and local politicians. In this way, the project moved from an opportunity for social interaction to one that challenged dominant negative social representations of the community held by outsiders and began to become a form of social action.

It was through a process of dialogue and local action that members of the community began to question their circumstances, to articulate their needs and begin to develop the community arts projects. The results of these projects were a source of great community pride which promoted substantial wider discussion. However, as previously emphasised, the success of such local action needs to be considered with reference to the support or otherwise of the immediate social environment, its history and culture, the character of the leadership offered and the broader political climate within which the action is located.

Social environment

Community health activists are aware of the limitations of focusing solely on singular and localised projects. They often report that while community residents can be enthused by local activities they are frustrated at the obstacles to broader social change. As Campbell et al. (2010) recently noted,

> In final project write-ups, wider social hierarchies (based on factors such as gender or socio-economic status) are depicted most often as obstacles to long-term project sustainability and to the 'scale-up' of innovative project strategies to other similar communities. Such final reports often conclude that such power hierarchies are too entrenched for small scale groups of marginalized people to mount an effective and sustainable fight against their ill-effects. (p. 963).

Campbell et al. continued, 'such projects are frequently successful in building the "voice" of the poor, but less successful in building "receptive social environments"' (p. 963). They argued that community health activists should turn their attention to exploring broader social movements that can create such 'receptive social environments'. This is a major challenge for health psychologists who have as of yet given limited attention to the processes involved in these larger social movements. Campbell et al. define 'voice' as the capacity of poor people both to develop critical analyses that link their poverty to wider social inequalities and to articulate forceful demands on the basis of these critical understandings. 'Projects develop voice through providing transformative social spaces for dialogue in which poor people are able to engage in critical thinking about the social roots of what might previously have been regarded as individual problems' (p. 963). This is the typical work of the community activist, but the challenge is to move beyond this local development of critical thinking and action. Campbell et al. illustrate the process of building receptive social environments within which this local social action can move to a higher level through an analysis of a number of collective health movements. These movements were able to build this receptive social environment by a) uniting a broad range of people behind its objectives and b) promoting a moral symbolic agenda for change.

Such a process of building a supportive social environment can occur at the local as well as at a broader level. The arts can play an important role in building such a supportive social environment through mobilising large numbers of people and articulating a moral agenda. An example is the work we did in promoting awareness of the occupational health hazards within the deep-sea fishing industry (Murray & Tilley, 2006). Traditional approaches focused on promoting safety awareness among individual fish harvesters. Such an approach mirrored the victim-blaming approach condemned by Ryan 40 years ago. Our approach was to engage whole communities in this process and to highlight a wider agenda for safety action. This involved a variety of community arts activities including plays, concerts and exhibitions. An important part of this project was the songs that we developed with local residents. In one community we worked with a folk singer who drew upon interviews conducted with fish harvesters and developed a series of songs about fishing and safety. When played at local concerts and on the radio, these songs had a powerful echo in fishing communities and contributed to developing a receptive social environment. However, despite substantial local and national interest, for various logistical and funding reasons, it was not possible to extend this project further. This illustrated the tensions often experienced by scholar activists between the success of local social action and longer-term social change.

In the CALL-ME project there have been attempts to move from short-term local action to engage the local council in developing a more supportive social environment for activities by older residents. The local council promoted a range of media events to highlight the problems faced by older people and helped to organise a variety of social activities for them. In this case, a department within the council played the advocacy role of larger social movements by promoting a popular city-wide agenda of social inclusion for older people and thus providing a supportive environment for sustaining local neighbourhood successes. However, the recent cutbacks in government funding for local services has seriously jeopardised this support, further illustrating the challenges faced by local community health activists.

Change narrative

Central to the process of social change is the leadership provided and the articulation of a new collective story by and with the community. The role of leadership in all forms of social action is central. The leader can inspire, support and challenge community members (Morris & Staggenborg, 2004). As already mentioned in the commentary on the work of Lykes, stories can be an important means by which the leader can engage the community and encourage reflection. Storytelling has often been consigned to the sideline in discussions about social change – they are often considered a diversion from practical issues. But stories convey the history and trajectory of a community as well as provide a guide to future action. As Selbin (2010) argued,

> ... often we use them [stories] not just to narrate our lives [...] but to tell, to share news, information and much more: to guide, to warn, to inspire, to make real and possible that which may well be unreal and impossible. Stories allow us to imagine the transformation of our lives and our world. (p. 3)

In his review of collective movements of change, Selbin concluded that 'the crucial factor in explaining how and why revolution persists is the stories of revolution, rebellion, and resistance we tell' (p. 3). Within the community one of the roles of the critical educator is to work with the community to reflect on and critique their experiences and begin to develop a change strategy which takes the form of a story of potential – what can be done. Selbin stressed 'the importance of the articulation of compelling narratives and stories in any meaningful effort at change' (p. 194). Political movements can be galvanised around vivid stories of potential change. Consider the case of the civil rights movement in the United States which was epitomised in Martin Luther King's 'I have a dream' speech which lasted only 14 minutes but continues to reverberate. Similarly powerful folk songs such as Woody Guthrie's 'This land is your land' can enthuse millions. The lyrics can be drawn upon by politicians. For example, Barak Obama used the phrase 'It's been a long time coming but tonight change has come to America' on the day of his election victory, drawing from Sam Cooke's civil rights anthem 'A change is gonna come'. In Britain there is a long tradition of political songs (Lynskey, 2011). An example is Billy Bragg's 'Between the wars' which invigorated supporters of the miners' strike with his call, 'I'll give my consent to any government/that does not deny a man a living wage'.

Certain community narratives can also play a reactionary role by excluding people from involvement in activities such that it becomes the role of the community activist to challenge such narratives and to develop alternatives. This is not an easy task since communities have shaped their identities around such narratives, and they are often reinforced through songs and images. The gradual assertion of new narratives can often be subverted by older tales of reaction. The scholar–activist is aware of this clash of narratives and how they can inhibit the process of change. It is through a combination of forms of local action, alternative narratives and trusted leadership that communities can begin to explore new ways of working and living.

Political context

While community action can enthuse and excite large numbers of people we also need to consider the broader political context within which it develops and whose interests are primarily served by its promotion. The recent growth of interest in community activism by conservative politicians has contributed to sustained reflection about its basic assumptions. Internationally this debate has been fanned as versions of participatory community action have been adopted by world development agencies as a means of imposing globalisation and the interests of multinational corporations. Thus rather than working to promote the interests of marginalised community members this approach can become a means of concealing a bigger transnational agenda (Kindon et al., 2007). It can become a means not of challenging established power interests but rather of pushing responsibility back on the poor and excluded. As Kindon et al. have stated,

> while participatory approaches seek socially and environmentally just proc-
> esses and outcomes, they none the less constitute a form of power and can
> reproduce the very inequalities they seek to challenge. (p. 2)

It is for this reason that Cooke and Kothari (2001) described participation as the 'new tyranny'. By this they meant that rather than challenging structural inequalities participatory projects have often ignored the workings of the system and as such contributed to its maintenance.

Historically, critical psychologists have emphasised the importance of reflexivity. This has meant different things to different researchers, but broadly it is the concern to reflect upon our practice in the collection and in the interpretation of data collected. In the case of scholar activists, issues of reflexivity become more important since it is concerned with multiple issues from the research/action, the interpretation of data, the use of data, the relationship with the community etc.

In her account of the work of scholar activists, Pain (2003) identifies three broad approaches. The first approach involves a deliberate attempt to combine social activism with academic research. Both interconnect with the other such that the politics informs the research and vice versa, and they are both infused with a social justice agenda. There are many challenges to this approach as the scholar–activist tries to satisfy two agendas – to be a good academic and a good social activist. The second approach is the more participatory approach where the academic uses participatory methods to engage the 'subjects' actively in the research. This approach criticises the traditional social research method as being dominated in agenda and method by the academic researcher. The dominant participatory approach is one that espouses some form of PAR. While formally this approach is emancipatory, in practice the academic researcher may be frustrated on a variety of levels including obtaining funding, engaging the community, leaving the community, the character of outputs etc.

The third approach is that concerned with policy and in particular how critical scholars can contribute to the development of critical social policy and practice. Often scholar activists are anxious about being integrated into powerful social agencies by discussion of policy. But here the challenge is to involve the community participants in the movement for policy change.

The critical scholar–activist can move between these different approaches depending upon the time, the place, the opportunity etc. The danger is to become over-involved in local projects to the neglect of awareness of the larger socio–political context. An important part of this process is the extent of critical engagement with the broader political agenda.

There is an ongoing need for scholar–activists to connect local action with the broader socio-political and cultural context and within an ongoing process of critique and reflection (Murray & Poland, 2006). Thus rather than imposing a fixed agenda the researchers work with members of groups, communities and broader social movements to excavate and challenge the structures that disempower them and exclude them from power.

Lott and Bullock (2007) have identified a range of such broader activist strategies. They begin by stressing the need to reject individuating theories of poverty and wealth as was emphasised by Ryan 40 years ago. To this we can add opposition to the process of collective victim-blaming whereby we can denigrate whole groups or communities. Instead we need to consider who benefits from this process of victim-blaming and how they can be challenged through various forms of social critique and action. Such challenges can vary in magnitude over time and place but behind them is a common commitment to social justice (Murray, Nelson, Poland, Maticka-Tyndale & Ferris, 2004).

Critical health psychologists today can learn from the many struggles of disenfranchised people over the years. By working at different levels and with different social groups and movements they can contribute more actively to the development of a more equitable and healthier society. Through connecting critical scholarly and activist traditions they can not only be involved in deconstructing oppressive discourses but also be engaged in different forms of collaborative challenge and resistance to symbolic and material oppression.

Key points

1. Community psychology aims to work with groups and communities to transform their living and working conditions through local and broader collective action.

2. Community health action aims to enhance the health and quality of life of groups and communities through collective action and requires such action to move beyond localised activities to promote a more sustainable social environment.
3. Critical health psychology draws attention to the broader socio-political context within which health and illness are located and the need for various forms of health action to challenge health injustice and to promote health and well-being.

REFERENCES

Albee, G. (1969) 'Who shall be served?', *Professional Psychology: Research and Practice*, 1, 4–7.

Campbell, C., Cornish, F., Gibbs, A. & Scott, K. (2010) 'Heed in the push from below: how do social movements persuade the rich to listen to the poor?' *Journal of Health Psychology*, 15, 962–71.

Campbell, C. & Murray, M. (2004) 'Community health psychology: definitions and challenges', *Journal of Health Psychology*, 9(2), 179–88.

Chamberlain, K. (2000) 'Methodolatory and qualitative health research', *Journal of Health Psychology*, 5, 285–96.

Cooke, B. & Kothari, U. (2001) *Participation: the new tyranny?* London: Zed Books.

Corcoran, T. (2009) 'Second nature', *British Journal of Social Psychology*, 48, 375–88.

DuBois, B. (1983) 'Passionate scholarship: Notes on values, knowing and method in feminist social science', in G. Bowles & R. Klein (eds) *Theories of Women's Studies* Boston: Routledge, pp. 105–16.

Fals Borda, O. & Rahman, M. A. (eds) (1991) *Action and Knowledge: Breaking the Monopoly with Participatory Action Research* New York: Apex.

Fishbein, M. & Ajzen, I. (1975) *Belief, Attitude, Intention and Behavior: An Introduction to Theory and Research* Reading, MA: Addison-Wesley.

Freire, P. (1970/1993) *Pedagogy of the Oppressed* New York: Continuum.

Gerassi, J. (ed.) (1971) *Camilo Torres, Revolutionary Priest: His Complete Writings and Messages* London: Penguin.

Gutierrez, G. (1971) *A Theology of Liberation: History, Politics and Salvation* Maryknoll, NY: Orbis.

Jovchelovitch, S. (2007) *Knowledge in Context: Representations, Community and Culture* London: Routledge.

Kindon, S., Pain, R. & Kesby, M. (2007) 'Connecting people, participation and place', in S. Kindon, R. Pain & M. Kesby (eds) *Participatory Action Research Approaches and Methods: Connecting People, Participation and Place* London: Routledge.

Lott, B. & Bullock, H. E. (eds) *Psychology and Economic Injustice: Personal, Professional, and Political Intersections* Washington, DC: APA Books.

Lykes, M. B. (1997) 'Activist participatory research among the Maya of Guatemala: constructing meanings from situated knowledge', *Journal of Social Issues*, 53(4), 725–46.

Lykes, M. B., Banuazizi, A., Liem, R. & Morris, M. (eds) (1996) *Myths about the Powerless: Contesting Social Inequalities* Philadelphia, PA: Temple University Press.

Lynskey, D. (2011) *33 Revolutions Per Minute: A History of Protest Songs* London: Faber & Faber.

Marks, D. F. (2002) 'Freedom, power and responsibility: contrasting approaches to health psychology', *Journal of Health Psychology,* 7, 5–19.

Martin-Baro, I. (1994) *Writings for a Liberation Psychology: Ignacio Martin-Baro* (A. Aron & S. Corne (eds) Cambridge, MA: Harvard University Press.

Matarazzo, J. (1980) 'Behavioral health and behavioral medicine: frontiers for a new psychology', *American Psychologist*, 35, 807–17.

Morris, A. D. & Staggenborg, S. (2004) 'Leadership in social movements' in D.A. Snow, S.A. Soule & H. Kiriesi (eds.) *The Blackwell companion to social movements* Oxford: Blackwell, pp. 171–96.

Murray, M. & Chamberlain, K. (eds) (1999) *Qualitative Health Psychology: Theories and Methods* London: Sage.

Murray, M. & Campbell, C. (2003) 'Living in a material world: Reflecting on some assumptions of health psychology', *Journal of Health Psychology*, 8, 231–36.

Murray, M. & Crummett, A. (2010) "I don't think they knew we could do these sorts of things": social representations of community and participation in community arts by older people', *Journal of Health Psychology*, 15, 777–85.

Murray, M. & Poland, B. (2006) 'Health psychology and social action', *Journal of Health Psychology*, 11, 379–84.

Murray, M., Nelson, G., Poland, B., Maticka-Tyndale, E. & Ferris, L (2004) 'Assumptions and values in community health psychology', *Journal of Health Psychology*, 9(2), 315–26.

Murray, M. & Tilley, N. (2006) 'Promoting safety awareness in fishing communities through community arts: an action research project', *Safety Science*, 44, 797–808.

Pain, R. (2003) 'Social geography: on action-oriented research', *Progress in Human Geography*, 27, 649–57.

Potter, J. (2010) 'Contemporary discursive psychology: Issues, prospects, and Corcoran's awkward ontology', *British Journal of Social Psychology*, 49, 657–78.

Ryan, W. (1971/76) *Blaming the Victim* New York: Vintage.

Selbin, E. (2010) *Revolution, Rebellion, Resistance: the Power of Story* London: Zed Books.

Webster, M. & Buglass, G. (eds) *Finding Voices, Making Choices: Creativity for Social Change* Nottingham, UK: Educational Heretics Press.

CHAPTER 3

Changing Behaviour: Can Critical Psychology Influence Policy and Practice?

WENDY STAINTON ROGERS

Introduction

In the summer of 2010, on taking up the post of Secretary of State for Health, Andrew Lansley announced big changes in the way Health Services would be run. It would no longer be based, he announced, upon 'state regulation', but rather on 'social responsibility'. Most memorably he declared that he was not in favour of 'lecturing, nannying people or constantly legislating or taxing people' (as cited by Ramesh, 2010). Lansley immediately abolished the Food Standards Agency (FSA). He deplored, he said, the 'witch-hunt against saturated fats, salt and sugars' perpetrated by the previous government (Lansley, 2010). So he offered a deal to the food industry – no regulation of food content in return for food manufacturers funding a social marketing campaign to promote people taking greater responsibility in their habits and lifestyles.

This was precisely the time when I was writing this chapter, a few months into a new government, a coalition between our centre right party (Conservative) and a much smaller Liberal Democrat party. Times like this (Rex Stainton Rogers called them 'discursive hotspots') provide great opportunities for observing politico-text operating in relatively 'raw' form, not yet modulated and prettied up for consumption by the spin doctors, as inexperienced and often naive newly elected political appointees get to have their say after a long period in opposition.

In this chapter I will examine how critical psychologists can influence public policy and professional practice in the way that health services are delivered. In the face of the power that politicians can exercise, it can be easy to become disheartened. Nonetheless I strongly believe that critical psychologists must 'walk the walk' as well as 'talk the talk' of social justice. Our engagement, as academics, must not be confined to personal and parochial concerns about what we publish where. We must also engage beyond the academy in ways that have some hope of, for instance, reducing rather than increasing health inequalities. And our critique of mainstream psychology must go beyond challenging its 'wrong thinking' into a careful and convincing challenge to its 'wrongdoing' – such as providing a 'scientific' justification for unjust and inhuman policies and practices.

I will start with familiar ground: a summary critique of mainstream psychology's continuing preoccupation with social cognition models to explain health-related behaviour change. In parochial terms, these still dominate the field. This I will juxtapose against the recommendations made by NICE[1] (National Institute for Health and Clinical Excellence) on behaviour change interventions at individual, community and population levels. Social cognition health psychologists took part in their production, but here alongside academics and lay members from a diversity of disciplines and interest groups, of which I was one. The guidance produced tells a very different story. My final section, 'So is there any hope?' compares and contrasts the two, particularly the ideological themes and values underpinning each one, and their potential consequences. It ends with a call to action, for critical health psychologists to become more active in promoting values of equity, diversity and social justice.

Social cognition models of behaviour change

Some days I get very disillusioned. In preparing to write this chapter I nosed around in the social and health psychology journals to find out what's new in research into behaviour change. The truth is, not a lot. Tossing terms like 'reasoned action', 'planned behaviour' and 'stages of change' into search engines was truly disheartening. The 'high end' literature is still overburdened with studies tinkering around with these models. Predictably there were shed loads of data, beguilingly impressive algebra, sophisticated computer modelling. But look a little deeper and it's fool's gold: plaintive excuses for only being able to predict intention but not actual behaviour, the odd 'new' variable or three, or, worse, splitting up variables to give the impression of greater accuracy.

Early promise

Cognitive psychology played a crucial role in the development of critical psychology. It had its origins in the highly prescient work of Frederick Bartlett

(1932). Inspired by the game of 'Chinese whispers', he studied the distortions that people made when remembering stories and pictures. People's recall, he observed, reflected their attempts to make sense of what they had heard and seen. The stories got less fantastic, the pictures more familiar. Once they named a drawing (say, as a cat) the subsequent drawings made from memory became more and more cat-like. It was Ulric Neisser, though, in his book *Cognitive Psychology* (Neisser, 1966), who established cognitive psychology as a new-and-better paradigm (better, that is, than Behaviourism and Information Processing) for understanding the ways people's thinking affects their behaviour. The cognitive paradigm moved away from modelling people as mindless, machine-like beings driven by instinct, conditioning and learning. Instead it portrays people as purposive thinkers who strive to make sense of their social world and bring to this endeavour complex, sophisticated models-of-the-world which they use to interpret it and construct a social reality.

What went wrong

It is easy to see how, for some of us, cognitive psychology opened up the way into semiotics, social constructionism and then postmodernism. But, in my view, mainstream cognitive psychologists went down an unproductive blind alley. Their turn to 'cognitive algebra' models (Stainton Rogers, 1991, p. 55), while putting the 'person' back into personhood, ended up creating strangely austere beings: 'naive scientists' in attribution theory (i.e. hypothesis-testers working from hunches) and 'accountants' in theories of behaviour change (i.e. as data-crunchers calculating costs and benefits). These are so very Spock-like in character, operating only as rational, detached and objective beings. They are little removed from the 'strange Frankenstinian monsters' that Claxton (1987) observed in psychological laboratories of the time, consisting only of a brain, an eye to observe signals and a finger poised over a button, so precious to stimulus-response theory. A bit more human – but not much! I suspect these beings were not so much created in their own image but aspirationally (some have called it 'physics envy') within the Big-science-based ethos dominating psychology then and now.

But that is not all that went wrong. From the beginning critics from within psychology have complained about the model's poor showing in predicting behaviour. McGuire, for example, called it 'a scandal of social psychology' (McGuire, 1986, p. 92). What is so shocking is that this scandal persists today and shows absolutely no sign of abating.

As opposed to my anecdotal searches, Mielewczyk and Willig (2007) provide us with an elegant and thoroughgoing critique of social cognition approaches, especially in relation to their attempts to account for people's 'health threaten-ing' habits, life-styles and actions. They note,

> the overwhelming majority of the investigations conducted...have adopted a single theoretical framework and, as a result, a single methodological approach: the literature in this area is dominated by applications of models in which social cognitions such as attitudes and control beliefs are combined and assessed according to specific algorithms aimed at maximizing the propor-tions of variance explainable (by means of multiple regression analyses) in the performance of target health behaviours. (p. 812)

Earlier Ingham (1993) had described this as being like an adult who has to go through all manner of contortions to continue wearing the clothes they first bought as teenagers. Mielewczyk and Willig (2007) take up this metaphor with glee:

> social cognition researchers have been reluctant to abandon the old clothes, preferring instead to make repeated adjustments to their darts and waistbands (i.e. to the definition and measurement of their component variables) and to dress them up with a variety of beads, baubles and bangles (in the form of supplementary variables) in the ongoing struggle to improve both their fit and their appearance. (p. 812)

Back-stabbing, bravura and false modesty

Mielewczyk and Willig then go on to spell out what is wrong with this mod-elling and offer a critical psychological alternative. But before we look at that, it is worth noting that the social cognition camp is itself far from consensual. Vociferous infighting goes on in the journals, as proponents of the differ-ent models (or even different versions of the same model!) vie for credibility and dominance. As just one example, the *Stages of Change* or *Transtheoretical Model* (Prochaska & DiClemente, 1983) has been targeted for ridicule, with a stream of papers given titles like '*Breakthrough or bandwagon?*' (Ashworth, 1997); '*When popularity outstrips the evidence*' (Herzog, 2005); '*Back to the drawing board*' (Sutton, 2001); and '*Another nail in the coffin of the transtheo-retical model?*' (Sutton, 2005). If I were being cynical I might argue that this is something of a mock battle, motivated less by antagonism than playing a clever strategy in the publication-game. Or I might give my own identity meta-phor – the 'shark infested pool'. This is a world in which people behave like predators, fighting for territory and dominance in an academic world where 'survival of the fittest' is seen to be the best way to improve productivity and stimulate excellence in research. But those are other stories for other times and other places.

Interestingly, when not knocking the work of peers, many authors actually become quite disingenuous. An illustration here is a paper published in *Health Psychology* (an American, high impact factor journal – 3.69 – implying that the research reported is of very high value and significance). Authored by Sutton, McVey and Glanz it compares the efficacy of two social cognition theories: the *Theory of Reasoned Action* and the *Theory of Planned Behaviour*, through research on intended condom use by young people. Given its 'impact', the paper's aims are expressed in remarkably modest terms: 'We hope that the findings of this study will be of interest and value not only to health psychologists but also to policymakers, health educators, and others with responsibilities in the field of sexual health' (Sutton et al., 1999, p. 79).

Yet some serious problems are acknowledged: firstly, about the sample, 'one should be cautious about generalizing the findings beyond young people in England who are available and willing to complete a lengthy questionnaire on sexual health'; secondly, about not actually predicting *behaviour*, only intention, 'We are therefore unable to say from our data whether the factors that predict intentions to use condoms carry through to predict future behavior' (Sutton et al., 1999, p. 80). But the most candid admission is about the possibility that both models tested may be measuring the wrong variables. The study found that the best predictor of behavioural intention was, simply, young people's reports about their prior condom use. This outstripped all the variables in the two models. And so the authors coyly own up: 'beliefs based on personal experience, in contrast to those acquired through information from outside sources such as television programs, are likely to be highly resistant to change' (Sutton et al., 1999, p. 79).

Critical health psychology

Leaving aside the question why such a clearly flawed piece of research gets published in such a highly prestigious journal, it is clear from papers like this that there are, still, real problems with the cognitive algebra models. Critical psychologists argue that the reason why these models have such trouble predicting 'health behaviour' is because health behaviour is a fabrication – a made-up phenomenon. Health behaviours are theorised and written about as if they are 'easily identifiable, unitary entities whose meaning does not change across the diverse contexts and settings within which they may be carried out' (Mielewczyk & Willig, 2007, p. 824). But they are not: take 'condom use' as studied by Sutton and his colleagues – decoupled from time and place, salience and meaning. Are we really to believe that it is a single kind of action with a single kind of cause? That whenever and wherever it occurs, the same set of influences are in play?

Qualitative research in this field has come up with a whole host of reasons for not using condoms. They can be 'a moment killer' (Williamson et al., 2009):

> And then all the magazines that tell you they can become a fun part of fore-play. Lies! Lies! They're the worst things. I've been having sex since I was 14 years old and I still can't put one on somebody properly. ('Kathy' quoted in Williamson et al., 2009, p. 564)

Not using condoms in a committed relationship can scream 'I don't trust you':

> Because it's a very tricky thing, there's pride and there's suspicion and there's jealousy and there's all these terrible things, all mixed up together, and these are the things that kill a marriage, and therefore it's very delicate ground that you are treading on. (Cited in Willig, 1995, p. 81)

Just these two examples say it all, for me at least. There are plenty more. Mielewczyk and Willig (2007) sum it up very elegantly when they propose that,

> instead of attempting to predict the occurrence of de-contextualized, behav-iourally defined health-related actions (such as 'smoking behaviour' or 'safe sex'), it may be more productive and more meaningful to focus on the wider social practices of which such actions form a part. ... [T]his would mean recog-nizing that health-related behaviours acquire their meaning and significance on the basis of their relationship to the particular social practice of which they form a part and that, therefore, what appears to be the 'same' behaviour can take on radically different meanings within different contexts. (p. 829)

They then go on to argue for research methods and forms of analysis that provide an entrée into the social practices within which actions like smoking a cigarette or using a condom are performed.

Nice work

NICE is the British government-sponsored body responsible for providing national guidance on the promotion of good health and the prevention and treatment of ill health. In 2006 I was invited to become a member of a NICE 'Behaviour Change' Programme Development Group (PDG) with a remit to

LIVERPOOL JOHN MOORES UNIVERSITY
LEARNING SERVICES

prepare recommendations on '[t]he most appropriate means of generic and specific interventions to support attitude and behaviour change at population and community levels' (NICE 2007a).

At the time of writing, NICE provided guidance in three areas. It is best known (some would say notorious) in Health Technologies where NICE makes recommendations on which drugs and other treatments are sufficiently cost-effective to be provided within the NHS. The effectiveness of treatments (based on systematic review evidence) is balanced against their costs. The second area is Clinical Practice. Our work on behaviour change was in the third, Public Health. We had a broad remit, given that Public Health concerns the health of the overall population, encompassing services ranging from sanitation to transport, housing to leisure and exercise.

On its website (http://guidance.nice.org.uk/PH6) NICE states that its guidance 'is developed using the expertise of the NHS and the wider healthcare community including NHS staff, healthcare professionals, patients and carers, industry and the academic world'. The full process is described in detail on that site, and is highly transparent – you can download the documents involved in the process including PDG members, minutes of meetings and copies of all the consultations and reports involved in the process.

The work of the Programme Development Group

The PDG is at the centre of the process. Our job was to systematically review evidence provided to us, develop recommendations on the basis of this evidence, and contribute to making plans for dissemination. Chaired by Professor Mildred Blaxter, a highly respected sociologist with particular knowledge of (and powerful concern about) health inequalities, the PDG was made up of a mix of three lay representatives of patient groups and academics, with expertise in epidemiology, health economics, psychiatry, medicine, public health, public policy and social research. There were four health psychologists (one co-opted) with specific expertise in behaviour change – two committed to mainstream, social cognition approaches, one with his own model and me, a long-standing antagonist and critical health psychologist. We were actively managed by a number of NICE staff who themselves had academic expertise in the field, led by the Director of the project, Professor Mike Kelly, also a sociologist, with a special interest in health inequalities (see, for example, Killoran et al., 2006).

After an initial training session on how to systematically judge evidence, subsequent meetings were devoted to discussing reports commissioned by NICE on evidence about behaviour change. We started with the standard NICE format, meta-analytical reviews using two key criteria: relevance to the UK situation and standard evaluation of research designs (usually called the 'gold standard', starting with the highest score for fully randomised, double-blind controlled trials). The meta-analytic reviews considered were on: interventions in general; road safety and environment-related behaviour; resilience, coping and salutogenic behaviour; the influence of social and cultural contexts; and the main social cognition models (Health Belief, Reasoned Action, Planned Behaviour and Trans Theoretical/Stages of Change). There was a vast amount of paper, and a series of lengthy meetings.

Considering this evidence proved extremely frustrating for the group. We soon found that there was very little publicly available quantitative data on behaviour change at population and community levels. Even with the extensive research on interventions at individual level, there proved to be very little conclusive evidence. The majority of studies reviewed were poorly designed and conducted, and often used unsophisticated variables (e.g. mere presence or absence of the intervention, but with no data on quality). Demographic data were limited, with almost none on health inequalities. Most studies only measured indirect outcomes (e.g. compliance with the programme). Most were very short term (over a matter of months at most). The group expressed concern about the restricted analytical approach, which explicitly excluded qualitative research.

The recommendations

Yet we did, in the end, produce the recommendations required of us. There was, however, no big fanfare when they were launched – there was little in them that appeared at all contentious. Indeed, on first sight, they look banal, especially in their short form (NICE, 2007b). In summary, they advise planning interventions and programmes properly and in partnership with local communities, ensuring that practitioners are competent and trained and evaluating what gets done – nothing new, simply already well-established, standard 'good practice'.

However, a closer look at the full version (NICE 2007a) offers some oddities and surprises. The glut of social cognition research hardly gets a mention. It is hugely overshadowed by other, much stronger, messages about the importance of the 'socioeconomic and cultural context' in which behaviour change takes place, and, especially, the need to 'identify and attempt to remove social, financial and environmental barriers that prevent people from making positive changes' (NICE, 2007b, p. 4). This emphasis is hardly surprising given the membership of the Development Group and the people influential in the Public Health section of NICE. But it also reflects something more. These documents show a real sense of unease about the conceptual and theoretical underpinnings of mainstream psychology's highly individualising theories.

The recommendations make some acknowledgement that 'a number of concepts drawn from the psychological literature are helpful in planning work on behaviour change with individuals' (NICE, 2007a, p. 10). These are set out in Principle 4 (NICE, 2007b, p. 5). However, broadly the verdict was that 'the evidence of psychological models was found to be limited', and this was evident in the recommendations.

The short version stresses the need to 'specify the theoretical link between the intervention or programme and its outcome', insists that it is essential to 'clearly justify any models' used in planning interventions and says they must be 'based on best available evidence'. This message is underlined by the specific recommendation to 'disinvest... if there is good evidence to suggest they are not effective'.

To get to grips with why there is such unease, it is worth quoting in full some of what the full report has to say about social cognition models:

> The psychological literature is extensive and provides a number of general models of health behaviour and behaviour change. However the research literature evaluating the relevance and use of these models is inconsistent. For example, it includes multiple adaptations of particular models, poor study designs and studies that fail to take account of confounding factors. Having considered some of the more commonly used models of health behaviour, the PDG concluded that the evidence did not support any particular model (although some have more evidence of effectiveness than others). (NICE, 2007a, p. 9)

There is not space here to examine in detail what the recommendations have to say about the individual models considered, but it is hardly flattering. But there was another reason for the reticence in the recommendations. While the PDG recognised, for instance, that there was good evidence that advice from healthcare staff can make a real difference, they had considerable anxiety about the ethics of endorsing actions that could well *increase* inequity in health outcomes.

A change of strategy

How to 'narrow the health inequalities gap' (NICE, 2007a, p. 44) was, throughout our deliberations, a central preoccupation. Examining the commissioned 'gold standard' evidence reviews gave us no insight, and proved frustrating for many members of the group and the NICE staff who worked with us. Consequently, fairly late in the day and in the face of close and rigid deadlines, we nonetheless decided to free ourselves from NICE's standard procedures and gave ourselves permission to look elsewhere. We explored work directly related to the question of whether interventions increase health inequalities. We dipped into a variety of qualitative studies. And we brought in some sociological theory – for example, Bourdieu's ideas of *habitus*, various kinds of *capital* (social, cultural) and the diversification of *social fields* (Bourdieu, 1993).

The PDG took a turn that parallels that taken by critical health psychology, away from a preoccupation with social cognition and quantitative research, and into theorisation and research into the way health-related practices (like eating and driving) operate within the overall practices of everyday life.

> Instead of producing persuasive messages in order to change participants' beliefs about health behaviours and their consequences, we would need to design interventions which assist individuals in unpacking the meanings and functions of health-related practices. (Mielewczyk & Willig, 2007, p. 829)

Mielewczyk and Willig (2007) also make the point that these practices 'are involved in the constitution of our (social and self) identities and any change in such practices is likely to have implications for our experience of ourselves as social actors and as selves' (p. 831). They illustrate this by reference to work describing how some people who loose a lot of weight do not feel 'like themselves' any more, and so find themselves in a 'no-person land' (English, 1993). Alternatively, by contrast, giving up smoking can be made easier by seeing oneself as an 'ex-smoker', a new identity where smoking was something done by an 'old self' (Willms, 1991).

So is there any hope?

Taking part in the NICE Behaviour Change PDG was both a satisfying and a frustrating experience. It was satisfying, as a critical psychologist, to have been part of a decision-making process that recommended to the NHS and other agencies, governmental and non-governmental, that produced recommendations like this one:

> Work in partnership with individuals, communities, organisations and populations to plan interventions and programmes to change health-related behaviour. The plan should:
>
> • be based on a needs assessment or knowledge of the target audience
> • take account of the circumstances in which people live, especially the socio-economic and cultural context – aim to develop – and build on – people's strengths or 'assets' (that is, their skills, talents and capacity)

- set out how the target population, community or group will be involved in the development, evaluation and implementation of the intervention or programme

(NICE, 2007b, p. 2)

To me these reflect the core principles of critical health psychology – a pursuit of social justice and a respect for diversity. Particularly this is about policy and practice in planning and delivering services that reject the 'shark infested pool' worldview, a market-driven world in which the people served by health services are no longer 'patients' but 'customers' who can 'choose'. The ethnographic philosopher, Mol (2008), provides a lucid and informative critique of this approach. As she notes,

> The nineteenth-century public health efforts that succeeded in making cities easier to survive did not take the form of pamphlets admonishing individuals to live more hygienic lives. Sewers and drains were built; the supply of food was submitted to rules of hygiene; and health inspectors were appointed. (p. 68)

Instead the NICE guidance we produced is redolent with awareness of the smug and self-interested ways in which power can be exercised in medical encounters as much as in health-care policy-making. In simple language it chides, by implication, those who stigmatise individuals and groups who fail to comply.

Back to another new government minister, Ann Milton, who, on taking office advised family doctors and nurses to tell people they are 'fat' rather than 'obese', as this would be more likely to persuade them to take responsibility for losing weight. In an interview with the BBC she said, 'If I look in the mirror and think I am obese, I think I am less worried [than] if I think I am fat'(cited by Ramesh, 2010).

Being part of the PDG was frustrating simply because we (those of us concerned about health inequalities) knew how hard it would be to change the behaviour of those with the power to change public health policy and practice. There are so many other interests at stake, and not only directly (such as professional self-interest, the market forces within and beyond the NHS, and simply that held by those more able to capitalise on what is on offer). These forces operate within the academia too, and in the media.

Telling better stories

If I were to make one optimistic suggestion, I am increasingly convinced it is this: we have to tell better stories. I have been inspired by Donna Haraway's perceptive take on the importance of story-telling within academic work as a means of changing the way people see the world: 'The story quality of the sciences ... is not some pollutant that can be leached out by better methods ... . The struggle to construct good stories is a major part of this craft' (Haraway, 1986, pp. 79–80). She wrote this as part of an argument about theorisation in science. What makes a theory popular, she says, is not about being good at explaining the data. It is about telling good stories – stories that intrigue and capture our interest, stories that 'ring true'. Tell a good story and people will take notice. But to do this you have to be a story-teller, a job only some people can do. In her own originary discipline, primatology, the study of apes and monkeys, she observed that early theories explaining primate evolution were men's stories: they were all about dominance, hierarchy, territory and winning (i.e. shark-filled-pool stories). These dominated primatology until women were no longer relegated to being lowly research assistants and allowed to become professors. Only then did stories get told about the evolutionary advantages of communally shared care, nurture and co-operation.

Perhaps she was a bit too optimistic in her analysis. The shark-filled-pool story certainly seems to be widely and increasingly popular these days. It is densely woven into the audit-culture-speak that governs so much of public life today. Terms like performance-based funding, quality benchmarks, outcome measures and esteem factors have insinuated themselves, like a fungus, penetrating through the texts and praxes of the academia as well as healthcare, justice, social care and all sorts of other services and systems. While sold, imaginatively and cleverly, through stories all about choice and choosing, it would be hard to find a storyline more proficient for chipping away at principles of equity and social justice.

Here I take inspiration from Ann Game, and her exhortation to 'rewrite the texts of the culture':

> ... writing as transformation provides the opportunity to reformulate the question of social change. Reading a text is a writing practice, and in this lies the possibility of a rewriting of texts of the culture, in the now. A deconstructive strategy is a positive strategy of transformation: undoing is simultaneously an unmaking and making, a process without end. (Game, 1991, p. x)

Against my foray into today's social algebra literature proving direly 'same old, same old', reviewing recent work in critical health psychology and beyond was a joy – talk about good stories! What frustrates me now is that such work has such a tiny audience. Mainstream health psychologists ignore it, since it has no value within performance-based assessment. But more importantly, a mass media which abounds in cleverly told 'wonders of science' stories relegates 'inspiration through deconstruction' stories to the arts. Hidden away there these stories are defined as 'entertainment for the elite' rather than having anything serious to contribute to health-care policy and practice.

We have to do something about this. I included my account of how the NICE Behaviour Change recommendations were negotiated in this chapter as both a warning and as a call to action. Optimistically, it was satisfying to have contributed to telling a story about working with communities and the importance of tackling health inequalities. Pessimistically, our story got almost none of the media interest that NICE pronouncements usually achieve, and nothing compared to politicians' ill-considered sound bites. If we are going to have any real impact on policy and practice, then we must marshal our storytelling skills, and get them told in ways and in places that will attract attention. If Michael Moore can do it, so can we.

Key points

1. The poorest and most deprived individuals and communities suffer much more illness, incapacity and early death than those whose economic and social circumstances are better. Yet current public health policy in the UK increasingly locates the causes of ill-health in individuals' failure to take responsibility. If we are to tackle health inequalities, this has to change.
2. Cognitive algebra explanations of how to change the way people behave dominate mainstream health psychology, even though they are ineffective. These too focus on individual responsibility for 'behaviour change'. Change is also needed here – towards more sophisticated insights into the 'situated social practices' that constitute people's actions in relation to their health.
3. Critical health psychologists need to get better at telling good stories – ones that challenge the 'blame it on the individual' explanation of health inequality, and instead convince policy makers and the public that there are more practical, cheaper and more effective ways to improve everybody's health.

NOTE

1. It is worth noting that by the time I came to doing final corrections on this piece, NICE had become de-clawed, losing its power to specify the medications that could be prescribed in NHS treatment, on the basis that limits on their effectiveness did not justify their high costs.

REFERENCES

Ashworth, P. (1997) 'Breakthrough or bandwagon? Are interventions tailored to stage of change more effective than non-staged interventions?' *Health Education Journal*, 56, 166–74.

Bartlett, F. C. (1932) *Remembering* Cambridge: Cambridge University Press.

Bourdieu, P. (1993) *The Field of Cultural Production* New York: Columbia University Press.

Claxton, G. (1987) 'Beliefs and behaviour: why is it so hard to change?' *Nursing*, 3, 670–73.

English, C. (1993) 'Gaining and losing weight: identity transformations', *Deviant Behavior: An Interdisciplinary Journal*, 14, 227–41.

Game, A. (1991) *Undoing the Social: Towards a Deconstructive Sociology* Buckingham: Open University Press.

Haraway, D. (1986) 'Primatology Is Politics by Other Means', in R. Bleier (ed.), *Feminist Approaches to Science* New York: Pergamon Press, 77–118.

Herzog, T. A. (2005) 'When popularity outstrips the evidence: comment on West', *Addiction*, 100, 140–41.

Ingham, R. (1993) 'Old bodies in older clothes', *Health Psychology Update*, 14, 31–36.

Killoran, A., Swann, C. & Kelly, M. (eds) (2006) *Public Health Evidence: Tackling Health Inequalities* Oxford: Oxford University Press.

Lansley, Andrew, 7 July 2010, 'A new approach to public health', Speech to the UK Faculty of Public Health Conference. http://www.dh.gov.uk/en/MediaCentre/Speeches/DH_117280

McGuire, W. J. (1986) 'The viscissitudes of attitudes and other similar representational constructs in twentieth century psychology', *European Journal of Social Psychology*, 16, 89–130.

Mielewczyk, M. & Willig, C. (2007) 'Old clothes and an older look: the case for a radical makeover in health', *Theory and Psychology*, 2007, 17, 811.

Mol, A. (2008) *The Logic of Care: Health and the Problem of Patient Choice* Abingdon: Routledge.

Neisser, U. (1966) *Cognitive Psychology* New York: Appleton Century Crofts.

NICE (2007a) 'Behaviour Change at individual, community and population levels', NICE Public Health Guidance 6. http://guidance.nice.org.uk/PH6/Guidance/pdf/English

NICE (2007b) 'Behaviour Change, Quick Reference Guide', NICE Public Health Guidance 6. http://www.nice.org.uk/nicemedia/live/11868/37925/37925.pdf

Prochaska, J. O. & DiClemente, C. C. (1983) 'Stages and processes of self-change in smoking: toward an integrative model of change', *Journal of Consulting and Clinical Psychology*, 51, 390–95.

Ramesh, R. (2010) 'Food Standards Agency to be abolished by health secretary', *Guardian*, 12 July 2010.

Ramesh, R. (2010) 'Doctors should tell people they are fat, not obese, minister says', *Guardian*, 28 July 2010.

Stainton Rogers, W. (1991) *Explaining Health and Illness: An Exploration of Diversity* Hemel Hempstead: Harvester Wheatsheaf.

Sutton S. R. (2005) 'Another nail in the coffin of the transtheoretical model? A comment on West', *Addiction*, 100, 1043–45.

Sutton, S. R. (2001) 'Back to the drawing board? A review of applications of the transtheoretical model to substance use', *Addiction*, 96, 175–86.

Sutton, S., McVey, D., & Glanz, A. (1999) 'A comparative test of the Theory of Reasoned Action and the Theory of Planned Behavior in the prediction of condom use intentions in a national sample of English young people', *Health Psychology*, 18, 72–81.

Williamson, L. M., Buston, K. & Sweeting, H. (2009) 'Young women and limits to the normalisation of condom use: a qualitative study', *AIDS Care*, 21(5), 561–66.

Willig, C. (1995) '"I wouldn't have married the guy if I'd have to do that": heterosexual adults' constructions of condom use and their implications for sexual practice', *Journal of Community and Applied Social Psychology*, 5, 75–87.

Willms, D. G. (1991) 'A new stage, a new life: individual success in quitting smoking', *Social Science and Medicine*, 33, 1365–71.

Part II

Social Identities, Intersectionality and Advancing Health Psychology

Social Class, Socioeconomic Status and 'Health-Risk' Behaviours: A Critical Analysis

KATY DAY

Introduction

Inequalities in health connected to social class or 'socioeconomic status' have been well documented. Research has shown that those belonging to 'lower socioeconomic groups' tend to have poorer health profiles and are subject to higher mortality rates than those from higher up the socioeconomic scale (see Richter et al., 2006). This is said to hold true even in more prosperous populations (see, for example, Evans et al., 1994). Social and economic inequalities have dramatically increased in Britain in the past 30 years (see Dorling et al., 2007) and so unsurprisingly, health disparities connected to social class have become more pronounced (Businelle et al., 2010). It is therefore clear that class and inequality should be central to the concerns of health psychologists, despite suggestions in some quarters that class had disappeared or was no longer relevant as long ago as the 1980s (see, for example, Gorz, 1982). Yet social class has received less attention from psychologists than other social categories such as gender, race and ethnicity (Reimers, 2007). When psychologists have acknowledged and studied social class, the result has often been that the working-classes and their behaviours are problematised, thus flagging their status as 'Other' in psychological research (see Bullock & Limbert, 2009). This chapter critically reviews recent mainstream psychological literature on socioeconomic status and health-risk behaviours, the images and ideas that this literature promotes and the possible impact that this has upon our understandings of class and health. The chapter then moves on to discuss critical psychological perspectives. It also explores contemporary critical research on working-class identities, drinking and diet and considers what this research can offer existing debates. The chapter concludes by highlighting future directions for critical research on social class and health.

'Why do poor people behave so poorly?'
Cognitivism, neo liberalism and classism

Within the mainstream health literature, class tends to be understood and defined in terms of 'socioeconomic status'. Socioeconomic status (or SES for short) is determined by measures such as a person's income level (or the income level of the 'head of household' in which they live), occupation and educational attainment. Research into inequalities in health has tended to focus on those of 'lower SES' and has sought to identify the biological, behavioural and psychological factors that contribute to disparities in health. For example, being from a 'disadvantaged background' has been associated with 'negative cognitive-emotional factors' such as hostility, anxiety and depression which have all been found to have a negative impact on health (see, for example, Hatch & Dohrenwend, 2007). The predominant focus though has been on 'health-risk behaviours', defined as 'habits or practices that increase an individual's likelihood of poor health outcomes' (Goy et al., 2008, p. 314). For example, lower SES has been linked to a range of health-risk behaviours such as smoking, poor diet, physical inactivity and heavy drinking (see, for example, Wardle & Steptoe, 2003). Here, inequalities in health status are conceptualised in terms of differentials in individual health behaviours and lifestyle patterns (see, for example, Richter et al., 2006). Put more simply, working-class people, from this perspective, tend to be unhealthier because they do not take adequate care of their health and make poor choices. Indeed, a research paper by Lynch et al. (1997) is actually entitled 'Why do poor people behave poorly?'

In attempting to answer this question, health psychologists have drawn heavily on social cognitive psychology. They have identified and investigated health-related perceptions, beliefs and attitudes as determinants of health-behaviour, pointing to differences according to socioeconomic group membership (see, for example, Lee et al., 2008). For example, research into 'health locus of control' (beliefs about the factors controlling one's health) and 'self-efficacy' (the extent to which the individual feels that they have the ability to perform a given behaviour or achieve a given outcome) has found that people from lower socioeconomic groups tend to hold beliefs that result in them making poorer behavioural choices. Examples include a belief that health status is due to chance rather than being under the individual's control (see, for example, Wardle & Steptoe, 2003) and that people's health is controlled largely by environmental and social factors rather than personal and lifestyle factors (see, for example, Lemyre et al., 2006), the implication being that the latter is not a valid belief. Such beliefs, it is proposed, contribute to a sense of helplessness and discourage efforts on the part of working-class people to maintain a healthy lifestyle (see, for example, Lee et al., 2008). Unsurprisingly then, current health-risk reduction and health promotion interventions target the health behaviours of those from lower SES groups and the beliefs and attitudes believed to underpin these behaviours (Myers, 2009; van der Plight, 1996). Once again, working-class people have been characterised as problematic, with the failure of such interventions being blamed on those who have been targeted by these. For instance, one claim (excuse) has been that those from the working-classes are more resistant (presumably than middle-class people) to behaviour change (Lynch et al., 2007).

Walkerdine (2002) argues that psychology has played a special role in promoting the neo liberalist notion (which she contends is a fiction) of choice. Neo liberalist discourses (Rose, 1999) are said to be widespread in late capitalist societies and emphasise individualism, agency and the possibility of personal transformation. Similarly, Crawford (2006) argues that a good citizen is one who is widely regarded as taking personal responsibility for their health. Such discourses are detectable in the literature reviewed above wherein health inequalities are conceived of in terms of the lifestyle/behavioural choices that (working-class) people make (thus assuming that they have choices). As discussed, the reasons for, or causes of, these choices are typically located within the individual in the form of cognitions, and there is an assumption that these (along with the behaviours that they unpin) can be altered or modified (although as outlined previously, such interventions are often unsuccessful). What becomes an 'absent present' within these discourses (and the literature reviewed above) are notions of poverty, inequality and class oppression (Ringrose & Walkerdine, 2008). There is some acknowledgement in the mainstream literature that class-related stressors (for example, poverty) and discrimination may play an important role in health disparities. However, such factors have, to date, been under researched and even when acknowledged, are typically treated as 'bolt on' variables in an overall conceptual model rather than pervasive and central issues that need to be tackled in social and political ways (see Myers, 2009).

Further, such individualism/neo liberalism has important implications for notions of responsibility and blame. If we accept that people have a high degree of agency over their behaviours, have choices and can (relatively easily) change, then what follows is that (working-class) people become held as ultimately responsible and blameworthy for any harm that they suffer. A study by Ringrose and Walkerdine (2008), examining 'self-improvement' and lifestyle programmes on British television, may be illuminating here. They found that the subjects to be transformed in such programmes are usually working-class women who are depicted as insufficiently self-regulating, excessive and as making unhealthy lifestyle choices which in turn impact the health of their children. A central aim of such programmes is often to 'shame' these women into making changes/better choices, and they invite voyeuristic disgust on the part of the viewer (see Tyler, 2008 for a discussion of 'class disgust' in contemporary Britain). This disgust, I would argue, is bolstered by neo liberalism. Such discourses may be played out in health settings and in the interactions between health professionals and patients/clients. For example, a recent documentary on 'teen excess and the NHS' (screened April 2009) featured footage of young (mostly working-class) people getting drunk and being admitted to hospital as a result and interviews with middle-class health professionals such as doctors. The young people in the programme were depicted as a significant drain on public resources. Indeed, Businelle et al. (2010) describes the primary motivation behind interventions aimed at reducing health-risk behaviours as 'to ultimately reduce the burden of [smoking-related] disease' (p. 262), the implication being that the 'burden' refers, at least in part, to the financial burden on the 'public-purse'. In addition, the often-repeated argument presented by the health professionals interviewed in the programme was that individuals who engage by *choice* in destructive health-behaviours such as heavy drinking are not worthy (or are certainly less worthy) of NHS treatment than 'others' (for example, the elderly). Such views may result in 'class-biased' health-care delivery which in turn can contribute to and bolster long-lasting health inequalities (Poulton et al., 2002).

Before moving on, I would like to summarise the dominant images and messages that can be gleaned from contemporary neo liberalist discourse on class and health, including that noticeable within the mainstream psychological literature and British media. Firstly, there is a widespread and uncritically accepted notion that the working-classes characteristically engage in health-risk behaviours. It is perhaps important to point out here that there is mixed empirical evidence surrounding SES and some types of health-risk behaviour. For example, some studies have suggested that those from lower socioeconomic groups (particularly young people) are sometimes *less* likely to engage in health-risk behaviours such as problem-drinking (see Richter et al., 2006; Kuntsche et al., 2004), possibly due to a lack of financial resources to support this. Secondly, (working-class) people are conceptualised as having choices and all too often as making the wrong ones with regards to their behaviours and how they live their lives. The causes for poor health behaviours/choices are seen as residing mostly within the individual and therefore modifying these 'internal' factors has been the central aim of interventions. Thirdly, those who engage in health-risk behaviours (and the person who does so is usually portrayed or imagined as working-class) are regarded as a drain on public resources. This, along with notions of individualism and agency, bolsters classism or what Tyler (2008) describes as 'class disgust'. Mainstream psychology has played a pivotal role in promoting the images and discourses described above. This is not to suggest that mainstream health psychologists have deliberately set out to blame vulnerable people and place sole responsibility for health onto individuals (see Lee et al., 2008). However, critical psychologists are concerned with the outcomes or consequences of theorising, empirical claims and actions (for example, interventions) rather than the intentions of individual psychologists. It is to critical psychology that the discussion now turns.

Critical perspectives and research on social class and health: context, identity and resistance

There is not one single 'critical approach' that is readily definable and employed by everyone working in the field of critical psychology (Chamberlain & Murray, 2009). As such, it makes more sense to refer to 'critical approaches' in the plural as this takes account of the variety of methods and agendas that currently exist. However, there appear to be a number of common values, practices and discontentments that are shared by many critical psychologists. Firstly, critical psychologists largely reject the individualism inherent in mainstream psychological work. In the case of health psychology, this individualism results in a lack of acknowledgment and under-theorisation of the social and cultural aspects of health and illness (see Chamberlain & Murray, 2009). Mainstream health psychologists have variably acknowledged the roles of social environment (see, for example, Virtanen et al., 2007) and social relationships (see, for example, Sorensen et al., 2004) as mediating factors in the relationship between SES and health-risk behaviours. However, these have been treated as just that: factors or variables that can be separated from, and are often regarded as secondary to, individual cognitive processes. For example, in the study by Sorensen et al. (2004), social support provided through the individual's relationships was theorised as being important in smoking cessation primarily because it increases self-efficacy. 'Social environments' typically refer, within the mainstream literature, to the individual's immediate surroundings, such as the neighbourhood in which they live and local area characteristics such as crime rates (see, for example, Virtanen et al., 2007). The concern is with these environments as determinants of individual health behaviour in a linear fashion.

In contrast, critical psychologists regard our actions and experiences as inseparable from the surrounding social context and social relations. 'The social' therefore is not treated as an additional variable in an overall model within critical health psychology; rather there is a belief that health-related phenomena can *only* be understood meaningfully if studied within the social contexts of everyday life. For example, it is within our everyday social interactions with others that we construct and reconstruct our under-standings of health and related practices (Chamberlain & Murray, 2009), and these understandings are then 'played out' in particular contexts. For instance, critical psychological research on alcohol consumption within working-class communities has provided support for the notion of collect-ive, heavy episodic drinking (particularly at weekends) as a social 'norm' associated with 'release' from everyday demands and pressures, providing opportunities for social bonding and camaraderie and displays of 'tough-ness' (see, for example, Burns, 1980; Day, 2003; Day et al., 2003). The meanings associated with alcohol consumption here may be very different from those operating in other classed contexts, such as drinking at a dinner party or with business associates. Indeed, it has been argued that smoking and alcohol consumption should be regarded as social and cultural norms or practices rather than personal habits or individual behaviours, especially as class-related patterns of consumption vary according to time and place (see Borrell et al., 2000).

Accessing the (often localised) understandings and meanings associated with health practices has therefore been an important goal of critical health psychology. This has been achieved mainly through the use of qualitative research methods which involve listening to people's voices and stories and the meanings that various practices have for them. This is especially import-ant where marginalised groups such as the working-classes are concerned. Rarely, within the health psychological literature to date, have opportunities been offered to working-class people to communicate their experiences and identities. Rather, (as outlined previously) working-class people have been treated simply as a demographic group whose behaviours and attitudes have been measured and correlated. They have been 'spoken for' (Tyler, 2008, p. 32) rather than listened to. Listening to people's voices is essential if we are to gain richer, more contextualised understandings of the reasons why people engage in the types of health practice that they do.

Further, critical psychologists often seek to theorise beyond the local level by contextualising local meanings, practices and values within a broader soci-etal context. The social, political and economic conditions prevailing at any one time, in any given society, have an impact upon a range of health-related phenomena. For example, following on from the discussion presented above on drinking within working-class communities, scholars such as Burns (1980) and Canaan (1996) have suggested that heavy drinking and drink-related violence amongst working-class boys and men can be meaningfully understood in the context of social constructions of masculinity which allow for these as ways of validating masculine identities. Further, other, perhaps more 'socially sanctioned' means of validating masculinity, such as owning material possessions that indicate social status (for example, an expensive car) and the hard physical labour characteristic of industries traditionally associated with the working-classes (for example, the coal mining industry that has all but disappeared in the UK), are/have become blocked to these boys and men in many instances. Decreased levels of physical activity amongst the working-classes can similarly be understood in the context of post-industrial societies in which most people who are employed now work in the communications and service industries (see Ringrose & Walkerdine, 2008). This has meant that physical activity has become built into (working-class) people's everyday lives to a lesser extent and is now largely a (costly and often inconvenient) leisure pursuit (see Borrell et al., 2000). Such literature demonstrates the limitations associated with seeking to understand health-risk behaviours in decontextualised and individualistic terms.

This is not to suggest, however, that critical psychologists simply fall back on socially deterministic analyses of health and illness and regard people as the passive subjects of social conditions, dominant ideals and social/cultural norms. Rather, critical psychologists employing discursive approaches such as discourse analysis have been interested in the ways in which people interpret, negotiate and resist (as well as reproduce) dominant discourses. For example, a study by Woolhouse, Day, Rickett and Milnes (2012) examined the discourses employed by working-class girls and young women (aged 11 to 19 years) from South Yorkshire around food, eating and the body in focus group settings. One point of discussion was the social stigma attached to 'fatness' evident in the following excerpt:

Anna: also, also a lot of people think if you're bigger, then you obviously don't have a very successful job, you're a slob, you sit on your arse all day, you don't do anything for yourself

Jean: there's an image that comes with like overweight people isn't there?

Anna: a lot of people do that, you know if you saw a big fat woman walking down the street un you looked at her un you'd think, 'God look at the state of you!'

Anna: it always upsets me when people are right stereotypical about, like, 'God, she's right fat', un I'm just like

Jean: so what?
Anna: so what? So what if she's fat? So what if she's got...

The speakers demonstrate an awareness above that being overweight is often associated with the working-classes or being of 'lower socioeconomic status' ('people think that if you're bigger then you obviously don't have a very successful job, you're a slob, you sit on your arse all day'), thus demonstrating how widespread such discourses are. The participants directly question and challenge such 'stereotypical' assumptions, and one participant even describes these as 'upsetting'. Indeed, some critical researchers such as Tyler (2008) have called for work on social class that analyses the role of emotions, especially as 'class disgust' and the reactions that this provokes (as indicated here) are emotionally charged. Although only a brief example, this draws attention to the impact of dominant (classed) constructions of fatness which are evident (as previously discussed) in the mainstream literature and the media (see Pieterman, 2007 for a critical discussion of constructions of fatness). Interestingly, the 'fat person' is imagined here as a woman. This may possibly be because, as demonstrated by Ringrose and Walkerdine (2008) and discussed previously, the unhealthy/overweight subjects of ridicule in the media are usually working-class women (see also Tyler, 2008). Chamberlain and Murray (2009) argue that critical psychological work can play an important role in challenging problematic dominant constructions by publicising 'critical consciousness' such as that indicated in the above extract. This also suggests that there may be opportunities for social transformation/resistance that actively includes working-class people.

The participants in this study also talked about their failure to follow a 'healthy' diet on occasions (or as one participant put it: 'all salads an like') because they associated this with a form of vain, middle-class femininity defined (in part) by a preoccupation with appearance that they wished to distance themselves from. The image of the salad-eating 'girly girl' that they discussed (and derided) was co-constructed between the participants as 'pink, pretty and *posh*'. Once again there is evidence of resistance to normative images and discourses around femininity that are class based (see Bordo, 2003). Publicising such discursive activity can help respond to Walkerdine's (1996) call for work which challenges stereotypical images of working-class femininities as conformist and passive. This rejection of 'middle-class' practices and values can also be seen in the work of Tomsen (1997), on alcohol consumption and drink-related violence amongst working-class men. Tomsen (1997) characterises these activities as a form of 'social protest' against socially dominant, middle-class values such as restraint and respectability. Such work invites an understanding of 'health-risk' practices such a failure to follow a healthy diet and heavy, episodic drinking as socially meaningful and as bound up with the construction of working-class identities that are constructed rela-tionally (see, for example, Gough & Edwards, 1998), or 'against' other groups such as the middle-classes in an attempt to consolidate a sense of self.

Summary and future directions for critical research on class and health

This final section of the chapter shall summarise and crystallise some of the points and arguments made previously. Firstly, in critiquing mainstream approaches to disparities in health, I would like to argue for an analysis of social class in the psychological literature rather than a reliance on the more narrow definition of 'socioeconomic status'. Of course, a person's occupa-tion and income are often important indicators of their access to material resources and social power. However, class encompasses much more than this including (as illustrated) experience, identity, values and discourse. A per-son from a working-class background may become middle-class (according to SES indicators) as a result of, for example, higher education, but still iden-tify themselves as working-class due their background, life experiences and sense of disconnection with middle-class 'ways of being/living'. Examining how people position themselves within classed discourses and understanding how these intersect with discourses around gender, race, ethnicity, region-alism and sexuality (amongst others) may be more illuminating to (health) psychologists than gathering detached, surface information about socio-economic variables and how these correlate with health-behaviours. That is not to say that there is no value in knowing how frequently something occurs (see Parker, 2007), such as rates of various health-risk behaviours amongst different social groups. However, Walkerdine (1996) has called for more hol-istic and contextualised approaches to the study of class which recognise the complex interplay of the different facets of this, and this is essential if we are to develop meaningful understandings of how class relates to health. In add-ition, there is research evidence suggesting that being from a working-class background can be a disadvantage health wise regardless of socioeconomic status in adulthood and so 'upwards-mobility' does not always mitigate or reverse the adverse effects of 'low childhood socioeconomic status' (Poulton et al., 2002). Again, this points to the problems associated with using current socioeconomic status as a marker of class and the complexity of the relation-ship between class and health.

Further, there is a need for more critical work on class and health because, as outlined at the start of the chapter, class has been neglected in relation to other social categories. Some of this work also needs to focus on class groups other than the working-classes. There is evidence that people from across social classes suffer health wise in unequal capitalist societies that emphasise and value individualism and destructive competition (albeit not to equal degrees). For example, Subramanian and Kawachi (2006) found negative health profiles for both 'advantaged' and 'disadvantaged' individuals in the United States. This has been explained as one result of the stresses and strains associated with living in a 'winner-takes-all economy' and the negative impact that this has on social cohesion (Belle & Doucet, 2003). It would therefore be misleading to imply that social inequality and the class system *only* impact negatively on the health of 'poorer' people. In addition, some problematic health practices such as those associated with 'eating disorders' (for example, self-starvation), have been depicted in the literature as 'middle/upper-class' ones (Thompson, 1994). Thompson argues that this literature belittles the experiences of white middle-class women by depicting 'eating disorders' as self-inflicted and as resulting from privilege, wealth, vanity and self-absorption. Such discourses can be detected in the talk of the working-class girls and women who took part in the Woolhouse et al. (2012) study cited previously. As discussed, the social construction of class and class identities occurs relationally. For example, Thompson (1994) further agues that this depiction of 'eating disorders' as a white, middle-class women's syndrome underpinned by appearance and bodyweight concerns is linked to oppositional constructions of working-class women as unconcerned with appearance and insufficiently self-regulating and therefore not susceptible to eating disorders. As such, examining representations of the middle-classes and their health practices can also reveal how the working-classes are positioned/represented and the possible implications of this (although, as outlined above, this is not the only reason for conducting research with middle-class participants or focusing on constructions of middle-class health practices). Therefore although this chapter has focused largely on research involving working-class participants, I would argue that critical health psychology should widen its focus to include other, less disadvantaged class groups. This will help to respond to a 'call for action' on the part of some scholars whereby critical health psychologists act as agents of change in challenging (and not simply describing) social inequalities. By identifying the class system as widely problematic, as a problem for society more generally (and not just as a problem for those who 'lose out' in this system), we may make progress in taking our political agendas to a wider audience, including those (for example, policy and decision makers) who may be instrumental in helping to invoke social change.

Key points

1. Research indicates that those from 'lower socioeconomic groups' have poorer health outcomes than those of higher socioeconomic status (SES).

2. Understandings of social class within mainstream health literature are generally in terms of SES, with much research focusing on 'health-risk behaviours' associated with SES. Those of lower SES are often conceptualised as making poor health choices and characterised as engaging in health-risk behaviours.

3. Health psychologists have predominantly used social cognition to explain health 'choices', specifically highlighting the role of attitudes and beliefs. However, what is missing in much of this literature and broader views about working-class lifestyles and behaviour are notions of poverty, inequality and class oppression, with notions of individual responsibility and blame predominating.

4. A critical health psychology approach emphasises that class is much more than SES, encompassing experience, identity, values and discourse. It also highlights how class intersects with other social identities.

5. This chapter also highlights the need to focus on class groups other than the working-class as particular health implications have been identified for other groups. This broader focus will help to identify endemic problems with the class system which can be brought to the attention of those who have the power to instigate social change.

REFERENCES

Belle, D. & Doucet, J. (2003) 'Poverty, inequality and discrimination as sources of depression amongst US women', *Psychology of Women Quarterly*, 27, 101–13.

Bordo, S. (2003) *Unbearable Weight*, 10th Anniversary edn, Berkeley: University of California Press.

Borrell, C., Domínguez-Berjón, F., Pasarín, M. I., Ferrando, J., Rohlfs, I. & Nebot, M. (2000) 'Social inequalities in health related behaviours in Barcelona', *Journal of Epidemiology and Community Health*, 54, 24–30.

Bullock, H. E. & Limbert, W. M. (2009) Class, in D. Fox, I. Prilleltensky & S. Austin (eds) *Critical Psychology: An Introduction*, 2nd edn, London: Sage.

Burns, T. F. (1980) 'Getting rowdy with the boys', *Journal of Drug Issues*, 10, 273–286.

Businelle, M. S., Kendzor, D. E., Reitzel, L. R., Costello, T. J., Cofta-Woerpel, L., Li, Y., Mzas, C. A., Vidrine, J. I., Cinciripini, P. M., Greisinger, A. J. & Wetter, D. W. (2010) 'Mechanisms linking socioeconomic status to smoking cessation: a structural equation modelling approach', *Health Psychology*, 29(3), 262–273.

Canaan, J. (1996) '"One thing leads to another": drinking, fighting and working-class masculinities', in M. Mac an Ghaill (ed.) *Understanding Masculinities: Social Relations and Cultural Arenas*, Milton Keynes: Open University Press.

Chamberlain, K. & Murray, M. (2009) 'Critical health psychology', in D. Fox, I. Prilleltensky & S. Austin (eds) *Critical Psychology: An Introduction*, 2nd edn, London: Sage.

Crawford, R. (2006) 'Health as a meaningful social practice', *Health: An Interdisciplinary Journal for the Social Study of Health, Illness and Medicine*, 10, 401–20.

Day, K. (2003) *Women and Alcohol: Contemporary Discourses Around Femininity and Leisure in the UK*, unpublished doctorate thesis, Sheffield Hallam University.

Day, K., Gough, B. & McFadden, M. (2003) 'Women who drink and fight: a discourse analysis of working class women's talk', *Feminism and Psychology*, 13(2): 141–58.

Dorling, D., Rigby, J., Wheeler, B., Ballas, D., Thomas, B., Fahmy, E., Gordon, D. & Lupton, R. (2007) *Poverty, Wealth and Place in Britain, 1968 to 2005*, Joseph Rowntree Foundation, http://www.jrf.org.uk/publications/poverty-and-wealth-across-britain-1968–2005, date accessed 27 July 2010.

Evans R. G., Barer, M. L. & Marmor, T. R. (1994) *Why Are Some People Healthy and Others Not?* New York: Aldine de Gruyter.

Gorz, A. (1982) *Farewell to the Working Class*, London: Pluto.

Gough, B. & Edwards, G. (1998) 'The beer talking: four lads, a carry out and the reproduction of masculinities', *Sociological Review*, 46(3): 419–35.

Goy, J., Dodds, L., Rosenberg, M. W. & King, W. D. (2008) 'Health-risk behaviours: Examining social disparities in the occurrence of stillbirth', *Paediatric and Perinatal Epidemiology*, 22, 314–20.

Hatch, S. L. & Dohrenwend, B. P. (2007) 'Distribution of traumatic and other stressful life events race/ethnicity, gender, SES and age: a review of the research', *American Journal of Community Psychology*, 40, 313–32.

Kuntsche, E., Rehm, J. & Gmel, G. (2004) 'Characteristics of binge-drinkers in Europe', *Social Science and Medicine*, 59, 113–27.

Lee, J. E. C., Lemyre, L., Legault, L., Turner, M. C. & Krewski, D. (2008) 'Factor analytic investigation of Canadians' population health risk perceptions: the role of locus of control over health risks', *International Journal of Global Environmental Issues*, 8(1/2), 112–31.

Lemyre, L., Lee, J. E. C., Mercier, P., Bouchard, L. & Krewski, D. (2006) 'The structure of Canadians' health risk perceptions: environmental, therapeutic, and social health risk perceptions', *Health, Risk and Society*, 8, 185–95.

Lynch, J. W., Kaplan, G. A. & Salonen, J. T. (1997) 'Why do poor people behave poorly? Variation in adult health behaviours and psychosocial characteristics by stages of the socioeconomic life course', *Social Science and Medicine*, 44, 809–19.

Myers, H. F. (2009) 'Ethnicity- and socio-economic status-related stresses in context: an integrative review and conceptual model', *Journal of Behavioural Medicine*, 32, 9–19.

Parker, I. (2007) 'Critical psychology: what it is and what it is not', *Social and Personality Psychology Compass*, 1(1), 1–15.

Pieterman, R. (2007) 'The social construction of fat: care and control in the public concern for healthy behaviour', *Sociology Compass*, 1/1, 309–21.

Poulton, R., Caspi, A., Milnes, B. J., Thompson, W. M., Taylor, A., Sears, M. R. & Moffitt, T. E. (2002) 'Association between children's experience of socioeconomic disadvantage and adult health: a life-course study', *The Lancet*, 360, 1640–45.

Reimers, F. A. (2007) *Putting It All Together: A Content Analysis and Methodological Review of Intersections of Class, Race and Gender in the Counselling Literature*, doctoral dissertation, Texas Woman's University. *Dissertation Abstracts*, 68, 1B.

Richter, M., Leppin, A. & Gabhainn, S. N. (2006) 'The relationship between parental socio-economic status and episodes of drunkenness among adolescents: findings from a cross-national survey', *BMC Public Health*, 6, 289–98.

Ringrose, J. & Walkerdine, V. (2008) 'Regulating the abject: the TV make-over as a site of neo-liberal reinvention towards bourgeois femininity', *Feminist Media Studies*, 8(3), 227–46.

Rose, N. (1999) *Powers of Freedom: Reframing Political Thought*, Cambridge: Cambridge University Press.

Sorensen, G., Barbeau, E., Hunt, M. K. & Emmons, K. (2004) 'Reducing social disparities in tobacco use: a social-contextual model for reducing tobacco use among blue-collar workers', *American Journal of Public Health*, 94(2), 230–39.

Subramanian, S. V. & Kawacki, I. (2006) 'Whose health is affected by income inequality? A multilevel interaction analysis of contemporaneous and lagged effects of state income inequality on individual self-rated health in the United States', *Health and Place*, 12, 141–56.

Thompson, B. W. (1994) *A Hunger So Wide and So Deep*, Minneapolis: University of Minnesota Press.

Tomsen, S. (1997) 'A top night: social protest, masculinity and the culture of drinking violence', *British Journal of Criminology*, 37(1), 90–102.

Tyler, I. (2008) '"Chav Mum Chav Scum": class disgust in contemporary Britain', *Feminist Media Studies*, 8(1), 17–34.

van der Plight, J. (1996) 'Risk perception and self-protective behaviour', *European Psychologist*, 1, 34–43.

Virtanen, M., Kivimäki, M., Kouvonen, A., Elovainio, M., Linna, A., Oksanen, T. & Vahtera, J. (2007) 'Average household income, crime, and smoking behaviour in a local area: the Finnish 10-town study', *Social Science and Medicine*, 64, 1904–13.

Walkerdine, V. (1996) 'Subjectivity and social class: new directions for feminist psychology', *Feminism and Psychology*, 6, 355–60.

Walkerdine, V. (2002) 'Psychology, post modernity and neo-liberalism, keynote address to the Politics of Psychological Knowledge Conference', Free University of Berlin.

Wardle, J. & Steptoe, A. (2003) 'Socioeconomic differences in attitudes and beliefs about health lifestyles', *Journal of Epidemiology and Community Health*, 57, 440–43.

Woolhouse, M., Day, K., Rickett, B. & Milnes, K. (2012) '"Cos girls aren't supposed to eat like pigs are they?" ' Young women negotiating gendered discursive constructions of food and eating', *Journal of Health Psychology*, 17, 46–56.

CHAPTER 5

Men's Health: Thinking about Gender Mainstreaming and Gender Sensitive Services

CHRISTINE HORROCKS

Introduction

I have for a number of years collaborated with the National Health Service (NHS) in the UK assisting in supporting the evaluation of community-based health interventions. Like others working on and around community development projects I was not too surprised when an evaluation study I was working on revealed that those 'choosing' to participate were predominately women. Yet why was I unsurprised, and furthermore, are there strategies that can be employed to bring about change? Possibly low levels of male participation were linked to differences in employment patterns but in an area of high unemployment, still men were noticeably uninvolved (Horrocks et al., 2008). Given that the aim of community development participation is to enhance social justice, equity, empowerment and sustainability (Uphoff, 1991) ignoring men's non-participation seems incongruous. In relation to the evaluation, a consideration of the process of engagement and the projects that were in existence gave some indication of why men were not participating. Many of the projects had a distinctly female focus, for example, support groups for breast-feeding and 'mother and baby'[1] groups while others were at times of the day that excluded those in full-time work. Nonetheless, on projects that were more generic (healthy walks, ill-health support groups) and accessible, men were still observed to be a distinct minority in terms of participation. This observation, of men's failure to access health interventions, links into the themes of this chapter where I explore health inequalities and growing concerns regarding men's health. Approaches that have been adopted to address gender inequalities in health will be considered, placing these in a frame of reference that explores men's health, social action and change.

Health inequalities and the 'crisis' in men's health

In developed countries there is now mounting interest in men's health with Gough and Robertson (2010) making the point that this attention is long overdue. This viewpoint is based upon seemingly overwhelming evidence regarding men's health inequalities with statistics revealing a gap in mortality between men and women (White & Cash, 2004). In the UK the average life expectancy for men is approximately four years less than for women (Office for National Statistics, 2006) with suicide rates three times higher for men (Office for National Statistics, 2003). Indeed, when compared with women, men are twice as likely to develop and die from the ten most common cancers affecting both sexes (Men's Health Forum, 2004). Figures also show that men are significantly more likely than women to be overweight or obese (National Centre for Social Research, 2004). Thus, men are consequently much more likely than women to suffer from the co-morbidities of overweight and obesity including cancer, coronary heart disease and metabolic syndrome (Villegas et al., 2003). Also, it is consistently reported that men are much less likely to visit their GP than women (see for example White & Johnson, 2000; Galdas et al., 2004) and are more likely than women to drink alcohol, smoke tobacco and eat a less healthy diet (National Centre for Social Research, 2004). Peter Baker, the then chief executive of the Men's Health Forum (MHF), argues for a 'gender sensitive' approach to policy development and service provision with local health planning aiming to address men's health issues as part of a consideration of gender as a health determinant (Men's Health Forum, 2006).

The growth of the women's health movement in the 1960s and 1970s brought about systematic and interdisciplinary studies of gender and health. Most of this early work revolved almost exclusively around women (see Sabo, 2005), although, the rethinking of gender that was initiated by feminist scholars and activists stirred an exploration of men's health and masculinities. What's more it is claimed that, despite evidence of men's health inequalities, policy makers and health professionals have in the past paid very little attention to men's health risks and unequal outcomes (Courtenay, 1998). This duality of evidence and inaction has led to claims that there is a men's health 'crisis' that needs to be addressed, with men being particularly vulnerable to a range of health problems that need to be tackled. However, the notion of 'crisis' is not new with previous claims around masculinity and crisis linked to disruptions in the traditional system of gender relations, with men being problematically positioned within a changed social context. This 'crisis' assumes that men are confused and insecure because of a combination of widespread disapproval of traditional displays of masculinity and feminism's successful assault on male privilege (see for example Horrocks, 1994; Clare, 2000). Blaming feminism for this crisis is seen to be part of backlash politics which sees feminism as a monolithic form with no acknowledgement of 'feminisms'' diversity of interests and theoretical positions (Pease, 2006). Similarly, suggesting an all encompassing, somewhat universally overburdened and assaulted form of masculinity further creates unhelpful binary positions which fail to engage with, and acknowledge, socio-economic, socio-cultural and relational health determinants.

Gaining a critical understanding regarding the disparity in morbidity and life expectancy between men and women is a highly complex task. It is commonly known that many diseases affect men and women disproportionately. Biomedical theory and practice usually focuses on sex differences in reproductive systems with women presumed to be at a disadvantage due to the health risks associated with pregnancy and childbirth. However, despite what might be seen as a biological advantage, there are very few societies in which men, as an inclusive category, have a longer life expectancy than women. Perhaps, surprisingly, given the plethora of evidence showing men's health inequalities, Schofield (2000) maintains that there is considerable confusion surrounding understandings of men's health. The emergence of men's health as a theme of public concern is based upon what she refers to as a *margins of difference* understanding whereby men's health disadvantage is assumed based upon oversimplified interpretations of statistically significant differentials in men's and women's health outcomes. Here, using *sex* as the biological variable, the focus is on the margin of difference between group averages or rates. It is fairly obvious to appreciate that relatively small differences among minority populations of the larger grouping category (sex) may produce significant results. The implication of this observation is that *all* men do not experience health disadvantage but rather socioeconomic factors, lifestyle, ethnicity and other social and cultural factors intersect and have a determining influence on men's, and indeed on women's health.

Lifestyle and men's health

Lifestyle is a frequently used term that, in a broad sense, refers to the ways in which individual men and women live their lives and this includes engaging in specific behaviours. Lifestyle is frequently linked to individual health with health promotion, preventative medicine and health research targeting certain behaviours (smoking, over eating, drinking excessively) aiming to bring about individual behaviour change. At this individual level men's behaviours are attributed as 'lifestyle choices' whereby activities that may have adverse detrimental consequences for men's health are based upon decisions *they* have made. Thus men are unequivocally seen as responsible for their behaviour and any ensuing impact on their health and well-being as seen in the popular media. For example, Macrae (2010), writing in the Daily Mail Online, says, 'Unhealthy lifestyles and a "stiff upper lip" make men up to 70 per cent more likely to die from cancer than women, doctors have warned.' Similarly, in the *Independent*, it is men's reluctance around accessing healthcare that is problematised; hence it is claimed that 'men are generally more reluctant than women to seek the advice of their GP and they are more likely to engage in activity which puts them at a higher risk of having a catastrophic health event – including drinking alcohol to excess, smoking and maintaining a poor diet' (Cavaglieri & Knight, 2009). Quite startlingly in this article, men are later characterised as 'laggards', and thus the message is unmistakably one that positions men as choosing to behave in specific ways that can have detrimental effects on health, or possibly even worse, being too idle to take proactive steps to engage in health promoting behaviours. Hence, using this popular view of men's responsibility for their health, with reference to the community development health interventions referred to earlier, men were *choosing* not to participate in activities that may have benefitted their health and well-being.

With regard to men's unhealthy lifestyles and behaviours, many commentators suggest that 'hegemonic masculinity' has a part to play. The concept of 'hegemonic masculinity' provides a relational and socially constructed concept of men, masculinities and lifestyle. As Gough (2010, p. 125) explains hegemonic masculinities refers to, 'gender ideals which predominate in a given cultural context...which specify hierarchical relations between men, and between men and women'. This draws on notions of 'doing gender' whereby gender is not viewed as a set of traits residing within individuals, but something people do in their social interactions. As such, sex as a category, and its meanings, are given concrete expressions through social relationships and the historical context, with socially organised power relations structuring interactions. Masculinity and femininity are understood as fluid, relational and situated constructs. However, hegemonic masculinity is argued to be the dominant form of masculinity, constructed in relation to more subordinate and marginal masculinities such as those that surround homosexual and non-white men (Connell, 1995; Whitehead & Barrett, 2010). Unsurprisingly, heterosexuality is a fundamental signifier of hegemonic masculinity and, when refined, we discover that authority, control, independence, competitiveness, individualism and aggressiveness are also emphasised practices (Messerschmidt, 1993). This is not to suggest that there is no variation; men are social actors and thus they construct varieties of masculinities through a range of practices. Goodey (1997) also suggests it is useful to think of experience across the life course, explaining that the demands of hegemonic masculinity are diverse and ever changing, needing to be contextualised in relation to class, race, age, sexuality and any number of other intersecting variables. However, it is still undeniable that hegemonic masculinity shapes a sense of reality for most men with speech, dress, activities, relationships and behaviours conforming to particular social signs of masculinity that are associated with, while not necessarily always conforming to, this dominant form.

Hitherto, rather than being conceptualised as an individual choice, with men positioned as morally responsible, or indeed irresponsible in relation to their health, this theoretical position recognises gender as a situated social and interactional accomplishment. If we view gender as an accomplishment, and thus situated conduct, our attention shifts from individualised accounts to a concentration on interactional and institutional practices. Hence, gendered forms of behaviour, or to use the more specifically moralising term, 'lifestyles', are concrete expressions of the precise social relations and contexts in which they are embedded. Rather than men choosing certain behaviours they are participating and coordinating their activities to do gender in ways that recognise their 'accountability'. West and Zimmerman (1987), when offering a detailed analysis of doing gender, discuss the importance of social frameworks whereby we locate activities relative to others comparing like with unlike. Consequently, our actions are 'often designed with an eye to their accountability, that is how they might look and how they might be characterized' (p. 136). Drawing on Garfinkel's (1967) work, they highlight the 'omnirelevance' of sexual status showing how virtually any activity can be assessed as to its womanly or manly nature. There are normative expectations for doing gender, and in many respects this is unavoidable, arguably sustaining essentialist accounts of differences between men and women. Enactments that might resist normative, hegemonic forms of masculinity require an acknowledgement of their accountability and an understanding of how such actions will be interpreted and remarked upon in the social contexts of men's lives. For example, if most men hide or mask feelings of depression then identifying as a man experiencing depression is seen as non-normative because it is not frequently observed. Emslie et al. (2006, p.2249) tell of men's depression journeys as involving the potential for, 'multiple insults to their sense of masculinity' with some men describing being labelled as 'weak'. This said, other men in Emslie et al's study interestingly drew upon hegemonic masculinity to rebuild their own masculinity, conceptualising their depression as a heroic struggle that made them stronger. This speaks to the power of this idealised form of masculinity and potential opportunities to resist and re-enact constructions of masculinity.

Gender mainstreaming and developing gender sensitive services

Over recent years there has been a move towards 'gender mainstreaming' which is a globally accepted strategy for promoting gender equality. Mainstreaming involves ensuring that gender perspectives, and attention to the goal of gender equality, are central to all activities including health policy development, research, advocacy/dialogue, legislation, resource allocation, and planning, implementation and monitoring of programmes and projects (The United Nations Economic and Social Council, 1997). Mainstreaming includes gender-specific activities and affirmative action, whenever women or men are in a particularly disadvantageous position. Interestingly, Wilkins, Payne, Granville and Branney (2008) make the following observation:

> Where biological explanations are inadequate, health planners and policy makers have to come to realise that differences in outcome between men and woman are often an indicator that health services are varying in effectiveness between the sexes. (p. 8)

When using effectiveness as the defining feature of their position, they refer to the usage of health services, recognising that this is not just about people 'choosing' to engage but also relates to the extent to which services meet the needs of both men and women. The authors go on to say that a key principle of their work is that once problems with service delivery and service use are acknowledged it can be seen that the differential impact on the health status of men and women is an inequality stemming from decisions made by health policy-makers and directly related to the planning and organisation of health services. Given explanations for men's health outcomes rooted in particular forms of masculinity and lifestyle, this might seem to be a somewhat simplistic or unsustainable claim. However, if we take on board the ideology of gender mainstreaming, justifiable affirmative action and thus the responsibility of health-care policy and practice to promote health equality then it becomes clear that offering gender-sensitive services would involve working towards tackling harmful forms of masculinity and unhealthy lifestyles.

Consequently, Payne (2009) stresses that the gender gap in health might be addressed by tackling the differences between men and women in their use of preventative health care, their health behaviours and their access to health-care and treatment. She outlines a range of strategies that have been used to address the differential needs of men and women: *regulatory*, including legislation designed to counter discrimination; *organisational*, including gender mainstreaming and gender-related budgeting; and *informational*, whereby gender-sensitive indicators are developed to measure progress. This systems-based approach resonates with the Equality Act 2006 which imposes a 'duty' on all public agencies, including the NHS, to take gender into account when planning and delivering services. However, as already touched upon, inequality is a straightforward measure of difference that does not necessarily reflect a situation that needs to be, or is capable of, being changed. For example, men and women's inequalities when accessing certain types of health screening actually reflect biological differences rather than any form of injustice. Hence, when taking gender into account, the focus is on 'equity' whereby fairness in the distribution of resources is based upon demonstrable need.

Doyal (2000) put the aspirations of gender equity into a very succinct practical strategy where the way forward is, 'to ensure that the two groups have equal access to those resources which they need to realize their potential for health' (p. 932). Health is essential to well-being and to overcoming other effects of social disadvantage; the Strategic Review of Health Inequalities in England Post 2010 (The Marmot Review, 2010) takes up the point that health inequalities which could be avoided by reasonable means are unfair. Nonetheless, how do these inequalities occur and to what extent are they inequities? Many might argue that men as a social group are not socially disadvantaged – indeed quite the reverse. Men as a social group disproportionately have access to a host of resources that place them at a distinct advantage both materially and more subjectively. While men may be exposed to increased risks due to the need to affirm their gender identities they also obtain major benefits. Gender equity will require the removal of privileges that are embedded in all aspects of social and economic organisation. A further challenge may be to engage at a critical level with the theoretical and practical application of gender-sensitive services. Interestingly, Robertson et al. (2008), when undertaking a systematic review of health promoting interventions targeting men, found that many of the interventions were sex specific rather than gender specific. That is to say, they aimed to prevent diseases unique to men, for example, prostate cancer. Some interventions were ostensibly targeting men by, for instance, taking services to men's places of work or other locality-based male-oriented spaces such as sports clubs. However, only three interventions were specifically designed with men in mind. Given limited evidence it would be premature to suggest that targeting health promotion interventions at men, compared with interventions aimed at men and women, would be more effective. This said, it would seem prudent, given the evidence of men's health inequalities, to think creatively about how men interact with, and why they might use or resist, health-promoting interventions and healthcare more generally.

Men's health and a dialogical exchange

Drawing on the work of Bakhtin (1986), it is possible to reflect on gender equity by situating men's health within an arena that offers some tangible accounts of action and change. Instead of viewing men's health-related behaviours within the domain of an individualising ideology of personal choice and motivation, we can begin to explore the assertion that human action is situated, relational and participatory. Bakhtin argues that the self develops through an ongoing dialogue with others and with the external world, and is 'something that arises not prior to intersubjective exchange but as a dynamic product of that ongoing exchange' (Booker & Juraga, 1995, p. 16). Thus for Bakhtin who we are is always emergent in conversation and dialogue:

> To become a self one must speak, and in speaking, one must use words that have been used by others. In using words that echo with the voices of others, one must take a position with respect to those others...Bakhtin argues that becoming a self involves positioning oneself with respect to other speakers whose words (and relational stances, characteristic acts, and viewpoints) one ventriloquates. (Wortham, 2001, p. 147)

Importantly, the idea of taking a position with respect to others relates to notions of accountability and doing gender. Men ventriloquate normative forms of masculinity, with dominant accounts of hegemonic ideals being a significant part of the dialogical exchange. Thus, the dialogical self is neither psychologically or socially located; instead what is proposed is that lived experience is characterised by linguistically mediated exchanges between persons and the social world. Therefore the stories we tell about our lives and our experiences are always a function of both self and other. Here 'authorship' is key; the self is not seen to be the product of a single voice but instead emerges as a process of interaction among 'authoritative' and 'internally persuasive' discourses (Bakhtin, 1981). Bakhtin's authoritative and internally persuasive discourses distinction relates to the extent to which the individual claims authority and responsibility for what is being said and done. Is the person merely 'reciting by heart' the prevailing authoritative discourse or are they 'retelling in one's own words' (Bakhtin, 1981, p. 341)? Therefore, as Holquist (1990, p. 18) says 'the very capacity to have consciousness in based on *otherness*' (emphasis in original). This otherness shows the importance of the relational sphere and the implicit importance of accountability when trying to understand and tackle men's health outcomes. Therefore, there exists the potential to implicate other, less obvious, actors and conditions that might enhance or inhibit the change process. Returning to messages in the popular media, the following is a quote from an edition of Men's Health magazine:

> If you're a man, then you're a gambler. Statistically, you are more likely to die before your partner simply because you are genetically more likely to do bloody stupid things. When it comes to the differences between the sexes, we're the ones more inclined to break the speed limit, fight in pubs, smoke ... all of which kill us early ... as a man, you need a bit of risk. (May 2005, p. 100)

Crawshaw (2007) explains that this is a form of direct address, in that the text is speaking explicitly to the reader as a man, presumably with an assumption that promoting normative conceptualisations of hegemonic masculinities satisfies the needs of the readership. Hence, in a magazine that purports to promote 'Men's Health', the dialogical exchange is one of 'heteronormativity' (Butler, 1999), with risk-taking presented as an all embracing lifestyle. Also embedded with this quote is the glorification of a biological imperative that is seemingly driving men to their doom. Worryingly, Sullivan, Smith and Matusov (2009) explain that an authoritative discourse is 'any discourse which can legitimately (from the participant's point of view) control and direct the discourse and the participants' action and ideas without the participants questioning this control, direction, action and ideas' (p. 330). This authoritative discourse is conditional upon establishing and maintaining an internally persuasive discourse as a voice speaking that cannot be ignored and must be attended to. Nonetheless, although widely accepted and influential, such discourses can be adapted, modified, challenged and changed.

For example, Seymour-Smith's (2010) research exploring men and women's involvement in cancer self-help groups offers a telling account of the authoritative discourse guiding men's participation and its interactional adaptation. In her discursive analysis it is the negotiation around hegemonic ideals that is interesting. The analysis identifies 'interactional trouble' with men reluctant to be accountable as the more normative attendees at self-help groups which are characterised as 'touchy-feely', 'coffee morning' encounters. Thus 'blokes don't like that sort of thing' and as Seymour-Smith surmises they find ways to negotiate and 'legitimate' their participation. Nonetheless, with research revealing that men are far less likely to attend self-help and support groups and seek emotional support (Robertson and Fitzgerald, 1992), it seems justifiable to argue that in order to tackle this inequity more needs to be done to make such groups appealing for them. The important message from her research is that gender-sensitive health promotion can work with the prevailing hegemonic authoritative discourse by appealing, and potentially conforming to these masculine ideals. The men in her study legitimated their involvement by resisting problematic identities around being in receipt of support, preferring a more action-oriented account, and changed the name of their group by removing the troubling 'self-help' aspect from their group identity. Hence, gender-sensitive health promotion can accommodate and negotiate the authoritative discourse of hegemonic masculinity. Payne (2009) acknowledges that taking account of gender differences between men and women's behaviours may mean that specific strategies are more successful. She also states that, 'men's underuse of some services...needs to be recognised and addressed' (p. 1). The danger is that 'gender sensitive' becomes synonymous with avoiding any level of confrontation or challenge to the totalising discourse of hegemonic masculinity. Thus the underlying reasons for not accessing health services, or resisting engaging in health promoting behaviour, go unaddressed. Consequently, the stereotype of men being resistant to normative, some might say feminised, forms of emotional engagement is maintained even though men may indeed be participating in this kind of expressive exchange.

Strategies involving working specifically with hegemonic masculinities to bring about men's health-promoting behaviours have been explored and critiqued by Gough (2010). Here a series of health promotion materials sponsored by Haynes, a publisher more usually associated with car manuals used for servicing and repairing automobiles, deploys the familiar format of the manual to deliver health messages to men. This format adopts the everyday stereotype of men's affiliation with cars, providing what might be viewed as a gender-sensitive approach. As Gough explains, the text in the manual, which is aimed at overweight and obese men, reproduces hegemonic ideals, with men's bodies depicted as machines with hard exteriors. Great care is apparently taken to avoid individual blame, and opportunities to question the inherent dangers in specific behaviours are not taken but rather alcohol consumption and unhealthy eating are normalised with masculine identities preserved. It is conceded that the manual includes a wealth of information that serves to educate the reader, possibly adhering to the belief that men have a very functional view of their bodies thus respond better to health-care interventions that offer facts and figures (White, 2001). On the one hand, the avoidance of an individualised, moralising and perhaps self-defeating approach to tackling men's health inequalities seems understandable and even laudable. There is sensitivity to gender as a socially embedded practice with masculinity for men needing to be respected and protected. However, is this what gender sensitive means? Still, with no challenge to the authoritative discourse of hegemonic masculinity there is ostensibly very little need for men to make any real adjustments to their existing practices. If equity, in terms of tackling socially unjust and unfair disparities, is to be an aspiration then avoiding any challenge to the authoritative discourse of hegemonic masculinities while targeting men is possibly a form of tokenism. There is the appearance of inclusive practices that are aiming to promote men's health, but this is false in that there is a continuation, and indeed shoring up of identities that are in many respects detrimental to men's health.

One of Bakhtin's central philosophical arguments is that *monologism*, or one voicedness, represents the shutting down of dialogue. A monological stance seems evident in some aspects of what might be characterised as gender-sensitive health promotion. There is no dialogical exchange in taking services to men – of course this is a sensible way to circumvent men's resistance but it does not involve any discussion around why men are not using other normative routes to services. There is a level of dialogical exchange when adapting health-care services to fit in with the monological voice of hegemonic masculinity. This adaptation and accommodation, as outlined by Seymour-Smith, arguably offers potential for change, whereas the use of highly detrimental stereotypes, while avoiding any critique described Gough (2010) suggests the shutting down of dialogue. Still, within Bakhtin's (1984) body of work, he discusses and elucidates occasions and periods when 'frank' exchanges occur. He introduces his literary theory of the 'carnivalesque' that draws on the Renaissance carnival culture which involved the 'temporary suspension of all hierarchic distinctions and barriers...and the prohibitions of usual life' (p. 15). Within this tradition of the carnivalesque people are able to mock authority with carnival, celebrating 'temporary liberation from the prevailing truth and from established order' (p. 255). The ambition of the carnival is to reveal, undermine and even obliterate the hegemony of any ideology that seeks to have the final word about the world. Thus through carnival, ideas and truths are tested and contested, and the authoritative voice is de-privileged and other voices set free, opening up opportunities for renewal and regeneration.

Sullivan, Smith and Matusov (2009), by drawing on Bakhtin's analysis of Socratic dialogue, articulate some of the dialogical exchanges that can be entered into to refute and challenge cherished beliefs such as hegemonic masculinity. Within a carnival-fuelled atmosphere of 'praise-abuse', in and among offering praise, a series of lowly comparisons and irony (reduced laughter) can be used to subvert beliefs and dominant ideologies. But there are dangers; people's beliefs are enmeshed with their identity. Therefore, care needs to be taken that the point of 'praise-abuse' is not to offend but to enable free debate. The point of this device would be to avoid the often hierarchical critique prevalent in much health promotion, replacing this with supportive criticism that strips hegemonic masculine ideology of some of its authority. It would not seem too difficult to, on the one hand, praise the stoicism that prevents some men from seeking health-care while at the same time gently mocking the outmoded image of the bygone Victorian patriarch that such stoicism conjures up. Equally, it would not seem too hard to bring low some of the worst excesses inherent in the early quote from the Men's Health magazine. Indeed, it would be insulting to imagine that most men involved in such a dialogical exchange would not see the irony in a 'Men's Health' publication that apparently subscribes to a deterministically gloomy scenario where they have a risky lifestyle and inevitably die early. There is a need to 'drag the going truths into the light of day' (Bakhtin, 1984, p. 11), to cross-examine and more openly question, not only the worst excesses of hegemonic masculinity, but also the resultant naïve stereotypes suggesting that all men are essentially disinterested in taking care of their health.

Conclusion

Gender is not only a women's issue, as without doubt men and women's differential health outcomes cannot be separated from the politics of gender. It is to the credit of men's health activists to note that inequalities in men's health outcomes are not being correlated or positioned as oppositional to women's health outcomes. Certainly, the picture is complex being impacted upon by biological, socio-cultural, economic and a host of other factors, and thus straightforward explanations and solutions are by no means readily available. Doyal (2000) identifies three positions in the health and politics of gender. The first is rooted in claims that there is a need to return to more traditional models of masculinity thus calling a halt to challenges to men's sense of identity and associated well-being. It is tempting to say that this is both undesirable and impracticable and claims that this would benefit both women and men seem somewhat incredulous. Laying aside this initial reaction it would be naïve to believe that this position would not have some support among certain groups. The second position is referred to as a 'woman-centred' approach (Sabo & Gordon, 1993) as there is a recognition that unreconstituted masculinity can be detrimental to both women's and men's health. Here the route to gender equity in health is to reconstitute masculinity and to embrace behaviours that are associated with femininity, therefore making life healthier for both men and women. Even so it is simplistic to suggest that men can easily demonstrate and perform masculinity differently, as to do so would require some transgression of socially structured gender ideals. The final position, which is a broadly feminist approach, recognises the importance of material and institutional practices. The introduction of the Equality Act 2006 and the development of local procedures are of course to be welcomed and hopefully will bring about institutional processes that offer a much clearer picture of health inequalities and intersections with gender. Also, having a gender-sensitive approach to health-care services recognises that men and women differ in terms of sex and gender and therefore appropriate interventions can be developed. However, it would seem unwise to merely avoid any active and interactive engagement with authoritative discourse of hegemonic masculinity. Evidently Bakhtin's carnivalesque does not offer a panacea in terms of change and social action.

However, it offers a more morally defensible route to incremental change than one that either avoids or perpetuates the underlying causes of many men's health inequities. The edifice of hegemonic masculinity will not crumble any time soon but without laying bare some of the more damaging aspects it will be business as usual and nothing will change.

Key points

1. There is a growing interest in men's health that reflects evidence outlining a range of health inequalities, for example; men have on average a shorter life expectancy, are twice as likely to develop and die from the ten most common cancers affecting both sexes and access health-care advice less readily.
2. Differences in health outcomes, in particular those relating to gender, are often framed as 'lifestyle choices' with men characterised as implicitly responsible for behaviour that may have detrimental consequences for their health. However, such explanations fail to take account of societal pressures which shape and guide gendered behaviour.
3. Health-care providers are required to be mindful of gender equality as a goal when developing and delivering services hence demonstrating action to overcome gendered health inequalities. This contemporary context needs to be considered – does taking some forms of action collude with the societal pressures imposed by dominant forms of masculinity?
4. Gender mainstreaming in healthcare requires more than the taking of simplistic measures that might improve men's access to health-care. These may be effective in the short term but they will do little to challenge the underlying reasons for some of the gendered, men's health inequalities.
5. In this chapter notions of 'doing gendered' are outlined with Bahktin's ideas around 'dialogism' employed to show how dominant and potentially harmful authoritative forms of masculinity can be carefully explored and challenged. It should be acknowledged that this may offer no direct solution to men's health inequalities but alongside other forms of action it does represent a more critical and responsible approach to what is a somewhat intractable issue.

NOTE

1. The term 'mother and baby' group was not actually used and indeed should be avoided as it excludes fathers and other carers. Nonetheless, the groups which were targeted as offering support for those caring for infants and pre-school children were observed to be almost exclusively attended by 'mothers and babies' or at the very least mothers and female carers.

REFERENCES

Bakhtin, M. M. (1981) *The Dialogic Imagination: Four Essays by M. M. Bakhtin*, (ed.) M. Holquist, trans. C. Emerson & M. Holquist, Austin: Texas University Press.

Bakhtin, M. M. (1984) *Problems of Dostoevsky's Poetics* ed. and trans. C. Emerson, Manchester, Manchester University Press.

Bakhtin, M. M. (1986) *Speech Genres and Other Essays* (eds) C. Emerson, M. Holquist, trans. V .M. McGee, Austin: Texas University Press.

Booker, M. K. & Juraga, D. (1995) *Bakhtin, Stalin, and Modern Russian Fiction: Carnival, Dialogism, and History*. London: Greenwood Press.

Butler, J.P. (1999) *Gender Trouble*. London: Routledge.

Cavaglieri, C. & Knight, J. (2009) 'Men ignore financial fall-out of ill health: if you get sick, you can lose your income', *Independent*, http://www.independent.co.uk/money/insurance/men-ignore-financial-fallout-of-ill-health-1698521.html, Sunday, 7 June 2009.

Clare, A. (2000) *On Men: Masculinity in Crisis*, London: Chatto and Windus.

Connell, R. W. (1995) *Masculinities*, Berkeley: University of California Press.

Courtenay, W. H. (1998) 'College men's health: an overview and a call to action', *Journal of American College Health*, 47(3), 279–90.

Crawshaw, P. (2007) 'Governing the healthy male citizen: men, masculinity and popular health in Men's Health magazine', *Social Science and Medicine*, 65(8), 1606–18.

Doyal, L. (2000) 'Gender equity in health: debates and dilemmas', *Social Science and Medicine*, 51(6), 931–39.

Emslie, C., Ridge, D., Zeibland, S. & Hunt, K. (2006) 'Men's accounts of depression: reconstructing or resisting hegemonic masculinity?' *Social Science and Medicine*, 62, 2246–57.

Galdas, P. M., Cheater, F. & Marshall, P. (2004) 'Men and health help-seeking behaviour: literature review', *Journal of Advanced Nursing*, 49(6), 616–23.

Garfinkel, H. (1967) *Studies in Ethnomethodology*, Englewood Cliffs, NJ: Prentice-Hall.

Goodey, J. (1997) 'Boys don't cry: masculinities, fear of crime and fearlessness', *British Journal of Criminology*, 37(3), 401–18.

Gough, B. (2010) 'Promoting "masculinity" over health: a critical analysis of men's health promotion with particular reference to an obesity reduction "manual"', in B. Gough & S. Robertson, *Men, Masculinities and Health: Critical Perspectives*, Basingstoke: Palgrave Macmillan.

Gough, B. & Robertson, S. (2010) *Men, Masculinities and Health: Critical Perspectives*, Basingstoke: Palgrave Macmillan.

Horrocks, R. (1994) *Masculinity in Crisis*, London: Macmillan.

Horrocks, C., Kelly, N. & Perry, S. (2007) *Community Development Practice: Tackling Health Inequalities.* Report prepared for NHS Wakefield.

Holquist, M. (1990) *Dialogism: Bakhtin and His World*, London: Routledge.

Macrae, F. (2010) 'Cancer death risk is 70% higher in men: "stiff upper lip" and lifestyle raise the danger'. *Daily Mail* Online, http://www.dailymail.co.uk/health/article-1259049/Cancer-death-risk-70-higher-men-Stiff-upper-lip-lifestyle-raise-danger.html, last updated 24 March, 2010.

Men's Health Forum (2004) *Getting it Sorted: A Policy Programme for Men's Health*, London: Men's Health Forum.

Men's Health Forum (2006) *The Report of the Gender Equity Project*, London: Men's Health Forum.

Messerschmidt, J. W. (1993) *Masculinities and Crime: Critique and Reconceptualization of Theory*, Lanham, MD: Rowman and Littlefield.

National Centre for Social Research (2004) *Health survey for England 2003*, Report commissioned by the Department of Health, http://www.dh.gov.uk/en/Publicationsandstatistics/Publications/PublicationsStatistics/DH_4098712

Office for National Statistics (2003) *Social Trends 33*, London: Stationery Office.

Office for National Statistics (2006) *Social Trends 36*, London Stationary Office.

Payne, S. (2009) *Health Systems and Policy Analysis: How Can Gender Equity Be Addressed through Health Systems?* Policy Brief 12, World Health Organisation.

Pease, B. (2006) 'Governing men and boys in public policy in Australia', in G. Marston & C. McDonald, *Analysing Social Policy: A Governmental Approach*, Cheltenham: Edward Elgar Publishing Limited.

Robertson, L. M., Douglas, F., Ludbrook, A., Reid, G. & van Teijlingen, E. (2008) 'What works with men? A systematic review of health promoting interventions targeting men', *BioMed Central Health Services Research*, 8, 141.

Robertson, J. M. & Fitzgerald, L. F. (1992) 'Overcoming the masculine mystique: Preferences for alternative forms of assistance among men who avoid counseling', *Journal of Counseling Psychology*, 39, 240–46.

Sabo, D. (2005) 'The study of masculinities and men's health: an overview', in M. Kimmel, J. Hearn, & R. W. Connell (eds) *The Handbook of Studies on Men and Masculinities*, Thousand Oaks, CA: Sage.

Sabo, D. and Gordon, G. (1993) *Men's Health and Illness: Gender, Power and the Body*. London, Sage.

Schofield, T. (2000) 'What does "gender and health" mean?' *Health Sociology Review*, 11 (1–2), 29–38, http://www.un.org/documents/ga/docs/52/plenary/a52-3.htm

Seymour-Smith, S. (2010) 'Men's negotiations of "legitimate" self-help group identity', in B. Gough & S. Robertson, *Men, Masculinities and Health: Critical Perspectives*, Basingstoke: Palgrave Macmillan.

Sullivan, P., Smith, M. & Matusov, E. (2009) 'Bakhtin, Socrates and the carnivalesque in education', *New Ideas in Psychology*, 27, 326–41.

The Marmot Review (2010) *Fair Society, Healthy Lives: A Strategic Review of Health Inequalities in England Post-2010*, http://www.marmotreview.org/

The United Nations Economic and Social Council (1997) Report of the economic and social council for 1997*, United Nations, General Assembly, 52nd Session, http://www.un.org/documents/ga/docs/52/plenary/a52-3.htm

Uphoff, N. (1991) 'Fitting projects to people', in M. M. Cernea (ed.), *Putting People First: Sociological Variables in Rural Development*, New York: Oxford University Press.

Villegas, R., Creagh, D., Hinchion, R., OHalloran, D. & Perry, I. J. (2003) 'Prevalence of the Metabolic Syndrome in middle-aged men and women', *Diabetes Care* 26, 1781–85.

West, C. & Zimmerman, D. H. (1987) 'Doing gender', *Gender and Society*, 1(2), 125–51.

White, A. (2001) 'How men respond to illness', *Men's Health Journal*, 1(1), 18–19.

White, A. & Cash, K. (2004) 'The state of men's health in Western Europe', *Journal of Men's Health and Gender*, 1(1), 60–66.

White, A. K. & Johnson, M. (2000) 'Men making sense of their chest pain – niggles, doubts and denials', *Journal of Clinical Nursing*, 9, 534–41.

Whitehead, S. M. & Barrett, F. J. (2001) 'The sociology of masculinity', in S. M. Whitehead & F. J. Barrett, *The Masculinity Reader*, Cambridge: Polity Press.

Wilkins, D., Payne, S., Granville, G. & Branney, P. (2008) *The Gender and Access to Health Services Study: Final Report*, for Department of Health: Men's Health Forum.

Wortham, S. (2001) *Narratives in Action. A Strategy for Research and Analysis*, New York: Teachers College Press.

CHAPTER 6

Working without Sacrifice: Discourse, Femininity and Occupational Risk

BRIDGETTE RICKETT

Danger – women at work!

This chapter will begin by reviewing occupational health literature in relation to women, then move on to examine the main approaches from psychology that have been used to explain occupational health for women. The remainder of the chapter will be spent presenting understandings of women's health and safety at work that both views women's workplace health through a critical lens and allows us to make claims for action.

It may as well be stated from the outset that the story of women's health and safety at work is obscured by the stance taken within most occupational health research. This has assumed the male worker is the dangerous worker and the female worker the safe worker. In the UK, 2008/9 data reveal that accidents, injuries and work-related illnesses caused 29.3 million lost work days (Health and Safety Executive (HSE), 2010), while worldwide, 'on the job' accidents claim 2 million lives every year (International Labour Office, 2005). Statistics tell us that, in the UK, approximately 37% of workplace accidents, 48% of work-related illnesses and injuries, almost 50% of the most common work-related illnesses (musculoskeletal disorders) and a staggering 70% of stress and anxiety (HSE, 2010) occurs in women. However, Messing (1998) has argued that the collating of such data has left women's experiences invisible or, as she describes it, 'one-eyed'. For instance, figures are often marred by gender-insensitive data gathering techniques (Messing, 1997), hazards for women can be unknown and safety is commonly defined through male-dominated occupations (Vogel, 2003). A demonstration of these problems is the finding that while injury rates are commonly determined by successful compensation claims, there is something of a systemic gender bias in that ill-ness/injury claims associated with traditionally male-dominated work are sig-nificantly more likely to be successful than those associated with traditionally female-dominated work (Messing et al., 2000). In addition, Messing (1997) has reported that accident rates for women are artificially lowered when cal-culated, as women often work fewer hours than men so the probability of hav-ing an accident is lower. As feminists have long pointed out (see for example, Gilligan, 1982), assuming a male standard positions men as the reference point with women either ignored or compared unfavourably against such a 'standard'.

What light can psychology shed on occupational safety for women?

Occupational and health psychologists have also fallen foul of similar assump-tions to those discussed above regarding occupational health and safety. This is despite the establishment of conferences (for example, The International Conference on Safety and Well-Being at Work, held by the Centre for Hazard and Risk Management), annual seminars (for example, The International Seminar on Occupational Accident Research, Saltsjöbaden, 1983) and jour-nals (for example, The Journal of Occupational Health Psychology) dedicated to the subject of improving the health of the 'workforce'.

A brief historical reading of the rise of occupational health psychology gives us a clue as to why this may be the case. In the first part of the twentieth cen-tury an academic interest in workplace safety emerged which emphasised the need to take into account the 'human factor'. This was promoted by the grow-ing number of occupational psychologists. At the same time, health and safety legislation was absent from much industrialised work which was dominated by working-class men and becoming more reliant on heavy machinery. As such, accident and injuries were rife and a real social and economic issue. This, together with the introduction of state-sponsored compensation (for example, The Workers Compensation Law, 1910 in the US) created a social and political impetus for psychologists (see for example, Forbes, 1939) to argue for a need to take the psychological characteristics of workers into account when explaining occupational health and safety, with the worker being positioned firmly as 'the industrialised man'. Modern day psychological interest in health and safety at work can be read as growing from this historically positioned perspective on occupational safety, with most research focussing on 'the industrialised man' and the 'human factors' associated with him (Perez, 2008). In addition to this, the focus of much of the recent occupational literature has been on work stress which emanates mainly from studies with male populations.

In Macik-Frey et al.'s (2007) review of the occupational health literature we learn that the majority of research published in the previous 15 years has had work stress as its main focus. This literature is mainly concerned with the individual's perceived levels of stress and how this may affect adherence to safety practices or to making mistakes, leading to an accident (see for example, Levenson et al., 1980). Work stress is usually measured either via global measures (for example, The Maslach Burnout Scale; Maslach & Jackson, 1981) or more specific measures (for example, The Job Satisfaction Scale; Warr et al., 1979). Here, stress arising from the work environment is generally conceived of as resulting from high levels of occupational workload and/or low levels of occupational control that may lead to accidents or failure to enact safety practices.

This research on workplace stress has made some clear contributions to academic thinking on occupational safety. For example, it has provided an emphasis on occupationally situated well-being and has allowed an understanding of the interconnectedness between the mind (feelings), body (practices), social (work conditions) and political (increased demands driven by economic forces). However, the majority of this research is based on male samples (Offerman & Armitage, 1993), leaving women's experiences ignored or only represented by professional women (see for example, Burke, 1996). In addition, critics (for example, Messing, 1997) have argued that standard psychometric measures used are derived from all male populations (for example, Karasek's, 1979, questionnaire on job demands). Secondly, from a paradigm standpoint, what this fascination has left us with is a 'work-stress victim' model of the individual who is viewed in isolation in relation to the political, historical and social world they inhabit. As such, Harkness et al. (2005) argue that research should move towards a conceptualisation of work stress that embraces agency and community and moves away from the positioning of work stress in terms of negativity, passivity and individualisation.

There has also been some consideration of workers' beliefs and attitudes, and the role these might play in determining their motivations to carry out safety practices (see for example, Purswell & Rumar, 1984). These include beliefs concerning safety (Donald & Canter, 1994), the status of a worker's general health which is thought to influence a person's experience of the threat posed by an unsafe behaviour, the controllability of safety behaviours and the amount of social approval there is for a behaviour (Vaughan, 1993). These are all thought to be important determinants of safety behaviour. However, the main criticism of this strand of research is that it positions a worker's thinking about health and safety against the 'scientific', and therefore, objective rationale behind messages from health and safety 'experts' in a particularly value-laden manner whereby a worker is seen to have 'faulty' ways of understanding her working world, and therefore is guilty of 'unsafe' working. This kind of theorising has led to safety reduction programmes that discourage reports from employees through a fear of being labelled as being guilty of such 'unsafe' thinking (Zoller, 2003). These messages often use what Perry (2003, p. 8) describes as 'the sacred language of science' which, it could be argued, can disempower people in paid work by discouraging questioning, resistance and agency in relation to their health and their general working conditions. As many writers have persuasively argued, to overcome this, what would be required is for 'cognitions' to be re-located into an approach which goes beyond attitudes and behaviour into a non-intra-psychic focus of the social and political realm of paid work (see for example, Edwards & Potter, 1992). Research examining the discourse around occupational risk has led the way in this area (see for example, Zoller, 2003; Sanders, 2004; Rickett, 2010).

In addition, there is a body of literature whose central focus is to argue that personality may influence the likelihood of engagement in safety practices in the workplace (see for example, Evans et al., 1987). Recent research has assessed the relationship between workers' scores on The Eysenck Personality Inventory (EPI: Eysenck & Eysenck, 1964) and the amount of precautionary practices exercised in the workplace (see for example, Cellar et al., 2001). In addition the 'big five' factors of personality (openness, conscientiousness, extraversion, agreeableness, and neuroticism) (John, 1990) have been studied both in isolation (Sutherland & Cooper, 1986) and together (Cellar et al., 2001) as predictors of both safety behaviour and accidents in the workplace. This paradigm is at the core of early human factors research (see Burnham, 2009) and shares the androcentric ideology in that it privileges socially desirable presentations of masculinity. Batalha (2006) argues that the big five personality measures do not reflect internal realities but rather the dominant norms around the performance of gender, in that people scoring favourably are much more likely to also score highly on measures of masculinity (Marusic & Bratko, 1998) and people scoring unfavourable are much more likely to score highly on measures of femininity (see for example, Francis & Wilcox, 1998). A second issue here is that this paradigm relies on the understanding that people are categorically and essentially different and does so in a particularly morally imbued manner, presenting a 'personality' that will not and cannot adhere to workplace understandings. This allows for an ideology to prevail around health and safety at work that is based on notions of deviancy. This leads Nadesan (2006) to suggest that the proliferation of these personality measures functions more to exclude and/ or control any unruly workers who don't fit the required, and value-laden standard, than to increase occupational health. Instead of 'scientific facts', this focus on the personality of a worker to explain occupational health can be understood as a discourse and one that 'separates the individual, breaks his links with others, splits up community life, forces the individual back on himself and ties him to his own identity in a constraining way' (Foucault, 1984, pp. 211–12).

How can occupational and health psychology make visible women's occupational health?

Overall then psychological research that has attempted to explain accidents, injuries and work-related illnesses has used individualistic understandings, assuming workers are male and presenting people at work in a disempowered manner. This may have functioned to both exclude any persons not fitting the (male) standard and control and police occupational spaces. That this body of research, along with much organisational research is 'gender blind' is now largely acknowledged due to influential critics such as Messing (1997; 1998). Indeed, UK agencies have now been reconstituted to target this flaw (for example, the TUC's reconvened Women's Health and Safety Working Group), while the World Health Organisation's Global Plan of Action on Workers' Health 2008–2017 has a number of targets aimed at creating more 'gender sensitive' research in this area. The publication from the International Programme on Safety Health and the Environment in its 'Right of Women to Safe Work' document (IPSHE, 2008) has specifically requested that research be gender sensitive in order to make visible both women's occupational risks and the gendered constructions of paid work.

In addition, there is now promising new research within the social sciences that may further these goals using more politically informed analyses. For example, Kosny and MacEachen's (2010) thoughtful, grounded theory approach to examining occupational risk for women working in non-profit organisations, revealed that many of the hazards present in the jobs are hidden from view (for example, 'empathy work' and 'emotional work'). They argue that the invisibility of certain types of female-dominated work is reflected in the exclusions and shortcomings of occupational health and safety systems designed to protect the health of workers (i.e. they do not consider or therefore protect emotional health and safety). Ahonen et al.'s (2010) research which used a phenomenological approach to explore the physical and psycho-social hazards facing women employed in domestic work, revealed a multitude of previously unrecognised risks, including psychological and social risk. While Hepworth and Murtagh's (2005) content analysis of the talk of women who worked in beauty therapy illustrated how power relations between employers and female employees can serve to compromise safety (i.e. the pressure that employers put on therapists to save time and money prohibited the adherence to health and safety practice).

A focus on discourse, gender identity and occupational risk

Writers such as Holmes and Schnurr (2006) have argued that a focus on gender identity is key to understanding workplace risk. One way in which this has been achieved is by focusing on discursive practices in the workplace. These have been argued to be a powerful tool in shaping organisationally accepted gender subjectivities, such that workers come to 'embody and enact organisationally privileged modes of practice, in turn achieving organisationally desired outcomes' (Halford & Leonard, 2006, p. 657). Recently, a growing body of research has examined the discursive manner in which female subjectivities are shaped, reproduced and resisted in the workplace (see for example, Rickett, 2010; in press; Collinson et al., 1990).

However, with some notable exceptions (for example, Teeler Sanders' work on constructions of gender and risk in sex work, 2004; Rickett, in press, 2010), research has remained relatively untouched by the recent theoretical interest in the cultural and political relevance of 'risk' (see, for example, Beck, 1992; Giddens, 1990), especially to understandings of female subjectivities in occupational spaces. While there have been some useful and thoughtful studies aimed at understanding the partnership between organisationally legitimised risk and socially accepted masculine identities in male-dominated work (see for example, Mitchell et al., 2001), few studies have examined how feminine identities are implicated in both the deployment and resistance of occupational safety discourse and practice.

For much of my research career one of my aims has been to address this imbalance. In doing so I have used poststructuralist feminist discourse analysis, with an aim to analyse how different ideas around femininity and occupational risk are variably taken up, reworked and resisted in talk by women who work in physically dangerous work places. In this research I have draw upon Foucault's notion of governmentality, where discourses around 'risky' situations in the workplace can be understood as strategies of social control and regulation (Foucault, 1984). Developing this particular understanding of risk I argue that employing a gendered understanding of occupational risk will allow feminist researchers to examine how women's work practices in 'dangerous' work spaces are both controlled and regulated through gendered constructions of workplace risk.

While through much of the 20th century women were excluded from many kinds of jobs under a prevailing rhetoric about the protection of women, they have continued to labour in a variety of risky and dangerous jobs (Gutek, 2001). In my research I have examined the way women talk about themselves and the risks they face. These women have been drawn from a range of work-spaces considered to be dangerous. These include women who work in care work and nursing (Rickett, 2010), women who work in policing (Rickett, 2008) and women who work in door supervision. Through carrying out this research I have concluded that within these data are overtly politicised accounts of women attempting to make themselves safe at work. For instance, I have been interested in women's work practices around preventing themselves from getting back damage (Rickett, 2010) and work practices in potentially violent situations to avoid bodily harm (Rickett, 2008; 2010). One of the conclusions I have come to is that attempts to avoid harm and damage to health by adhering to recommended practices are often compromised by organisationally shared understanding of what women are and what they are capable of doing in their roles. Moreover, my research indicates that often by striving to challenge unfair gendered expectations and ideologies that hinder being successful and respected in their jobs, women are often forced to compromise their health and safety at work.

The example of women working as door supervisors

In the UK, door supervisors are responsible for the safety and security of customers and staff in organisational settings such as pubs, bars, nightclubs and other licensed premises or at public events. Often referred to as being a 'Bouncer' (US) or a 'Crowd Controller' (Australia), door supervision work is one of the main jobs within the security industry. Over the past decade, despite being historically occupied by the male employee, there have been increasing numbers of women joining and working in the industry, and numbers appear to be rising each year; 15% of licensed door supervisors in the UK are now women (Security Industry Authority, 2010). Hobbs et al. (2007) argue that this increase goes hand-in-hand with the rise in the number of women engaging in the night-time economy of pubs and clubs in the UK.

This 'masculinist work' is a physically risky occupation in the UK's fast expanding night-time economy where violence is seen as 'tools of the trade' (Monaghan, 2002, p. 404). In light of this, my research used a poststructural and feminist-informed discourse analysis (Willot & Griffin, 1997), to gain an understanding of the risk of violence in door supervision work. In particular, the focus was on how women's work practices are both controlled and regulated through gendered constructions of workplace risk (Rickett, 2010). Data were collected via semi-structured interviews with six female door supervisors (aged between 22 and 30) working in different sites across the UK.

The following data extracts are quotations taken from the recorded and transcribed interviews. Please note all extracts are anonymised.

Extract 1:

> Erm, you kind of think you don't go into this job if you've got fingernails to break or the model looks to mess up, you know you're not scared of being hit, you can't go, it's not nice being hit but you can't go in showing you're scared. (Katie)

We can see from this extract that Katie, who has been a door supervisor for two years, is presenting the safe door supervisor as one who is both desexualised and defeminised. This presentation appears to be operating in two main ways. First, as a strategy that Katie uses to present herself as being protected from physical harm through the rejection of outwards signs of idealised femininity. Second, it as a way of reconciling herself to the consequences of such harm. This is done by either distancing herself from, or actively disguising traditional markers of working class femininity (having fingernails and good looks) while favouring understandings of fearlessness and emancipation (not being scared). This is an interesting rejection of what McRobbie calls the 'post feminist masquerade' (2007, p. 722). McRobbie argues that a masquerade of hyper-femininity that uses fashion and beauty markers serves to disguise femininity and does so via a discourse of choice which functions to mask her rivalry with men and the competition she may pose in male-dominated work. What we see here is a rejection of this masquerade. Instead hyper-feminine markers are seen as a danger and a limiter to successful enactment of occupational identities. This rejection could serve to contest ideology around the professional enactment of femininity that McRobbie argues can render feminist action a non-issue. I argue, along with McRobbie, that rejecting hyper-feminine markers may enable the 'unmasking' of any rivalry a female worker may have with her male co-workers enabling gender politics to be pushed to the forefront in workplace discourse and practice.

The next extract is from 'Angela', who has worked for over six years as a city-centre door supervisor.

Extract 2:

> Well, I mean on Monday night we had three door staff on, usually we would have five. Urm, we had two on the front door both men, me on the inside, and err the end of the night he turned round 'I've got eight numbers [telephone numbers from female customers] what have you got?' 'oh, I've got two black eyes!'. So it's like nice, thanks lads (laughs) you know they've had a great night chatting up all the girls and I've been inside sorting out all the problems. (Angela)

It seems that what 'Angela' is alluding to here is a highly heterosexual work-space where men fulfil the 'macho man' identity through 'chatting up' female customers. As such, women are either doing the work or being objectified through the enactment of these identities. For the women who do the work, this practice requires commitment through self-sacrifice, whereby women complete duties under any conditions to the detriment of themselves, in this example, the outcome is bodily harm. These notions of self-sacrifice through work draw on heavily gendered understandings of agency, with masculinity associated with agency and power, and femininity with self-sacrifice (Rickett, 2010; Devon, 2007). Indeed, Ussher has argued the feminised construct of sac-rifice is explicitly embedded in hegemonic constructions of idealised feminin-ity, which involves the positioning of women as emotional nurturers of others, necessitating 'self-renunciation', and being morally dichotomised between the 'good' and the 'bad' (Ussher, 2004, p. 254). This discourse then functions to further positions female door supervisor in the gendered and morally superior position of the 'good worker', the obedient worker in relation to her male col-leagues and the female customers. As my previous work (for example, Rickett, 2010) has recognised, the construct of the 'good worker' is often bound up in normative ideology of ideal subject positions. Here we are seeing gender norms, class norms and normative sexuality being simultaneously drawn upon to construct a 'good worker' that is distinctive not only from fellow male col-leagues, but many female customers that occupy the work-space.

Using this perspective allows us to view women's work-place health through a critical lens whilst enabling us to make claims for action around gendered power inequities. It does so by endeavouring to focus on research and prac-tice that benefits women in paid work and by illuminating gendered power-relations as a site for action.

An aim of this research is to view the person at work as being a part of her work and community life, the political climate she lives and works in and the way she is understood and understands herself as a woman. This allows for a shift from the 'internal world' of the worker and from the problematising and disempowering of the paid worker. This has enabled us to further understand both women's occupational risks and gendered constructions of women in work. Through the rich and illuminating accounts we can see that for women labouring in work that carries a high physical risk, their ability to be safe, successful at their jobs and be respected is challenged by power relations that shape work practices. It is these power relations that potentially disempower, exploit and make fraught the identity of the female worker. Therefore any attempts to make women in paid work safer must make visible the woman in paid work, view her in the social and political world she inhabits, challenge normative assumptions of womanhood and have at its core an aim of gender equality for women in the workplace.

The beauty of these accounts is that they enable us to see the complex negotiations and conflicts which surround dominant understandings of occupational safety. These ideas are charged with tensions and women made vulnerable by sometimes competing negotiations for occupationally and socially sanctioned power positions. Therefore, I argue it is through emancipating women from these power inequities that we can enhance the occupational health of women in paid work.

Key points

1. Traditional psychological research that examines workplace safety has used individualistic understandings, assumed workers are male, presented people at work in a disempowered manner and may have functioned to exclude any persons not fitting the (male) standard.
2. Recent, high profile and international legislative and governmental documents have specifically requested that future safety research be gender sensitive in order to make visible both women's occupational risks and the gendered constructions of paid work.
3. Authors have argued that a focus on women's identities will allow us to provide an account of women's safety and health at work that challenges some problems associated with traditional understanding of safety at work.
4. Recent critical psychological research tells us that women's attempts to avoid harm and damage to health by adhering to recommended practices are often compromised by organisationally shared understanding of what women are and what they are capable of doing in their roles.
5. Critical health psychology understandings help to enlighten and may assist in emancipating women from power inequities identified and therefore enhance the occupational health of women in paid work.

REFERENCES

Ahonen, E. Q., Lóez-Jacob, M. J., Vázquez, M. L., Porthé, V., Gil-González, D., Garcí, A. M., Ruiz-Frutos, C., Benach, J. & Benavides, F. G. (2010) 'Invisible work, unseen hazards: the health of women immigrant household service workers in Spain', *American Journal of Industrial Medicine*, 53, 405–16.

Batalha, L. (2006) 'The construction of gendered identities through personality traits', *Gay and Lesbian Issues and Psychological Review*, 2(1), 3–11.

Beck, U. (1992) *Risk and Society: Towards a New Modernity* London: Sage.

Burke, P. (1996) *Gender Shock: Exploding the Myths of Male and Female* New York: Anchor Book.

Burnham, J. C. (2009) *Accident Prone: A History of Technology, Psychology, and Misfits of The Machine,* Chicago, IL: University of Chicago Press.

Cellar, D. F., Nelson, Z. C., York, C. M. & Bauer, C. (2001) 'The five-factor model of safety in the workplace: investigating the relationships between personality and accident involvement', *Journal of Prevention and Intervention in the Community*, 22, 43–52.

Collinson, D., Knights, D. & Collinson, M. (1990) *Managing to Discriminate* London: Routledge.

Devon, J. (2007) 'The Experience of Agency in Women: Narratives of Women whose Mothers Achieved Professional Success and Recognition', *Dissertation Abstracts International: Section B: The Sciences and Engineering*, 68, 4132.

Donald, I. & Canter, D. (1994) 'Employee attitudes and safety in the chemical industry', *Journal of Loss Prevention in the Process Industries*, 7, 203–8.

Edwards, D., Potter, J. (1992) *Discursive Psychology* London: Sage.

Evans, G. W., Palsane, M. N. & Carrere, S. (1987) 'Type A behaviour and occupational stress: a cross-cultural study of blue-collar workers', *Applied Ergonomics*, 52, 1003–7.

Eysenck, H. J. & Eysenck, S. B. G. (1964) *Manual of Eysenck Personality Inventory* (5th edn, 1987) England: Hodder & Stoughton.

Forbes, T. W. (1939) 'The normal automobile driver as a traffic problem', *Journal of General Psychology, 20,* 471–74.

Foucault, M. (1984) 'Neitzche, Genealogy, History', in P. Rabinow (ed.) *The Foucault Reader* Harmondsworth: Penguin, pp. 138–64.

Francis, L. J. & Wilcox, C. (1998) 'The relationship between Eysenck's personality dimensions and Bem's masculinity and femininity scale revisited', *Personality and Individual Differences*, 25, 683–87.

Giddens, A. (1990) *The Consequences of Modernity*, Stanford, CA: Stanford University Press.

Gilligan, C. (1982) *In a Different Voice* Cambridge, MA: Harvard University.

Gutek, B. A. (2001) 'Working environments', in J. Worell (ed.), *Encyclopedia Of Women and Gender* New York: Academic Press, pp. 1191–204.

Halford, S. & Leonard P. (2006) 'Place, space and time: contextualizing workplace subjectivities', *Organization Studies,* 27(5), 657–60.

Harkness, A. M. B., Long, B. C., Bermbach, N., Patterson, K., Jordan, S., & Kahn, H. (2005) 'Talking about work stress: discourse analysis and implications for stress interventions', *Work and Stress*, 19, 121.

Health and Safety Executive (2010) *Health and Safety Statistics Highlights 2008/9.*

Hepworth, J. & Murtagh, M. (2005) 'Correct procedures and cutting corners: a qualitative study of women's occupational health and safety in a beauty therapy industry', *Australian and New Zealand Journal of Public Health*, 29, 555–57.

Hobbs, D., O'Brien, K. & Westmarland, L. (2007) 'Connecting the gendered door: women, violence and doorwork', *British Journal of Sociology*, 58(1), 21–38.

Holmes, J. & Schnurr, S. (2006) 'Doing femininity at work: more than just relational practice', *Journal of Sociolinguistics*, 10(1), 31–51.

International Labour Office (2005), 'Decent work – safe work', *XVIIth World Congress on Safety and Health at Work*, Orlando, USA.

International Programme on Safety Health and the Environment (2008) 'The right of women to safe work', *XVIII World Congress on Occupational Safety and Health*, 29 June–2 July, Seoul, Korea.

John, O. P. (1990) 'The search for basic dimensions of personality: a review and critique', in Paul McReynolds & James C. Rosen (eds) *Advances in Psychological Assessment*, 7, New York: Plenum Press.

Karasek, R. A. (1979) 'Job Demands, Job Decision Latitude, and Mental Strain: Implications for Job Redesign', *Administrative Science Quarterly* 24(2), 285–309.

Kosny, A. & MacEachen, E. (2010) 'Gendered, invisible work in non-profit social service organizations: Implications for worker health and safety', *Gender, Work and Organization,* 17(4), 359–80.

Levenson, H., Hirschfeld, M. A. & Hirschfeld, M. D. (1980) 'Industrial accidents and recent life events', *Journal of Occupational Medicine,* 22, 53–57.

McRobbie, A. (2007) 'Top girls? Young women and the post-feminist sexual contract', *Cultural Studies,* 21(4), 718–37.

Macik-Frey, M., Quick, J. C., & Nelson, D. (2007) 'Advances in occupational health: from a stressful beginning to a positive future', *Journal of Management,* 33(6), 809–40.

Marusic, I. & Bratko, D. (1998) 'Relations of masculinity and femininity with personality dimensions of the five-factor model', *Sex Roles,* 38, 29–44.

Maslach, C & Jackson, S.E. (1981) 'The measurement of experienced burnout', *Journal of Occupational Behaviour,* 2, 99–113.

Messing, K. (1998) *One-Eyed Science: Occupational Health and Women Workers* Philadelphia: Temple University Press.

Messing, K. (1997) 'Women's occupational health: A critical review and discussion of current issue', *Women and Health,* 25(4), 39–68.

Messing, K., Lippel K., Demers, D. & Mergler, D. (2000) 'Equality and difference in the workplace: physical job demands, occupational illnesses, and sex differences', *National Women's Study Association Journal,* 12, 21–49.

Mitchell, W. A., Crawshaw, P., Bunton, R. & Green E. (2001) 'Situating young people's experiences of risk and identity', *Health, Risk and Society,* 3(1), 217–34.

Monaghan, L. F. (2002) 'Hard men, shop boys and others: embodying competence in a masculinist occupation', *Sociological Review,* 50(3), 334–55.

Nadesan, M. H. (2006) 'Constructing paper dolls: the discourse of personality testing in organizational practice', *Communication,* 7(3), 189–218.

Offermann, L., & Armitage, M. (1993) 'The stress and health of the woman manager', in E. A. Fagenson (ed.) *Women in Management: Trends, Issues and Challenges in Managerial Diversity* Newbury Park, CA: Sage Publications.

Perez, J. M. (2008) 'Medicine and the sexual distribution of work: an analysis of the scientific discourse on the role of the "human factor" in improving performance at work (Spain, 1922–1936)', *Asclepio; Archivo Iberoamericano De Historia De La Medicina Y Antropología Médica,* 60(1), 103–28.

Perry, S. E. (2003) 'Inserting the human into human history: experiments with montage, experience, and discontinuous narrative in archaeological reportage', *Journal of the Graduate Students of Anthropology,* 5, 7–21.

Purswell, J. L. & Rumar, K. (1984) 'Occupational accident research: where are we going?', *Journal of Occupational Accidents,* 6, 219.

Rickett, B. (2010) 'Working without sacrifice: acceptance and resistance to dominant discourse around women's occupational risk', *Feminism and Psychology,* 20(2), 260–66.

Rickett, B. & Mason, A. (2008) '"This Job is not a 'Girly' Job": An Analysis of Accepted and Rejected Gender Identities in the Construction of the Police Woman', *The Psychology of Women Section of British Psychological Society Annual Conference* Windsor, UK.

Rickett, B. & Roman, A. (in press) '"Heroes and matriarchs": working-class femininities, violence and door supervision work', *Gender, Work and Organisation.*

Sanders, T. (2004) 'The risks of street prostitution: punters, police and protesters', *Urban Studies,* 41(8), 1703–17.

Security Industry Authority (2010), Information Booklet, Links Induction and Training Centre.

Sutherland, V. J. & Cooper, C. L. (1986) *Man and Accidents Offshore – An Examination of the Costs of Stress Among Workers on Oil and Gas Rigs* Colchester, Essex: London Press Limited.

Ussher, J. (2004) 'Premenstrual syndrome and self-policing: ruptures in self-silencing leading to increased self-surveillance and blaming of the body', *Social Theory and Health*, 2(3), 254–72.

Vaughan, E. (1993) 'Chronic exposure to environmental hazard: risk perceptions and self-protective behaviour', *Health Psychology*, 12, 74–85.

Vogel, L. (2003) The gender workplace health gap in Europe, ETU1.

Warr, P., Cook, J. & Wall, T. (1979) 'Scales for the measurement of some work attitudes and aspects of psychological well-being', *Journal of Occupational Psychology*, 52, 129–48.

Willott S. & Griffin. C. (1997) 'Wham bam am I a man, unemployed talk about masculinities', *Feminism and Psychology*, 7(1), 107.

Zoller, H. M. (2003) 'Health on the line: identity and disciplinary control in employee occupational health and safety discourse', *Journal of Applied Communication Research*, 31(2), 118–39.

CHAPTER 7

The Emancipatory Potential of Critical Approaches to Promoting Sexual Health: Exploring the Possibilities for Action

KATE MILNES

Introduction

In this chapter I will outline the main features of dominant social cognition to studying sexual health before moving on to consider their limitations and the benefits of adopting more critical approaches. I will argue that critiquing mainstream psychological research and taken-for-granted assumptions about gender, sex, sexuality and contraception is of vital importance because these are often disempowering or discriminatory and neglect the material, cultural and ideological context of people's sexual lives. As a result, it can be argued that interventions based upon them have limited potential for bringing about change or creating possibilities for action. For example, it has often been assumed that the apparent gap between women's attitudes towards condoms and their actual condom use can be explained in terms of their lack of assertiveness and as a result, many sexual health campaigns have attempted to raise women's assertiveness levels. Critical psychologists (e.g. Gavey & McPhillips, 1999) have noted the ineffectiveness of such campaigns because they are based on overly simplistic conceptions of the constraints on young women's ability to initiate contraceptive use.

I will argue here that taking a critical approach to sexual health promotion that conceptualises sex and sexual relationships as situated practices (see, for example, Bondi, 2003) rather than as individual behaviours creates possibilities for action whilst still acknowledging the constraints that cultural, structural and material contexts place on people's sexual lives. By furnishing people with an opportunity to deconstruct and critique dominant discourses around gender, sex and sexuality and providing spaces and resources for them to explore alternative discourses, I believe that critical approaches to sexual health promotion have the potential to engage people in an active process of negotiation with regard to their sexual health and well-being.

Mainstream approaches to sexual health

In terms of studying sexual health, mainstream psychological research has largely maintained a narrow focus on preventing unwanted pregnancies and sexually transmitted infections (STIs) through targeting what are perceived to be 'high-risk' groups and finding ways to reduce their sexual risk-taking behaviour. Social cognition has been used particularly extensively in this field (Boer & Mashamba, 2005). Within these kinds of approaches, it is assumed that people's attitudes, beliefs and perceptions enable us to predict their health-related behaviour or at least their *intended* behaviour (see also Chapters 1, 2, 3 & 4 for further discussion of the limitations of social cognition). Social cognitive studies of sexual behaviour often set out to test existing models of health behaviour but within the context of sexual health. Common models used in studies of sexual risk taking include the Health Belief Model (Becker, 1974), the Theory of Reasoned Action (Fishbein & Ajzen, 1975) and the Theory of Planned Behaviour (Ajzen, 1985). Specific models have also been developed for understanding HIV such as the AIDS Risk Reduction Model (see Catania et al., 1994).

It can be argued that these rational and 'epidemiologic' (Schensul, 1998) approaches have provided an insight into some of the factors underlying people's decisions (or intentions) to use (or not use) contraception. However, Mielewczyk and Willig (2007) point out that even where continued efforts have been made to increase the explanatory and predictive power of these models, the variance in behavioural outcomes left unaccounted for is routinely somewhere between 50 and 80 per cent (for example, Fekadu & Kraft, 2002; Godin et al., 2005), suggesting that they have only a limited capacity to explain or predict sexual behaviours such as contraceptive use. Furthermore, a number of researchers have pointed out that this kind of research has failed to consider how young people's understandings of sex and relationships are situated in the social and cultural locations in which their experiences take place. Contraception itself, for example, appears to have many meanings attached to it. Research has suggested that the use of contraception is seen by both women and men as a threat to intimacy, romance and love (Rosenthal et al., 1998; Watson & Bell, 2005) and as a sign of distrust and promiscuity (Hammer et al., 2006; Moore & Halford, 1999). Feminist researchers have also questioned whether it is valid to study sex and sexuality from a neutral standpoint (see, for example, Rich, 1980; Vance, 1984). They argue that since sexual relationships are inherently political, involving complex power relations, there must be some recognition of the role that powerful cultural ideologies about gender play in the formation of sexual identities and subjectivities. As a result, much feminist research has focused on the dominant constructions of female sexuality and the constraints that these constructions place on women's ability to ensure their own sexual autonomy and safety (see, for example, Willig, 1998; Gavey & McPhillips, 1999). Power issues have also been identified for young people in developing countries such as South Africa (Campbell et al., 2005) and for young gay men entering the gay community (Flowers et al., 1998).

To summarise, social cognition appears to have limited success in terms of providing an insight into people's sexual health behaviours, and it has been argued by critical psychologists that this is largely down to their individualistic focus. Rather than looking to discursive, structural or material factors as sources of sexual health 'problems', traditional health psychology approaches have conceptualised 'unsafe' or 'risky' sexual behaviour as an 'individual failure' to use contraception.

The conceptualisation of 'choice' in social cognition and in health promotion

The focus on attitudes and intentions within mainstream sexual health research reflects an assumption that the purpose of health promotion is to reduce people's risk-taking by encouraging them to make 'safer' decisions or choices. However, social cognition has been widely criticised for drawing upon (and also reinforcing) overly simplistic and individualistic conceptions of 'choice' (see, for example, Lyons & Chamberlain, 2006). The same criticism can be levelled at sexual health promotion materials. Indeed, this was something which struck me recently whilst analysing data collected as part of an ongoing study to explore the discursive construction of sex and sexualities in sexual health promotion websites. The analytic process utilises a form of poststructuralist discourse analysis outlined by Willott & Griffin (1997). An aim of poststructuralist discourse analysis of this kind is to explore the subjectivities, identities and possibilities that certain discourses make (un)available to people. One way in which this is done is through a consideration of the ways in which discourses 'position' people (for example, as powerful or vulnerable, active or passive, victims or perpetrators) or the ways in which people position themselves in relation to particular discourses (see Davies & Harré, 1990). Discussion of the latter has led to debates amongst critical psychologists and feminists about the extent to which people have control over which discourses they 'take up' or 'resist', with some scholars (see, for example, Wray, 2004) arguing that concepts like agency and resistance are underpinned by neo-liberal and individualistic notions of choice similar to those adopted in much mainstream research and theorisation. For an extended discussion of these debates in relation to a number of different health-related contexts see Day et al. (2010).

The analysis of sexual health promotion websites that I have been engaged in has highlighted the extent to which these sites draw upon neoliberal discourse to construct 'choice' in relation to sexual health and relationships. The pervasive ideology of neoliberalism posits that individual lives should take an 'entrepreneurial form' (Brown, 2003; Lemke, 2001) in the sense that as individuals, we should live our lives as though we are in control of our destinies (Rose, 1990; 1996), striving for autonomy and individual success. In other words, neoliberal ideologies suggest that as individuals we have the freedom to make our own choices and also a responsibility to make the 'right' choices (Davies, 2005; Walkerdine et al., 2001).

The four websites from which data were collected are Avert (an International AIDS charity), Likeitis (part of Marie Stopes International), TheSite (which offers information and support to young people on a range of issues including sex and relationships) and the NHS Choices website (which provides general information on conditions, treatments, local services and healthy living). These websites draw heavily upon neoliberal discourse to construct young people as having almost unlimited choices, and as being able to make rational and informed decisions about issues relating to sex and sexuality. Issues including when and/or whether to have sex, deciding what to do if one is pregnant, 'deciding upon' one's sexuality and how to 'come out' are constructed in a highly simplistic way as being matters of personal preference. For each of these issues, the websites stress that there are no 'rights' or 'wrongs' and that the individual must do what is 'right' or 'best' for them. For example,

> *There is no 'right' age to start having sex. What is important is choosing a time that is right for you.* (Avert)

> *There is no right or wrong way to be bisexual. You are the person who determines your sexuality.* (TheSite)

This neoliberal discourse positions individuals as the authors of their own destinies. On the face of it, this may appear to be a positive way of constructing young people by recognising that they are mature enough to make decisions about their own sexualities and sexual relationships and have the right to do so. Yet there are a number of problems with the way in which choice and agency are being constructed here.

Firstly, it can be argued that by constructing sexual health decision making as a solitary activity, in which no-one else can, or should intervene, this neoliberal discourse arguably shuts down the avenues available to young people for discussion and leaves them to make important sexual health decisions alone and in the context of a relative lack of information (see Ashcraft, 2006, for a discussion of this issue in relation to discourses of 'readiness' for sex).

A second problem with this neoliberal discourse is that in stating that young people can take control, make their own choices, decide what is right for them and 'do what [they] want to do' (Likeitis), this discourse carries a connotation that when things go wrong or do not go according to plan, this is either because they have made the 'wrong' choice (for example, decided that they were ready for sexual intercourse when actually they weren't) or because they are lacking in some quality required to take control such as confidence, maturity, self-esteem or assertiveness.

There are numerous extracts across the sites that imply that failing to be assertive enough, confident enough or have high enough self-esteem can result in regret, unwanted sex, unsafe sex and even violence. This example is typical:

> *Low self-esteem can be caused by many different factors. You might be lonely, or feeling unattractive or maybe you're being bullied. And if you don't feel confident, it means you can't say no and the vicious circle begins. You end up making bad decisions because you don't feel good about yourself. That's why you might have sex when you don't really want to ... In extreme cases, having low self-esteem makes you more vulnerable to abusive relationships. The majority of victims are girls whose lack of confidence attracts these controlling boyfriends.* (TheSite)

This arguably well-intentioned but nonetheless highly problematic discourse fails to acknowledge the role of structural and material factors in coercive sex and violence, constructing them instead as the consequences of young people's individual 'inadequacies'. Cruikshank (1996) identified a tendency in the United States to explain a wide variety of social problems as resulting from individuals' lack of self-esteem and argued that this is rooted in a neoliberal model of rationality. Lemke (2001) argues that the goal of the 'self-esteem movement' identified by Cruiskshank is '... to solve social problems by heralding a revolution – not against capitalism, racism, the patriarchy, etc., but against the (wrong) way of governing ourselves' (p. 202). Davies (2005) and Walkerdine et al. (2001) have also noted the implications of this kind of neoliberal discourse in terms of its tendency to demonise those who are dependent or who 'make themselves vulnerable' to victimisation by not scrutinising and regulating their behaviour sufficiently.

Another limitation of the neoliberal discourse employed by these health promotion websites is its problematic implication that choices (particularly those around sex and sexuality, issues which have long been associated with morality and immorality) are, or can be, made in some kind of moral vacuum. Modern Western societies are highly sexualised, highly consumerist, and highly technological and young people are bombarded with multiple and competing discourses about sex and sexuality from the media, parents, schools and peers (Addison, 2006). To suggest that, within this context, choices can be made that reflect only 'what is best for the individual' is to vastly oversimplify the context within which individuals learn about sex, make sense of who they are and who they are attracted to and live out their sexual lives.

'Choice' as constrained by discursive resources and structural/material contexts

Researchers such as Fine (1988), Kirkman et al. (1998) and Gavey and McPhillips (1999), who have taken a discursive approach to the study of sexual health, have argued that whilst people may have some degree of freedom or control over their sexual relationships and sexual health, the options open to people in negotiating their sexual lives will be shaped and constrained by the discursive resources available to them as well as the structural and material contexts in which those lives are lived out.

With regard to sexual health, one of the most obvious or visible ways in which people's sexual behaviour is regulated is through the widespread adoption of moralistic discourse which constructs certain sexual activities as safe or unsafe, good or bad, right or wrong, appropriate or inappropriate. In terms of the extent to which discourses of this kind make certain forms of sexual expression available or unavailable, it is important to acknowledge that this discourse is not neutral in terms of social categories like gender, race, class, or sexuality. As a result, the range of sexual activities that are constructed as, for example, good, or safe, or appropriate, will vary according to these factors so that some groups (for example, white, middle-class, able-bodied, heterosexual males) are afforded a wide range of sexual opportunities whilst other groups are furnished with very narrow definitions of what constitutes appropriate sexual behaviour for 'people like them'.

The most widely written about example of discourse that prescribes differential sets of behaviours as appropriate for different social groups is the range of highly gendered and essentialist discourses that construct male sexuality as active, driven and predatory and female sexuality as reactive and responsive. Willig (1998), for example, argues that these discourses have naturalised male promiscuity and female fidelity by suggesting that these behaviours are instinctive and serve particular evolutionary functions. In this sense, they have lent credibility to a 'sexual double standard' whereby sex outside of the confines of a committed relationship is permitted for men but not for women. I have written elsewhere about the ways in which young women that I interviewed about their sexual relationships attempted to challenge this sexual double standard by asserting their right to behave in the same way as their male counterparts (see Milnes, 2004; Milnes, 2010). For example, Natalie said:

> So I had... you know about eighteen months of being... you know, to me, having fun, to a lot of other people it was... being a tart or whatever, but I don't see it like that, not when... the male... can get away with it (laughing) as far as I'm concerned... you know, I'm just as equal as they are and if I wanna do that, then that's my choice you know.

However, whilst Natalie draws here upon the neoliberal discourse of choice discussed earlier to suggest that she can simply 'choose' to behave however she wants to sexually, she then went on to talk about how having a 'casual' sexual relationship with a friend had impacted negatively on how others perceived her:

> as far as I'm concerned it was an ideal... situation to be in because there was no strings attached and as far as I was concerned that was good... I remember I had a few comments off people, you know, 'oh don't you think it's a bit slaggy?'

It can be argued then, that whilst Natalie (along with a number of the other women I interviewed) felt that having multiple sexual partners or having sex outside of a monogamous long-term relationship were (or at least should be) viable options for her, she was not permitted to engage in these activities without others alerting her to their 'impropriety' for a young woman.

Moralistic discourses around sex and sexuality are particularly prevalent in Western societies. Although there is a widespread perception that in the past half century the media and society generally have gradually become more liberal and permissive with regard to sex, the representations of sex that we are bombarded with frequently transmit clear moral messages about who can (or should) engage in what kinds of sexual activities and under what circumstances. So, whilst we may live in a highly sexualised culture, the sexual subject positions that are available to us are limited and regulated by the dominance of moralistic discourses that warn us of the dangers of behaving 'inappropriately'.

Connell and Hunt (2006) argue that since the beginning of the twentieth century, rather than functioning 'in its own voice', morality has increasingly functioned through 'proxies', that is, through other forms of discourse including risk discourse resulting in,

> an apparently benign form of moralization in which the boundary between objective hazards and normative judgments becomes blurred…unlike standard moral judgments ('X is wrong') the normative dimension is not immediately apparent. Thus, 'having unsafe sex is risky' does not directly state that 'unsafe sex is wrong', but it lurks very near the surface. Thus, risk discourses provide an apparently utilitarian ground for regulatory intervention, but without appearing directly to institute a form of moral regulation. (pp. 40–41)

Moralistic discourses of this kind feature heavily on the websites that I have analysed (referred to earlier in this chapter). Despite the websites' widespread adoption of neoliberal discourse to construct young people as having almost unlimited choices, they also simultaneously adopt moral discourse that with varying degrees of transparency, constructs various actions, interactions and behaviours as right or wrong. These discourses are employed to warn young people of the dangers of having sex with the 'wrong' people, at the 'wrong' time, or for the 'wrong' reasons. For example,

> … *sex without any commitment or ties may sound appealing [but]… casual sex is not for everyone and there are many who would say it is wrong… Sex should be enjoyable for all concerned, whether it be in a long and loving relationship or in a one off drunken mistake with some vague face from your college… Casual sex can be risky, to not only a person's physical health but to their mental health also.* (Avert)

They are also employed to inform gay, lesbian and bi-sexual young people about the 'right' and 'wrong' ways to go about 'coming out' and to prescribe to bi-sexual young people what are acceptable/permissable ways of being bi-sexual:

> … *don't reinforce negative stereotypes… don't lead people on… Being bisexual might mean you feel attracted to guys and girls, but it doesn't give you license to be unfaithful to your partner.* (The Site)

In thinking about the implications of the moral discourse adopted in these websites, it is useful to consider the work of Shoveller and Johnson (2006) who argue that in their attempts to identify those young people who are 'at risk' or 'in need of help', public health practices have inadvertently divided groups of youth on the basis of their sexual behaviour into, for example, those who are risky and those who are safe or those who are responsible and those who are irresponsible. It can be argued that these websites discursively divide young people into those who make the 'right' choices (for example, only having sex within relationships or only with people that they have known for some time, waiting until they are ready, using contraception, not giving in to peer or partner pressure) and those who make the 'wrong' choices, with the latter being constructed as a risk both to themselves and to others.

To return to my earlier argument then, the way in which choice tends to be constructed in sexual health promotion materials (which is based upon the social cognition of the individual as a rational decision maker) is both problematic and overly simplistic. As illustrated here, it fails to acknowledge the difficulties and tensions that individuals are likely to experience in trying to exercise choice, resistance and agency in a highly moralistic context. My arguments here have not been intended to undermine the aim of many health promotion campaigns and materials, assuming that is, that their aims are to enable people to play a more active role in negotiating their sexual health and well-being. However, I believe that taking a more critical approach to sexual health promotion (one that conceptualises sex and sexual relationships as situated practices rather than as individual behaviours) creates much greater potential for people to adopt an active role in the negotiation of their sexual lives whilst still acknowledging the socio-cultural and material contexts in which those lives are lived and the constraints that this may place on their relationships, experiences and identities.

Moving forward: possibilities for action

One of the themes of this book is the debate around the extent to which, as critical health psychologists we should be concerned with critique and/ or action. My position in relation to this debate is that critique is, in itself, a form of action. Allen (2007) conceives of agency as something which 'appears in the spaces where contradictory discourses compete for the constitution of the subject' (p. 224); in other words, she argues that where we have multiple competing and contradictory discourses available, this affords us some agency in negotiating our position. Allen stresses that we do not simply 'choose' which discourse we position ourselves within, however, it can be argued that our access to discursive resources (which is likely to be constrained to varying degrees by structural and material factors) plays a part in our ability to resist dominant discourses. In terms of sexuality, this implies that attaining sexual agency would require individuals to have access to multiple discursive resources about sex and sexual identity. Whilst appearing on the face of it to be operating within a neoliberal framework, which encourages people to 'be themselves', 'take control' and make informed choices, it can be argued that health promotion materials (such as the websites discussed in this chapter) actually function to limit people's options by making available only a very limited number of discourses and by alienating and marginalising anyone who does not conform to very narrow standards of 'approved' sexuality.

I would argue that if we want to create possibilities for action we need to create spaces where agency can appear, that is, we need to create spaces that are accessible to more diverse groups and that provide a multiplicity of competing and contradictory discourses. These spaces (whether they be websites, online communities, classrooms, youth, women's, disability or LGBT groups) must afford people the opportunity to critique aspects of those discourses which they find constraining, limiting or oppressive and to construct new discourses which they find more liberating or empowering and which resonate more closely with their lived experiences.

Key points

1. Mainstream psychological approaches to studying sexual health have tended to be underpinned by an assumption that human beings are rational decision makers who weigh up the costs and benefits of taking various courses of action before deciding how to behave.
2. Sexual health promotion campaigns and strategies informed by mainstream psychological research often aim to support people in 'making the right choices' and 'being assertive' enough to stand by these choices.
3. Mainstream psychological approaches to sexual health are problematic for a number of reasons: they are based on an overly simplistic conceptualisation of 'choice', they frame the 'failure' to use contraception or protect one's own sexual health and well-being as an individual 'problem', and health promotion campaigns and resources often perpetuate highly moralistic and paternalistic discourses.
4. A critical health psychological analysis and interpretation of sexual health acknowledges the ways in which discursive, material and structural factors constrain the options available to people in negotiating their sexual lives, emphasises the role of complex power relations and cultural ideologies in the use (or non-use) of contraception and alerts us to the highly moralistic and paternalistic discourses which may serve to alienate many of those who are seen by health professionals as being most 'in need of help'.

5. Possibilities for action involve creating spaces which afford people the opportunity to critique aspects of those discourses which they find constraining, limiting or oppressive and to construct new discourses which they find more liberating or empowering and which resonate more closely with their lived experiences.

REFERENCES

Addison, N. (2006) 'Acknowledging the gap between sex education and the lived experiences of young people: a discussion of Paula Rego's The Pillowman (2004) and other cautionary tales', *Sex Education*, 6(4), 351–65.

Ajzen, I. (1985) 'From intentions to actions: a theory of planned behaviour', in J. Kuhl & J. Beckman (eds) *Action-Control: From Cognition to Behaviour* (pp. 11–39), Heidelberg: Springer.

Allen, L. (2007) 'Denying the sexual subject: schools' regulation of student sexuality'. *British Educational Research Journal*, 33(2), 221–34.

Ashcraft, C. (2006) 'Ready or not…? Teen sexuality and the troubling discourse of readiness'. *Anthropology and Education Quarterly*, 37(4), 328–46.

Becker, M. H. (ed.) (1974) 'The Health Belief Model and personal health behaviour'. *Health Education Monographs*, 2, 328–35.

Boer, H. & Mashamba, M. T. (2005) 'Psychosocial corbelates of HIV protection motivation among black adolescents) in Venda, South Africa'. *AIDS Education and Prevention*, 17(6), 590–602.

Bondi, L. (2003) 'A situated practice for (re)situating selves: trainee counsellors and the promise of Counseling'. *Environment and Planning A*, 35(5), 853–70.

Brown, W. (2003) 'Neo-liberalism and the end of liberal democracy', *Theory and Event*, 7(1), 119.

Campbell, C., Foulis, C. A., Maimane, S. & Sibiya, Z. (2005) '"I have an evil child at my house" Stigma and HIV/AIDS management in a South African community'. *American Journal of Public Health*, 95(5), 808–15.

Catania, J., Coates, T., & Kegeles, S. (1994), 'A test of the AIDS Risk Reduction Model: psychosocial correlates of condom use in the AMEN cohort survey'. *Health Psychology*, 13(6), 548–55.

Connell, E. & Hunt, A. (2006) 'Sexual ideology and sexual physiology in the discourses of sex advice literature', *Canadian Journal of Human Sexuality*, 15(1), 23–45.

Cruikshank, B. (1996) 'Revolutions within: self-government and self-esteem', in A. Barry, T. Osborne & N. Rose (eds) 'Foucault and political reason: liberalism, neo-liberalism and rationalities of government' (pp. 231–51). London: UCL Press.

Davies, B. (2005) 'The (im)possibility of intellectual work in neoliberal regimes'. *Discourse: Studies in the Cultural Politics of Education*, 26(1), 1–14.

Davies, B. & Harré, R. (1990) 'Positioning: the discursive production of selves'. *Journal for the Theory of Social Behaviour*, 20(1), 44–63.

Day, K., Johnson, S., Milnes, K. & Rickett, B. (2010) 'Exploring women's agency and resistance in health-related contexts'. *Feminism and Psychology*, 20(2), 238–41.

Fekadu, Z. & Kraft, P. (2002) 'Expanding the theory of planned behaviour: the role of social norms and group identification'. *Journal of Health Psychology*, 7, 33–43.

Fine, M. (1988) 'Sexuality, schooling and adolescent girls: the missing discourse of desire'. *Harvard Educational Review*, 58, 29–53.

Fishbein, M. & Ajzen, I. (1975) *Belief, Attitude, Intention and Behaviour: An Introduction to Theory and Research*. Reading, MA: Addison-Wesley.

Flowers, P., Smith, J. A., Sheeran, P. & Beail, N. (1998) '"Coming out" and sexual debut: understanding and the social context of HIV risk-related behaviour'. *Journal of Community & Applied Social Psychology*, 8(6), 409–21.

Gavey, N. & McPhillips, K. (1999) 'Subject to romance: heterosexual passivity as an obstacle to women initiating condom use', *Psychology of Women Quarterly*, 23(2), 349–67.

Godin, G., Gagnon, H., Lambert, L. D. & Conner, M. (2005) 'Determinants of condom use among a random sample of single heterosexual adults'. *British Journal of Health Psychology*, 10, 85–100.

Hammer, J. C., Fisher, J. D., Fitzgerald, P. & Fisher, W. A. (2006), 'When two heads aren't better than one: AIDS risk behaviour in college-age couples', *Journal of Applied Social Psychology*, 26 (5), 375–97.

Kirkman, M., Rosenthal, D. and Smith, A. M. A. (1998) 'Adolescent sex and the romantic narrative: why some young heterosexuals use condoms to prevent pregnancy but not disease', *Psychology, Health and Medicine*, 3(4), 355–70.

Lemke, T. (2001) '"The birth of bio-politics": Michel Foucault's lecture at the College de France on neo-liberal governmentality', *Economy and Society*, 30(2), 190–207.

Lyons, A. & Chamberlain, K. (2006) *Health Psychology: A Critical Introduction*. Cambridge: Cambridge University Press.

Mielewczyk, F. & Willig, C. (2007) 'Old clothes and an older look: the case for a radical makeover in health behaviour research', *Theory and Psychology*, 17, 811–37.

Milnes, K. (2004) 'What lies between romance and sexual equality? A narrative study of young women's sexual experiences', *Sexualities, Evolution and Gender*, 6(2-3), 151–70.

Milnes, K. (2010) 'Challenging the sexual double standard: constructing sexual equality narratives as a strategy of resistance', *Feminism and Psychology*, 20(2), 255–59.

Moore, S. & Halford, A. P. (1999) 'Barriers to safer sex: beliefs and attitudes among male and female adult heterosexuals across four relationship groups'. *Journal of Health Psychology*, 4(2), 149–63.

Rich, A. (1980) 'Compulsory heterosexuality and lesbian existence'. *Signs: Journal of Women in Culture and Society*, 5, 31–62.

Rose, N. (1990) *Governing the Soul: The Shaping of the Private Self*. London: Routledge.

Rose, N. (1996) *Inventing Our Selves: Psychology, Power and Personhood*. Cambridge: Cambridge University Press.

Rosenthal, D., Gifford, S. & Moore, S. (1998) 'Safe sex or safe love: competing discourses?' *AIDS Care*, 10(1), 35–47.

Schensul, J. (1998) 'Learning about sexual meaning and decision-making from urban adolescents', *International Quarterly of Community Health Education*, 18(1), 29–48.

Shoveller, J. A. & Johnson, J. L. (2006) 'Risky groups, risky behaviour, and risky persons: dominating discourses on youth sexual health'. *Critical Public Health*, 16(1), 47–60.

Vance, C. (1984) *Pleasure and Danger: Exploring Female Sexuality*. Boston: Routledge and Kegan Paul.

Walkerdine, V., Lucey, H. & Melody, J. (2001) *Growing Up Girl: Psychosocial Explorations of Gender and Class*, Basingstoke: Palgrave Macmillan.

Watson, W. K. & Bell, N. J. (2005) 'Narratives of development, experiences of risk: adult women's perspectives on relationships and safer sex'. *British Journal of Health Psychology*, 10(3), 311–27.

LIVERPOOL JOHN MOORES UNIVERSITY
LEARNING SERVICES

Willig, C. (1998) 'Constructions of sexual activity and their implications for sexual practice: lessons for sex education', *Journal of Health Psychology*, 3(3), 383–92.

Willott, S. & Griffin, C. (1997). '"Wham bam, am I a man?" Unemployed men talk about masculinities', *Feminism and Psychology*, 7(1), 107–28.

Wray, S. (2004) 'What constitutes agency and empowerment for women in later life?' *Sociological Review*, 52, 22–38.

PART III

MODERNISATION AND DEMOCRATISATION IN HEALTHCARE

CHAPTER 8

Taking the Lead: Authority and Power in the National Health Service

PAULA NICOLSON, EMMA ROWLAND,
PAULA LOKMAN AND REBEKAH FOX

Introduction

It seems that each time something goes awry in the British National Health Service (NHS) or any other organisation such as the British football team, the Labour Party, child protection services, the international cricket board or the Mexican government in their fight against drug trafficking, experts declare the need for 'leadership' (or conversely decry the failure of 'leadership'). Leadership is the ultimate panacea for twenty-first century institutions. But what exactly is being demanded by this cry?

Little has been written about leadership under the umbrella of 'health psychology', although increasingly other disciplinary groups, particularly sociologically informed business and management academics, are taking a critical position towards the traditional perspective that focuses on the psychological qualities inherent in a leader. Here we reconsider the findings from our recently completed four-year study of leading in the NHS. In this chapter we suggest how some of the recent thinking from a (broadly) critical social science perspective can inform advances in critical health psychology.

We bring into play the qualitative components of our mixed-method study of leadership in the NHS in which Paula N was the Principal Investigator and Emma, Paula L and Rebekah the researchers. The study itself was about the relationship of leadership to patient care across three NHS Trusts in the south of England (see Nicolson et al. 2010)., In what follows we look at the ways in which our methodological approaches led us to *look critically beneath the surface of our data* and the uneasy nexus of leadership/followership/context.

What we did and what we found

Our study employed in-depth interviews with 'story-telling'(Gabriel, 2000; Hannabuss, 2000), focus groups (Macnaghten & Myers, 2004), ethnographic observation (Delamont, 2004) and 'shadowing' (Czarniawska, 2008; McDonald, 2005). The aim was to gain a sense of what it was like to work in the NHS and how the work and organisation were given meaning(s). Data comprised digitally recorded and transcribed texts based on the interviews and focus groups as well as detailed notes from the ethnographic observations and shadowing, and all were subjected to different layers of thoughts, challenges and ideas between the time of the data collection, the report writing and this chapter.

Typically though we began to analyse the transcripts with a *thematic analysis* to identify what themes emerged from the definitions, while also making interpretations using critical discourse analysis (CDA) (Foucault, 1982) and narrative analysis (Czarniawska, 2010; Lokman et al., in press). In so doing we payed attention to what Gough has termed 'emotional ruptures' (Gough, 2004) in the texts which serve to illuminate some of the subordinated or unconscious information in the stories of the respondents and the subjectivity of the narrator (Frosh, 2003; Frosh et al., 2003; Hollway & Jefferson, 2000). From these we developed a sense of the unspoken, emotional and unconscious practices of both leadership and followership and how these intertwined within a context.

Advances in critical health psychology

Paula N, the psychologist in the group, considered that one important advance in critical health psychology is to manage and cross the boundaries with other disciplines something that psychology traditionally eschews. Emma and Rebekah are both cultural geographers with interests in health, the body, emotions, affect and psychoanalytical geographies and, for Rebekah in particular, human–animal relations. Paula L is a sociologist and anthropologist with an interest in phenomenologically informed understanding of social relations, in particular intersubjective knowledge construction and narratives.

As a team we worked closely together, and (mostly) we found that our skills and ideas proved complementary. Even so leadership shifted across time and activity. Most importantly perhaps though is that we continue(d) to work reflexively with the data, drafting and redrafting the report and chapters and papers that are emerging from this work (Barry, 2003; Nicolson, 2003).

Advances in critical health psychology have traditionally been identified with qualitative approaches to data collection and analysis. However there is not an immutable link between the two and increasingly qualitative psychology appears to be positioning itself alongside mainstream work setting out its own guidelines on how to do it 'properly' (e.g. Smith, 2004) thus falling into the trap of 'methodolatry' (Chamberlain, 2000). The capture and analysis of qualitative data however does open up possibilities for the scrutiny of taken-for-granted perspectives on 'what is going on' and how those involved (researchers and participants) make sense of and give meaning to their agency, processes and contexts.

Paula N, as a critical health psychologist, has also become increasingly convinced of the importance of psychoanalytic insights in the analysis of texts to explore the emotional worlds of organisations and the gendered and power dimensions of the relationships across the system. She therefore argues here that re-visiting psychoanalytic ideas (kicked into the wilderness by the exponential rise of experimental psychology since the 1960s and more recently neuropsychology) will show that they have much to offer critical research and thinking.

Contemporary leadership matters

The ongoing attempt to identify the characteristics necessary for effective leadership over recent years has been described as an 'obsession' studied more extensively than almost any other characteristic of human behaviour (Higgs, 2002; Tourish, 2008). Alimo-Metcalfe et al. (2007), in their comprehensive review of the literature, show that formal studies of leadership date back (at least) to the beginning of the twentieth century. They propose, that despite changes in the way leadership has been studied and the underlying epistemological stance taken by the researchers, 'in all cases, the emphasis has been on identifying those factors that make certain individuals particularly effective in influencing the behaviour of other individuals or groups and in making things happen that would not otherwise occur or preventing undesired outcomes' (p. 2). As 'many have pointed out, that in spite of the plethora of studies, we still seem to know little about the defining characteristics of effective leadership' (Higgs, 2002, p. 3). Even so this has not appeared to quell the appetite for pursuing an ideal of leadership, impelled by the changing demands of organisations echoed across public sector institutions such as the NHS. These changes are in part the result of technological advancements which impact upon clinical practices, demographic changes both of which have altered the strategic, structural, political and financial profile of health (and social) care (Tierney, 1996).

The tantalising questions remain though about what those factors might actually be and the significance of the context to understanding how certain characteristics might be more or less relevant or effective in particular organisations (Fairhurst, 2007; 2009; Liden & Antonakis, 2009; Uhl-Bien, 2006). One important set of findings suggests that leadership does have an effect on organisational performance – for good and for ill (Currie, et al. 2009; Schilling, 2009).

Thus it may be assumed that,

> Arguably, leadership is important in any organisation because [it] is needed to pull the whole organisation together in a common purpose, to articulate a shared vision, set direction, inspire and command commitment, loyalty, and ownership of change efforts. (Huffington, 2004, p. 31)

However,

> Leadership would be easy to achieve and manage if it weren't for the uncomfortable reality that without followership there could be no leadership except, perhaps for the delusional sort. (Obholzer, 2007, p. 33)

But how might it be understood critically?

In what follows we present data and discuss some key findings. These focus on,

1. transformational leadership, gendered leadership styles and emotion;
2. the crucial role of followers in the construction of leadership, power and authority; and
3. the importance of understanding leadership in its context, including the context of the mind.

Transformational leadership

Most discussed in theory and in practice over the past two decades has been the idea of *transformational leadership* (Bass, 1985), a model to explain ways in which a leader can be identified or trained to demonstrate the qualities that enable her/him to *perform beyond expectations*.

Transformational leadership then, is concerned with emotions, values and ethics, standards and long-term goals which include assessing followers' moves and satisfying their needs (Currie & Lockett, 2007; Day et al., 2006; Northouse, 2004).

Recognition that transformational leadership is not simply an individualistic model but one that *teams* can display (Day et al., 2006; Gronn, 2002; Sivasubramaniam et al., 2002) has shifted the concentration from individual leaders per se to a more diffuse and distributed model of leadership and organisation context.

What we realised as the study progressed was the central importance of *emotion* in the exercise of leadership which until relatively recently traditional research (and psychology in particular) has excluded.

Historical regulation: what makes a 'leader' and what makes 'leadership'?

One dramatic change over the past 20 and more years has been the image of the medical consultant in the public psyche. Thus the 'heroic' leadership of Sir Lancelot Spratt has been firmly (it seems) replaced by the team work in the TV series *Casualty* or *Holby City*. However the image of the rebel Dr. House (played by Hugh Laurie in an American TV series) is described as 'unorthodox' and 'radical' but most definitely a medical hero. Is this the type of leader that some might still long for? While the following comment was atypical of most people's definitions of what makes or fails to make a good leader it raises some interesting points about the contemporary regulatory discourses on leadership.

Thus one participant said of another[1],

> Now (Dr.) David is a really eccentric so he is not what you would naturally call a leader, erm but people are really respectful...Because he really cares for patients...And if he finds a junior doc, or nurse or anyone who is being unkind to an elderly patient then he is down on them like a ton of bricks but his, his patent commitment to medicine and clinical care just inspires admiration...And great affection hopefully. But he is very odd..... Yes. Erm, so he is like a one off so again there is no single person, you know there are, there are, there are different leadership styles which are appropriate in different situations but David of course could never be a chief exec, he just wouldn't be able to do it, so he would be hopeless there.

On the surface this might be explained as a judgement based on 'evidence' and a job description. However, focusing-in on the discursive and regulatory practices (Foucault, 1982) with which this extract engages, a different view can be taken. The respondent here, being asked to describe the qualities of leadership, begins by suggesting that taking patient care very seriously is 'eccentric' and the person who does that is a 'one off' and 'odd'. Paradoxically (it is suggested) David inspires affection and admiration but despite variety in leadership styles David would never make it to be CEO. Whether this is the case is irrelevant here because what is at stake are the ways in which discourses around 'leadership' and the qualities of the 'leader' *regulate conduct* setting normative behaviour through the discursive practices. There is little doubt that David would have been considered a leader (perhaps a leader in his field) during a different period when hospitals were smaller and perhaps when there was less specialisation in management.

What is worthy of note though is how David's 'old fashioned' leadership has apparently lost authority or at least is being subjected to an envious attack by someone invested in the 'new' style of leadership (for discussions of workplace envy, see Vidaillet, 2008; Stein, 2005). This example highlights the shifts in normative values supporting the idea that leadership is socially constructed rather than an 'innate' quality belonging to one individual.

Gender and leadership

While much has been written about the importance of understanding gender relations and leadership we identified it as an area that has attracted interest among policy makers and researchers, because the styles of leadership that are currently perceived to be the most effective, such as transformational and distributed, are believed to 'fit' more closely to 'feminine' styles of leadership. Fletcher (2004) notes that traditional 'heroic' leadership is usually associated with masculine traits (rather than men and women *per se*) such as individualism, control, assertiveness advocacy and domination, while 'post heroic' leadership traits (such as empathy, community vulnerability, collaboration) are more associated with feminine traits. Ford (2010) reconsiders the concept of *effective* leadership as a patriarchal model perpetuating an exclusionary and privileged view of the leader (metaphorically the 'father' figure).

Traditional research into gender, organisations power and leadership suggests that there are particular 'masculine' and 'feminine' leadership traits that are generally believed to characterise men and women's leadership styles (Rosener, 1990; Nicolson, 1996). Because women are widely believed to adopt a more democratic leadership style and men believed to adopt a more autocratic one, distributed leadership and concerted action in networked organisations may potentially be more conducive to those (women or men) who can adopt a more traditionally feminine relational style of leadership.

Furthermore, feminine styles are more akin to displaying social and/or emotional intelligence (Guy & Newman, 2004; Leon, 2005).

In reality, both men and women display a variety of 'masculine' and 'feminine' leadership styles, depending upon their individual personality, age, position and the situation involved (Cross & Bagilhole, 2002; McDowell, 2001). However, gender *expectations* influence perceptions and beliefs, and research suggests that subordinates are often more satisfied with leaders who behave in gender-typical ways than those who go against gender type (Rosener, 1990; Williams, 1993).

Indeed, women in explicit leadership roles often tend to be viewed less positively than men, in the belief that 'masculine' traits (competition, authority, lack of emotion) conform more to expectations of how a 'leader' should behave but not how a woman should (cf. the work of Broverman et al., 1970). The 'paradox' it seems persists in contemporary organisations so that some women leaders feel they have to behave in a 'masculine' way which frequently makes them appear rather heavy handed and/or as a 'bullying' because these behaviours do not fit with ideas about women (Eagly & Carli, 2003).

Most of the women and (some) of the men we spoke to during the study, made a point of denying that gender was an issue in today's NHS, indicating that they believed that women and men were treated equally, with an equal chance of success. However, several participants also mentioned gender differences in the negotiation of power and identities describing how either women or men were likely to gain advantage through use of their gender-typed styles (Lewis, 2000; Schnurr, 2008; West, 1984).

It seems gender and leadership remains a contradiction in people's minds but gender is a fundamental component of the discourses surrounding leadership in the NHS because of the demographic issues in clinical management and leadership (Evans, 1997; Gardiner & Tiggerman, 1999) and as we have shown in Chapters 4 to 7, role models and styles of leader/follower engagement have a major part to play in the transmission and exercise of leadership (Gill et al., 2008; Greener, 2007).

Women in senior managerial and/or professional positions either deny that being a woman is an issue for them or for their organisation or that they know what they had to do to prevent being seen as a senior '*woman*', rather than a senior leader.

Denying the impact of your own gender on how you are seen and how you manage and lead is not an easy position to maintain, and we observed some senior women working hard not to be seen as women even though at the same time they were arguing that *this behaviour was not necessary* because of the way 'things have changed'.

The researcher's observation of a senior female manager (Catherine) indicated that she thought that Catherine was trying to avoid being 'feminine' in her interactions. When the two interviewers were waiting to begin the interview, Catherine's PA came into the room with an important message but was shouted at in front of them. Thus in her notes one researcher judged that Catherine wanted,

> ...to indicate lack of interest and assume a position of superiority. Catherine was transgressing the boundaries of polite professional behaviour and attempting to define 'her' territory of the hospital. Answers to the questions were also defensive, perhaps indicating a lack of self-assurance. Despite the tough exterior she obviously felt a need to stamp her authority on people in order to maintain control of the situation. This may partially be related to her gender and need to appear 'more masculine than the men' in a competitive environment.

The researcher following on from her observational notes which included comments following the interview suggested that 'whilst she [Catherine] initially denied gender to be a relevant issue [for senior managers in the NHS], she then went on to make reference to "testosterone" and "the emotions of females" as problems in managing in her senior role'.
The relevant part of the interview transcript is below:

> *Q: Ok, so are men a problem? Are women a problem? Are there gender politics? Or am I just old fashioned there?*
> *A: I don't think there are anymore, I think there were. I mean when I was appointed, I could have been one of [only] four [senior] women, so the whole senior management was very...very 'suitish'. I don't think, no, I don't think it is a problem anymore. No, I think it is, if you talk to people in the north of England, they will say it's still a problem, and I think its a bit more of a problem to get females into acute trusts, big acute trusts, it's a bit of a climate difference. ...... I think there's a lot less testosterone around now, there's a sort of slightly...erm I mean I've got quite a young male management team.*
> *Q: Right*
> *A: I find the testosterone and sort of challenges a bit much from time to time.... So I mean from that point of view, it is quite interesting, it does manifest itself. As do emotions of females really. .....*

Catherine's somewhat aggressive, or at least uncompromising, behaviour witnessed by the researcher tended to soften after that and she added,

> *A: So I do think the answer to the question is that there are differences, but I don't think they're... they don't fundamentally affect how you do the job.*

The power of followers

In order to make sense of leadership, authority and power (individually and together), the role and experience of the 'follower' needs to be understood. The interconnections between power, authority and emotion play a complex part in understanding what leadership means to all those involved and in each organisational context. Leadership cannot be understood as something that can be observed and/or measured 'objectively'; it is not an essential 'quality' which resides in an individual but is socially constructed, meaning different things to different people at different times. Following Ford (2010) a more contemporary, appropriate and critical approach to the study of leadership 'pays attention to situations, events, institutions, ideas, social practices and processes that may be seen as creating additional repression or discursive disclosure' (Ford, 2010, p. 51).

To be specific Rioch (1975) and others had made the point that '"Leader" is a word which implies a relationship.... So the word "leader" does not have any sense without a word like "follower" implied in it'. (p. 159).

The relationship between leaders and followers might be more or less successful, and in order to be a follower a person needs (even on a very temporary basis) to 'give over' something of themselves (i.e. make themselves emotionally open) to the leader for the relationship to have meaning. Being a follower may be both (or either) passive or active, and there is the potential for the follower to engage and support, or subvert leadership (Bondi, 1997; Halton, 2007; O'Brien, 1994). Consequently, in order to analyse what it means to 'lead' in an organisation, understanding the practice(s) of emotional management alongside an analysis of power relations is fundamental (Grint, 2005; Schilling, 2009). For Foucault (Burrell, 1988; Foucault, 1982) power 'exists only when it is put into action, even if, of course, it is integrated into a disparate field of possibilities brought to bear upon permanent structures' (1982, p. 788). Thus, while organisations give formal power to relatively few leaders (including in a distributed model of leadership) consent is still required for the power to be maintained. Furthermore, 'the other' that is the one over whom power is exercised, needs to be 'recognised and maintained to the very end as a person who acts' (Foucault, 1982, p. 789).

Under the surface of leadership and followership: a moving experience?

For leadership in the NHS to be exercised effectively then there has to be an engagement between the leader and the followers (Macy & Schneider, 2008) and to understand fully how the engagement takes place, a degree of emotional engagement and/or attachment to the leader and to the organisational vision is fundamental (Riggio & Reichard, 2008; Rubin et al. 2005; Vince & Broussine, 1996).

The failure to take followers with you is made explicit here from the perspective of one (designated) leader:

> A^2: *I was forced upon them…*
>
> *Q: that's what I was going to ask. So presumably there was a lot of resentment I guess?*
>
> *A: Yes.*
>
> *Q: And how does it manifest itself?*
>
> *A: Erm, non-cooperation, making life difficult for you sometimes, people talking about erm sort of criticising you behind your back and erm playing silly games behind your back that makes management of other people more and more difficult. Erm you know, and yet we sort of have to fight another battle to win hearts and minds, when we, you know, don't really have the time to do that, we have got to have our focus on doing what we are meant to do, which is to manage patients and to manage our beds properly.*

This extract from the interview with someone whose role it is to lead change is revealing. The respondent recognises that he is not taking people with him and in his view, the followers appear to eschew co-operation. He also believes they are mocking him and that that mockery is contagious. He may or may not be able to evidence this, but that it is in his mind is potentially detrimental to his experience of leading in his organisation (Stein, 2005). Furthermore, instead of looking at himself, this respondent wants to push the blame for the leadership failures onto the followers or possibly does not even recognise he has failed (Klein, 1975; Segal, 1973).

In our study we found that having an influence and performing or 'doing' power was difficult to identify. A recurring theme was one in which there was a 'culture clash' between senior managers (who had the authority) and some clinicians who had power in some contexts through which they could subvert those in the leadership 'position' such as this deputy CEO:

> *A… a lot of the clinicians still think it's us and them and they forget why the managers might have been motivated to work here rather than sell houses as an estate agent. Erm, err, the erm, what I am sure about is that managers bring something to the party, that clinicians don't generally have, and when you work together you can achieve some amazing things.*
>
> *Q: Yeah. And can it be difficult to then, to work with the clinicians sometimes?*

A: Yeah it can be. But then they think you're on different planets, but they have all the tools if they don't cooperate and then nothing changes.

In this example the participant suggests that clinicians, 'on another planet' see the power/authority hierarchy as outside of their concern and 'do' their power through subversion and a performance of resistance and contempt for management.

In a complex organisation, such as the NHS, where layers of leadership are multiple, a leader will need to become a follower on occasions for collaborations to succeed. This requires the ability to shift between roles from those of power (leader) to those that take up others' authority (follower) (Obholzer & Roberts, 1994).

Organisation in the mind and under the surface

Contemporary research on the relationship(s) between leadership and context, in particular the development of qualitative approaches and discursive and social constructionist epistemologies (Grint, 2005; Uhl-Bien, 2006) emphasises how the context, culture, climate and/or structure of an organisation each have an impact on the performance of the people who lead it (Carroll et al., 2008; Goodwin, 2000; Michie & West, 2004).

The concept of the 'organisation in the mind' was a model developed originally in the early 1990s by organisational and group relations consultants working at the Grubb Institute, the Tavistock Centre and the Tavistock Institute of Human Relations, to refer to what an individual perceives mentally about how organisations, relations in the organisations and the structures are connected. 'It is a model internal to oneself... which gives rise to images, emotions, values and responses in me, which may consequently be influencing my own management and leadership, positively or adversely' (Hutton et al., 1997, p. 114, quoted in Armstrong, 2005, p. 4). In other words, when we talk about our colleagues, guess what the senior management are doing/ going to do and have fantasies about how well we fit, or don't fit, into the structure or system we do so in the context of the organisation we 'hold' in our mind which may or may not relate to that which other members of the organisation hold (Pols, 2005).

Organisations are experienced cognitively and emotionally by their members when they think about how their organisations work and are structured (see Armstrong, 2005; Morgan, 2006). As Stokes (1994) explains it, everyone carries a sense of the organisation in their mind but members from different parts of the same organisations may have 'different pictures and these may be in contradiction to one another. Although often partly unconscious, these pictures nevertheless inform and influence the behaviour and feelings of members' (p. 121).

Hutton (2000) talks about it as 'a conscious or pre-conscious construct focused around emotional experiences of tasks, roles, purposes, rituals, accountability, competence, failure, success' (p. 2). Morgan (2006) suggests that an organisation may serve as a 'psychic prison' in that the,

> ...patterns and meanings that shape corporate culture and subculture may also have unconscious significance. The common values that bind an organisation often have their origin in shared concerns that lurk below the surface of conscious awareness. For example, in organisations that project a team image, various kinds of splitting mechanisms are often in operation, idealising the qualities of team members while projecting fears, anger, envy, and other bad impulses onto persons and objects that are not part of the team (p. 226).

Some of this became apparent when talking to NHS staff about the leaders at various levels of their own Trusts and the NHS overall. So, when the respondent immediately below talks about the leader who has a 'really good understanding of the organisation or team' what exactly does that mean? How does that understanding come about? What do the team hold in mind about that particular leader?

Leadership is someone who has a really good understanding of the organisation or team, erm where it's going and where they imagine it to be going, so that sort of vision as well for their team, I think (Lead Clinical Non-medical Health Professional, T3).

This respondent, referring to the (frequently used) concept 'vision', also identifies this with the *imagination* the leader holds about where the organisation is going. This is not simply a matter of guesswork. It is an intellectual/cognitive and *emotional* sense of an organisation. Indeed to take this slightly further, as Gabriel and Schwartz (2004) propose, '... *what goes on at the surface of an organisation is not all that there is, and... understanding organisations often means comprehending matters that lie beneath the surface*' (p. 1).

Although not necessarily (in fact mostly not) made explicit, even the most clear thinking senior members of organisations hold an image of the organisation in mind, expressing their fantasy/belief/perception of the organisation based on conscious and unconscious knowledge (Halton, 2007).

So for instance for this CEO leadership is understood emotionally as it is,

> ...about the feel of the organisation and what it feels like in terms of how it delivers patient care. Yeah, erm. I can best illustrate that, and interestingly we were thinking about this earlier this morning, so as a group, the executives, we were talking about it. When you walk onto a hospital ward and there is real

leadership on that ward, you walk in and there are a number of signals that are given off, which give you a feel. Erm the place looks organised, it has a welcoming feel, the nurses on the ward and the clinical staff greet you as they come into contact with you. They know you from the previous interactions that you have had and when you sit there and listen to what is being said on the ward they will know that the patients, the visitors on the ward, the families that are coming in the junior doctors who are in there in that environment and all of that has a feel[3] of a well led ward (CEO).

The environment of the well-led ward (unit or organisation) is implicitly and unconsciously identified by all who engage with that organisation. The staff communicate effectively (visually, verbally and emotionally) so that the information required is passed on through managers, clinicians to colleagues, patients and relatives. This account, which preceded the extract that focused on strategy, directed to the best patient care for the greatest number of patients, expresses his ideas at an *emotional* level. He also suggests his senior colleagues agree with this. Signals are 'given off', you can 'feel' the organisation and how it delivers patient care and there is a 'welcoming feel'. He also talks about 'empirical' evidence in that staff know the patients, the ward looks organised; he remains convinced that there is a '*feel* of a well led ward'.

From a slightly different position, a deputy CEO quoted below also holds in mind the fantasy that a manager might think that they run an institution but that such a fantasy might get the manager into trouble. He is suggesting a vision of an organisation in which a manager has very little control, and proposes the need to gain a sense of *reality* by recognising this and taking responsibility for this organisation (Hirschhorn, 1997; Porter-O'Grady, 1995). His perception, again which has an emotional component, is one of a stressful contradiction – responsibility without power or control (de Vries, 2000).

> The minute, as a manager, you start to think that you do [run the service without accountability] ... erm then you're in trouble. Unfortunately you have still got the accountability for the service but you have very, very little control so it's a whole different leadership and managerial skill that is required I think in terms of recognizing that you have no control over what happens you know across this organisation across the N,000 beds here at [Trust], the thousands of people that go through the organisation everyday, what happens to them is completely outside of my control but if anything goes wrong it is absolutely my responsibility. And that is quite difficult (Deputy CEO).

Most recently Laughlin and Sher (2010) take up a version of this concept which they name the 'structure-in-the-mind' in their analysis of developing leadership in social care. They reassert, in their model, that not only the local stakeholders (staff and service users) have a sense of the organisation in the mind when considering, for instance, a particular Trust, but the range of stakeholders includes government bodies and service commissioners (in the round). They propose an inter-relationship between perceptions of communications from services (e.g. 'that you [management] don't listen and/or understand') and perceived communications from 'Head Office (or government or other bodies that control resources and practices) which include for example "just do it" "we know better" and "be rational"' (p. 9).

What is significant here, in the context of NHS leadership, is that the organisation and/or structure *in the mind* is where the leader and followers 'meet' emotionally as, similarly, do the various levels of leadership and governance bodies. It is a kind of 'virtual' space.

An example of this structure in the mind might be seen through the increase in stress for NHS employees detailad in a recent report by NICE (the National Institute for Clinical Excellence[4]) where it was revealed that staff absence caused by work-related stress costs the UK over £28 billion. It was proposed that a poor working environment characterised by bullying and poor management was at the heart of this problem[5] (Edwards & O'Connell, 2007). In a context where there is distributed leadership and a highly trained professional, multi-disciplinary workforce, such mismatches in how to run organisations and departments that lead to staff stress in these ways (e.g. being bullied and bullying) evoke questions about what is happening in the space between those who plan, govern and resource NHS Trusts and those who carry out the work. The emotional elements of leadership and followership relations seem to be neglected to everyone's disadvantage.

The idea of the organisation in the mind raises important questions of how leadership (good and bad) is transmitted across the NHS and its Trusts (Harrison & Carroll, 1991; Walsh & Ungson, 1991). Organisational cultures and climates are reproduced over time despite the coming(s) and going(s) of CEOs. However, organisations also *adapt* and *evolve* as a response to changes in leadership and outside influences (Morgan, 2006).

Conclusions

An important outcome of our work was to show that 'leadership' was a discursive construct and a social process rather than a characteristic or personality trait of an individual. Leadership, authority and power are thus fluid concepts so that what is understood as important in any organisational context is historically situated. Leadership understood in this way exists in a (potentially) problematic relationship to those who have formal roles which involve them in the exercise of leadership and to those who invest resources in training and selection of 'leaders'.

The research would not have happened and the report not written if we had not been able to distribute leadership across the team at various junctures. Also I believe that if there had not been an emotional engagement between us, at key points in the process, which enabled the shift of leadership then (again) we would not have achieved what we did. To reiterate also the Trusts and the SDO demonstrated similar dynamics, and it was not always possible to 'grasp' what was going on in these organisations at particular times, and we believe that these experiences are microcosms of 'real' organisational life which is frequently hidden in 'presentations' of the public face (Goffman, 1967). We consequently hope and intend that our research contributes to understanding how leadership might be exercised more effectively with a better understanding of the benefit to those who work in and are 'service' users of NHS organisations. However we also consider that we have contributed a critical perspective which challenges some of the taken-for-granted assumptions about what it is like to work in an NHS Trust.

Key points

1. Leadership has become a panacea for nearly every organisation but the meaning, practice and processes involved have not been considered. Despite the abundance of research the popular and professional concept remains contradictory in that it is still given the 'aura' of something magical while training is prosaic.
2. Emotionally and socially intelligent leadership are seen as an 'add on' something esoteric or even too feminine to be at the core of leadership selection and training. However without emotionally and socially intelligent leadership there is a strong possibility that leadership will either break down or fail to make a difference.
3. Senior women, despite the increase in their numbers in NHS organisations, on the whole experience more pressures than male leaders. Partly because they themselves try to behave 'as if' they were men. To do this they imitate what they see as male behaviour but inevitably get it wrong because there is more to being a man than the behaviour itself. Further there are still men (often from the post feminist generation) who think that women succeed because they have been favoured either because of sexual relationships or 'positive' selection.

NOTES

1. No identifying information is appropriate here.
2. Q = question and A = answer.
3. Respondent's emphasis.
4. An organisation established to oversee and provide guidance on clinical practice and cost and clinical effectiveness.
5. See news.bbc.co.uk/2/hi/health/8343074.stm and NICE web-site which has a power-point presentation.

REFERENCES

Alimo-Metcalfe, B., Alban-Metcalfe, J., Samele, C., Bradley, M. & Mariathasan, J. (2007) *The Impact of Leadership Factors in Implementing Change in Complex Health and Social Care Environments*, NHS.

Armstrong, D. (2005) *Organization in the Mind: Psychoanalysis, Group Relations and Organizational Consultancy* London: Karnac.

Barry, C. A. (2003) 'Holding up the mirror to widen the view: multiple subjectivities in the reflexive team', in L. Finlay & B. Gough (eds) *Reflexivity: A Practical Guide for Researchers in Health and Social Sciences* Oxford: Blackwell Science Ltd, pp. 214–28.

Bass, B. M. (1985) *Leadership and Performance beyond Expectations* New York: Free Press.

Bondi, L. (1997) *In Whose Words? On Gender Identities, Knowledge and Writing Practices* (vol. 22): Blackwell Publishing on behalf of The Royal Geographical Society (with the Institute of British Geographers), pp. 245–58.

Broverman, I. K., Broverman, D. M., Clarkson, F. E., Rosenkrantz, P. S. & Vogel, S. R. (1970) 'Sex-role stereotypes and clinical judgments of mental health', *Journal of Consulting and Clinical Psychology*, 34(1), 1–7.

Burrell, G. (1988) 'Modernism, Post Modernism and Organizational Analysis 2: The Contribution of Michel Foucault', *Organization Studies*, 9(2), 221–35.

Carroll, B., Levy, L. & Richmond, D. (2008) 'Leadership as Practice: Challenging the Competency Paradigm', *Leadership*, 4(4), 363–79.

Chamberlain, K. (2000) 'Methodolatry and Qualitative Health Research', *Journal of Health Psychology*, 5(May), 285–96.

Cross, S. & Bagilhole, B. (2002) 'Girls Jobs for the Boys? Men, Masculinity and Non-Traditional Occupations', *Gender, Work and Organization*, 9, 204–26.

Currie, G. & Lockett, A. (2007) 'A critique of transformational leadership: Moral, professional and contingent dimensions of leadership within public services organizations', *Human Relations*, 60(2), 341–70.

Currie, G., Lockett, A., & Suhomlinova, O. (2009) 'The institutionalization of distributed leadership: a "Catch-22" in English public services', *Human Relations*, 62(11), 1735–61.

Czarniawska, B. (2008) *Shadowing and other Techniques for Doing Fieldwork* (Abingdon, Oxfordshire: Marston Book Services).

Czarniawska, B. (2010) 'The uses of narratology in social and policy studies', *Critical Policy Studies*, 4(1), 58–76.

Day, D. V., Gronn, P. & Salas, E. (2006) 'Leadership in team-based organizations: on the threshold of a new era', *The Leadership Quarterly*, 17(3), 211–16.

Delamont, S. (2004) 'Ethnography and participant observation', in C. Seale, G. Gobo, G. J. F. & D. Silverman (eds), *Qualitative Research Practice* London: Sage, pp. 218–35.

Eagly, A. H. & Carli, L. L. (2003) 'The female leadership advantage: an evaluation of the evidence', *Leadership Quarterly*, 14(6), 807–34.

Edwards, S. L. & O'Connell, C. F. (2007) 'Exploring bullying: implications for nurse educators', *Nurse Education in Practice*, 7(1), 26–35.

Evans, J. (1997) 'Men in nursing: issues of gender segregation and hidden advantage', *Journal of Advanced Nursing*, 26(2), 226–31.

Fairhurst, G. T. (2007) *Discursive Leadership* London: Sage.

Fairhurst, G. T. (2009) 'Considering context in discursive leadership research', *Human Relations*, 62(11), 1607–33.

Fletcher, J. K. (2004) 'The paradox of postheroic leadership: An essay on gender, power, and transformational change', *The Leadership Quarterly*, 15(5), 647–61.

Ford, J. (2010) 'Studying leadership critically: a psychosocial lens on leadership identities', *Leadership*, 6(1), 47–65.

Foucault, M. (1982) 'The subject and power', *Critical Inquiry*, 8(4), 777–95.

Frosh, S. (2003) 'Psychosocial studies and psychology: is a critical approach emerging?' *Human Relations*, 56(12), 1545–67.

Frosh, S., Phoenix, A. & Pattman, R. (2003) 'Taking a stand: using psychoanalysis to explore the positioning of subjects in discourse', *British Journal of Social Psychology*, 42, 39–53.

Gabriel, Y. (2000) *Storytelling in Organizations: Facts, Fictions and Fantasies* Oxford: Oxford University Press.

Gabriel, Y. & Schwartz, H. (2004) 'Individual and Organisation', in Y. Gabriel, *Organisations in Depth* London: Sage.

Gardiner, M. & Tiggerman, M. (1999) 'Gender differences in leadership style, job stress and mental health in male- and female-dominated industries', *Journal of Occupational and Organizational Psychology*, 72, 301–15.

Gill, J., Mills, J., Franzway, S. & Sharp, R. (2008) '"Oh you must be very clever!" High-achieving women, professional power and the ongoing negotiation of workplace identity', *Gender and Education*, 20(3), 223–36.

Goffman, E. (1967) *Interaction Ritual. Essays on Face-to-Face Behavior.* Allen Lane: The Penguin Press.

Goodwin, N. (2000) 'Leadership and the UK health service', *Health Policy*, 51(1), 49–60.

Gough, B. (2004) 'Psychoanalysis as a resource for understanding emotional ruptures in the text: the case of defensive masculinities', *British Journal of Social Psychology*, 43, 245–67.

Greener, I. (2007) 'The politics of gender in the NHS: Impression Management and Getting Things Done™', *Gender, Work and Organisation*, 14(3), 281–99.

Grint, K. (2005) 'Problems, problems, problems: the social construction of "leadership"', *Human Relations*, 58(11), 1467–94.

Gronn, P. (2002) 'Distributed leadership as a unit of analysis', *Leadership Quarterly*, 13(4), 423–51.

Guy, M. E. & Newman, M. A. (2004) 'Women's jobs, men's jobs: sex segregation and emotional labour', *Public Administration Review*, 64(3), 289–98.

Halton, W. (2007) 'By what authority? Psychoanalytic reflections on creativity and change in relation to organisational life', in C. Huffington, D. Armstrong, W. Halton, L. Hoyle & J. Pooley (eds) *Working Below the Surface: The Emotional Life of Contemporary Organisations* London: Tavistock, pp. 107–24.

Hannabuss, S. (2000) 'Narrative knowledge: eliciting organisational knowledge from storytelling', *Aslib Proceedings*, 52(10), 402–13.

Harrison, J. R. & Carroll, G. R. (1991) 'Keeping the Faith: A Model of Cultural Transmission in Formal Organizations', *Administrative Science Quarterly*, 36(4), 552–82.

Higgs, M. J. (2002) *Leadership: the Long Line: a View on How We Can Make Sense of Leadership in the 21st Century*, Henley, UK: Henley Business School, University of Reading.

Hollway, W. & Jefferson, T. (2000) 'Eliciting narrative through the in-depth interview', *Qualitative Inquiry*, 3(1), 53–70.

Huffington, C. (2004) 'Introduction', in C. Huffington, W. Hatton, L. Hoyle and J. Pooley (eds) *Working below the Surface: The Emotional Life of Contemporary Organizations*. Tavistock Clinic Series, Hobbs, London.

Hutton, J. (2000) *Working with the Concept of Organisation in the Mind* London: The Grubb Institute.

Hutton, J., Bazalgette, J. & Reed, B. (1997) 'Organisation in the Mind', in J.E. Neumann, K. Kellner & A. Dawson-Shepherd (eds), *Developing Organisational Consultancy* London: Routledge, pp. 113–26.

Klein, M. (1975) 'Our Adult world and its roots in infancy (1959)', in *In the Writings of Melanie Klein: Envy and Gratitude and Other Works 1946–1963*, vol. 3, London: Hogarth Press, pp. 247–63.

Laughlin, R. & Sher, M. (2010) 'Developing leadership in a social care enterprise: Managing organisational and individual boundaries and anxiety', *Organizational and Social Dynamics*, 10(1), 1–21.

Leon, G. R. (2005) 'Men and women in space', *Aviation Space and Environmental Medicine*, 76(6), B84–B88.

Lewis, K. M. (2000) 'When leaders display emotion: how followers respond to negative emotional expression of male and female leaders', *Journal of Organizational Behavior*, 21, 221–34.

Liden, R. C. & Antonakis, J. (2009) 'Considering context in psychological leadership research', *Human Relations*, 62(11), 1587–605.

Lokman, P., Gabriel, Y. & Nicolson, P. (in press) 'Hospital doctors' anxieties at work: Patient care as intersubjective relationship and/or as system output', *International Journal of Organizational Analysis*.

Macnaghten, P. & Myers, G. 2004. 'Focus groups: the moderator's view and the analyst's view'. in *Qualitative Research Practice*. G. Gobo, J. Gubrium, C. Seale, & D. Silverman (London: Sage).

Macy, W. H. & Schneider, B. (2008) 'The meaning of employee engagement', *Industrial and Organisational Psychology*, 1, 3–30.

McDonald, S. (2005) 'Studying actions in context: a qualitative shadowing method for organizational research', *Qualitative Research*, 5(4), 455–73.

McDowell, L. (2001) 'Men, management and multiple masculinities in organisations', *Geoforum*, 32(2), 181–98.

Michie, S. & West, M. A. (2004) 'Managing people and performance: an evidence based framework applied to health service organizations', *International Journal of Management Reviews*, 5–6(2), 91–111.

Morgan, G. (2006) *Images of Organisation* London: Sage.

Nicolson, P. (1996) *Gender, Power and Organisation: A Psychological Perspective* London: Routledge.

Nicolson, P. (2003) 'Reflexivity, 'bias' and the in-depth interview: developing shared meanings', in L. Finlay & B. Gough (eds) *Reflexivity: A Practical Guide for Researchers in Health and Social Sciences* Oxford: Blackwell Science Ltd., pp. 133–45.

Nicolson, P., Rowland, E., Lokman, P., Fox, R., Gabriel, Y., Heffernan, K., Howorth, C., Ilan-Clarke, Y. and Smith, G. (2010) *Leadership and Better Patient Care: Managing in the NHS* HMSO: London.

Northouse, P. G. (2004) *Leadership: Theory and Practice* (3rd edn), Thousand Oaks, CA; London: Sage.

Obholzer, A. & Roberts, V. Z. (1994) *The Unconscious at Work: Individual and Organizational Stress in the Human Services* London: Routledge.

O'Brien, M. (1994) 'The managed heart revisited – health and social-control', *Sociological Review*, 42(3), 393–413.

Porter-O'Grady, T. & Krueger Wilson, C. (1995) 'Transitions and transformations: leadership in an emerging new world', in *The Leadership Revolution in Health Care: Altering Systems, Changing Behaviors* Gaithersburg, Maryland: Aspen Publishers, pp. 1–6.

Riggio, R. E. & Reichard, R. J. (2008) 'The emotional and social intelligences of effective leadership: an emotional and social skill approach', *Journal of Managerial Psychology*, 23(2), 169–85.

Rioch, M. J. (1975). '"All we like sheep..." [Isiah 53:6]: Followers and Leaders', in A. D. Colman & H. Bexton (eds) *Group Relations Reader*, vol. 1, Jupiter, Florida: A.K. Rice Institute, pp. 159–78.

Rosener, J. (1990) 'How women lead', *Harvard Business Review*, Nov–Dec, 119–25.

Rubin, R. S., Munz, D. C. & Bommer, W. H. (2005) 'Leading from within: the effects of emotion recognition and personality on transformational leadership behavior', *Academy of Management Journal*, 48(5), 845–58.

Schilling, J. (2009) 'From ineffectiveness to destruction: A qualitative study on the meaning of negative leadership', *Leadership*, 5(1), 102–28.

Schnurr, S. (2008) 'Surviving in a man's world with a sense of humour: an analysis of women leaders' use of humour at work', *Leadership*, 4(3), 299–319.

Segal, H. (1973) *Introduction to the Work of Melanie Klein* (New, enl. ed., London: Karnac and the Institute of Psycho-Analysis, 1988.

Sivasubramaniam, N., Murry, W. D., Avolio, B. J. & Jung, D. I. (2002) 'A longitudinal model of the effects of team leadership and group potency on group performance', *Group Organization Management*, 27(1), 66–96.

Smith, J. A. (2004) 'Reflecting on the development of interpretative phenomenological analysis and its contribution to qualitative research in psychology', *Qualitative Research in Psychology*, 1(1), 39–54.

Stein, M. (2005) 'The Othello Conundrum: The Inner Contagion of Leadership', *Organization Studies*, 26(9), 1405–19.

Stokes, J. (1994) 'Institutional chaos and personal stress', in A. Obholzer & V. Zagier-Roberts (eds) *The Unconscious at Work: Individual and Organisational Stress in the Human Services* London: Routledge.

Tierney, W. G. (1996) 'Leadership and postmodernism: on voice and the qualitative method', *Leadership Quarterly*, 7(3), 371–83.

Tourish, D. (2008) 'Challenging the transformational agenda: leadership theory in transition?' *Management Communication Quarterly*, 21(4), 522–28.

Uhl-Bien, M. (2006) 'Relational leadership theory: exploring the social processes of leadership and organizing', *Leadership Quarterly*, 17(6), 654–76.

Vidaillet, B. (2008) *Workplace Envy* Basingstoke: Palgrave Macmillan.

Vince, R. & Broussine, M. (1996) 'Paradox, defense and attachment: accessing and working with emotions and relations underlying organizational change', *Organization Studies*, 17(1), 1–21.

Walsh, J. P. & Ungson, G. R. (1991) 'Organizational memory', *The Academy of Management Review*, 16(1), 57–91.

West, C. (1984) 'When the Doctor Is a Lady – Power, Status and Gender in Physician-Patient Encounters', *Symbolic Interaction*, 7(1), 87–106.

Williams, C. L. (1993) *Doing 'Women's Work': Men in Nontraditional Occupations* Newbury Park, CA; London: Sage.

CHAPTER 9

Re-Visiting Pandora's Box: Primary Healthcare 'Directive' and 'Participatory' Practices with Women Experiencing Domestic Violence

VICTORIA LAVIS AND CHRISTINE HORROCKS

Introduction

Writing previously (Lavis et al., 2004) we drew upon the metaphor of Pandora's Box to consider emergent issues in UK primary healthcare, when responding and delivering services to women experiencing domestic violence.

This chapter revisits some of these issues and offers further elaboration. Making use of feminist and critical health psychology methods and ideologies we reveal practices which might perform transformatory functions in terms of improving health and benefitting participants (Creswell, 1998; Murray & Poland, 2006). In particular we highlight the emergence of two distinct practices which we have named 'directive' and 'participatory'. We intend to interrogate the origins of these differential practices, to reflect upon the subject positions they make available and the possibilities they afford for taking action. Significantly, the implications for both the women and health professionals will be targeted as areas of concern. Hence, throughout the chapter we illustrate how the exploration of 'directive' and 'participatory' practices offers insight into the consistently reported reluctance of health professionals to open the 'Pandora's Box' (see for example Sugg & Innui, 1992; McCauley, et al., 1998).

Yet we also demonstrate the centrality of integrated 'action orientated' services in providing an effective health care response for this group of service users.

Domestic violence and Pandora's box

The 2004 paper mentioned earlier, aimed to highlight some of the challenges and dilemmas arising from the re-positioning of domestic violence as a health, rather than 'merely' a social care issue (Department of Health (DOH), 2000a and 2000b). We drew on a metaphor which had been employed by health professionals in constructing their experience of responding to domestic violence as a 'Pandora's Box',

> I think that some physicians, and I, do the same thing, if you are very busy and have lots of patients waiting you just don't ask a question that you know is going to open a Pandora's box. Even if it crosses your mind, you don't ask. (Sugg & Innui, 1992, p. 3158)

The metaphor arises from Greek mythology. Pandora was the first woman, created by Zeus (King of the Gods) to punish another god, Prometheus, for helping mortal men. Zeus reportedly endowed Pandora with a 'deceptive heart', a 'lying tongue' and a box that she was forbidden to open. Eventually, out of curiosity, Pandora opened the box releasing into the world all manner of evils, sorrows, plagues and misfortunes. However, the remains of the box held one consolation – 'hope'. Obviously we would refute the negative and detrimental representation of women portrayed in the myth of Pandora's Box. Nevertheless, deploying the metaphor demonstrates a way of conceptualising the position of domestic violence within healthcare which is both meaningful and useful when trying to understand levels of reluctance around responding to women's distress and healthcare needs. The intention seems to be to keep the lid on the box as to do otherwise might release a range of sorrows and misfortunes. The question is whose misfortunes are these and where might the hope be for women who experience domestic violence?

A basic premise of our theoretical stance and critical engagement is that medicine is a commanding institution, which holds the power to claim 'truth' about a whole range of phenomena in social life, of which domestic violence is merely one (Lupton, 1997). This is achieved and illustrated, in part, by the practices of classification and diagnosis through which phenomena become medicalised (Armstrong, 1997). Medicalisation of social issues like domestic violence is problematic; as in practice medicalisation often leads to individualisation (Jeffrey, 1979; Waitzkin & Britt,1989; Lavis et al., 2004). By taking an individualistic stance, the complex health and social factors involved become redefined and thus accountable in terms of the individual woman's attributes. Hence, the woman is the difficulty to be solved rather than the complex social, cultural and material relations within which she is currently living her life. Indeed, making the individual the focus of the intervention is oppressive, serving to minimise and obscure the complexities of a life lived.

Crucially, we want to shed light on the relationship between power, knowledge and language which shapes and directs the health service response to domestic violence, and the implications of that relationship for health professionals and women experiencing domestic violence. Drawing on Foucault (1979, p. 1990) we maintain that medicine is a 'practice of power' which subjugates other knowledges to its own dominant truth. As Mishler (1984) explains the dominance of the medical discourse obscures the patients' lifeworld. Consequently, we suggest that women who experience domestic violence, and indeed health professionals who respond to domestic violence, are likely to have specialised and local knowledges that can become hidden or overpowered by other more dominant truths such as those articulated within the medical model. This said, more localised knowledge is to a certain extent being legitimated within healthcare, for example, the 'expert' knowledge of people with chronic ill-health has been recognised (DOH, 2001b). Also, the Department of Health report on the 'expert patient' (2001a) suggests an acceptance that some patients,

> ...can become key decision-makers in the treatment process. By ensuring that knowledge of their condition is developed to a point where they are empowered to take some responsibility for its management and work in partnership with their health and social care providers, patients can be given greater control over their lives. Self-management programmes can be specifically designed to reduce the severity of symptoms and improve confidence, resourcefulness and self-efficacy. (p. 5)

Key to this 'new approach' is respecting the skills and knowledge of patients, aiming to work in partnership. Even so the above quote makes it clear that this is not a partnership of equals. Rather there is the possibility of 'some' responsibility and 'greater' control. It is these relationships, boundaries and provisos that we want to consider in this chapter.

Brief overview of the research

The research we report upon aimed to explore the response of primary health care services to domestic violence within one case study area in the North of England. Specifically, the study sought to explore the construction(s) of domestic violence, the practices of responding this might precipitate and the multi-level experiences of those who live by and operate within such understandings. Adopting a case study design (Reinharz, 1992; Stake, 1998) meant viewing health services as a group or community and yet also a system, made up of different purposive elements: policy making, implementation, practical responding and patient experience. Thus, the participant groups included managers who developed and implemented healthcare policy, primary care health professionals who delivered services and women accessing health care services who were experiencing domestic violence. What was significant about the health professionals who self-selected to participate was that they all identified as having undertaken some further training in domestic violence. For many this was through a local integrated, health service-commissioned domestic violence support agency.

The research comprised three discrete stages of data collection: qualitative semi-structured interviews with policy makers, implementers of policy and health professionals; a quantitative survey to all health professionals within the District; and qualitative in-depth, unstructured interviews with women who had accessed health care services in relation to their experience of domestic violence. In this chapter we report on only the qualitative semi-structured and in-depth interviews.

The interviews were transcribed using the detailed discursive notation outlined by Parker (1992) and were subjected to a detailed Foucauldian Discourse Analysis following the guidance outlined by Willig (2001). This analysis included identifying discursive constructions, locating these constructions within wider discourses, considering the action orientation of the constructions, considering the subject positions made available, exploring the implications for action and practice, and the impact of subject positions on subjective experience. However, it is important to note that when undertaking this analysis there were tensions around Crossley's (2007) suggestion that there is 'chain of connection' between language and the experiencing self, where how a person thinks and experiences the world can be assumed to be associated with what they say or write. Drawing on a *critical realist* position we aimed to recognise the complexity of language and reality but nonetheless acknowledge a 'relationship' between how people narrate their world and their experiences (King & Horrocks, 2010).

The health professionals' accounts: avoidance and frustration

Whilst not explicitly using the metaphor of Pandora's Box, and also recognising the diversity of those working in this area, health professionals did, in their interviews deploy a variety of metaphors to describe their experiences of responding to domestic violence that evoked the myth. These included constructing responding as a 'horror' to be endured, a 'floodgate' to be kept closed and a 'can of worms', whose lid must not be lifted. These metaphors imply that domestic violence is experienced by health professionals as something which may release a flood of negative repercussions, suggesting that fear of these negative outcomes may influence their interactive practices when working with women. Indeed Edith[1], a general practitioner (GP), suggested that domestic violence was something she had, in the past, tried very hard to overlook, 'I didn't want to hear, so if (.)[2] there was anything, you know, these little hints you get, I would block them out and not ask further.' Moreover, she suggested that this 'overlooking' of domestic violence was common practice amongst health professionals,

> I think they are aware, I think they don't want to have anything to do with it, and (.) erm, they (4) wouldn't even refer to me (.) because they are aware where they can refer to. [Edith]

This 'overlooking' of domestic violence, hoping that the problem will go elsewhere, may offer some further insight into concern expressed regarding the lack of a consistent medical approach (Llewellyn et al., 1995; Warshaw, 1997, Lavis et al., 2004). The quality of the response that women receive is assumed to vary greatly dependent upon their geographic location and the presence or absence of any local initiatives for responding. Yet the interview data from the research reported here suggests that this variation may be as great 'within' a geographic area due to the individual practices of specific healthcare professionals when working with women. For example, Helen, in responding to the question 'How do you feel that the practice you are working in responds to domestic violence?', drew upon a discourse of inaction on the part of colleagues, constructing this as arising from a lack-of-awareness and not-knowing-what-to-do,

> At the moment I think they are very unaware erm (.) [Victoria: right] of the extent of it and I don't think many of them would question a woman if she presented and said 'I'm..' y'know that she was being abused. I really don't know, that they'd know what to do.

Moreover, the practice of 'overlooking' domestic violence, to which Edith alludes, appears to provide support for the arguments of a range of researchers that domestic violence-related symptoms are missed because health professionals are uncomfortable operating in this domain (see, for example, Llewellyn et al., 1995: Warshaw, 1997, Lavis et al., 2004).

A further concern evidenced in the health professional interviews, is that when health professionals did respond to domestic violence, their responses were prescriptive and directive. This is often premised on a lack of under-standing regarding the complexity of issues faced by women experiencing domestic violence (Landenberger, 1989; Lees, 2000). These concerns rever-berated in Helen's assessment of her previous practices when responding as a health visitor. As she said,

> Erm (2) and yes, when you first go in, y'know, you just want to say, 'get out of here'. Y'know, 'what are you doing?'

> I mean, I know my own attitude before I did erm (2) the course [domestic vio-lence training], was that I couldn't understand why women just didn't leave. I think that was such, y'know, I just couldn't imagine why they stayed. Having looked at that and read around a bit more I'm very well aware now, but I think there's still a lot of prejudice within most people. [Helen]

Offered here is a health professional collective account of frustration that women are often not compliant in removing themselves from a situation which impacts so significantly on their health and well-being (see, for example, Brown et al., 1993). However, Helen's account also claims that training can bring about a change in understanding the constraints and risks faced by women who experience domestic violence.

Power relations and constructions when responding to women

Unsurprisingly, given the anticipated sorrows and misfortunes constructed within the Pandora's box of domestic violence, the analysis showed that healthcare managers and health care professionals, when asked to explore the direct service level of responding to domestic violence, drew on a *prob-lem discourse*. For example, Louise, also a general practitioner, used negative metaphors to frame her historical experience of responding as a problem. In answer to a question about whether, 'in the period of time that you've been working in general practice, [she had] noticed any changes in the way that [she thought] about domestic violence', Louise mobilised the construction of responding-as-shooting-yourself-in-the-foot:

> because if you ask and you know you can't deal with it, then (.) you are shoot-ing yourself in the foot aren't you?(3)

Thus, even within the talk of constructing subjects who framed their current experience of responding as less problematic as a result of training, negative metaphors such as 'opening up the floodgates' were employed in framing prior experiences of responding, as Edith illustrates:

> Em and I was, I was completely, I was so shaken by the whole thing, erm (.) and em (.) and then, as a result of that I, I, I didn't want to hear, so if (.) there was anything, you know these little hints, you get, I would block them out and not ask further. Erm, and, and then one, one gets a bit more confidence and asks and opens the floodgates and (6) and now, I, I don't mind opening floodgates, in fact I, I do it quite, erm, even without being prompted I do it.

In line with the research literature which has sought to illustrate health care professionals' experiences of responding to domestic violence (Davis, 1984; Sugg & Innui, 1992; Richardson & Feder, 1996) this discourse served to construct domestic violence as problematic *for* the health professional. This said, a key construction within this discourse, 'responding-as-the-front-line', reveals the differential power relations within and between people working at different levels within health services. Utilising elements from a 'war' discourse, health professionals are framed as forming the '*front line*', operating '*on the ground*' and working without '*back up*' from their employers, the Primary Care Trusts. The following quote from June, one of the health professionals interviewed, is expressive of a range of similar constructions drawn upon by others who were interviewed: 'So down at the front line, we still have got, y'know this hardcore of professionals who are clamouring for the training ...'

Figure 1 aims to illustrate how such constructions potentially position those responding to domestic violence within health care services. We show

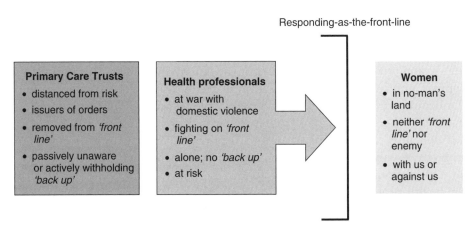

Figure 1 Illustrating subject positions within the construction of responding-as-the-front-line

words from participants' transcripts in italics and our own interpretations are presented in normal font. Through this analysis we argue that health professionals appear positioned as 'at war' with domestic violence, fighting '*at the front line*', alone and at risk. In contrast, the Primary Care Trusts (PCT) who employ/deploy them, are positioned as distanced from risk, the issuers of orders *not 'on the ground*' but removed from the '*front line*', isolated and safe. Further, it appears to position the PCT as either passively unaware of what is happening at the '*front line*' or actively withholding, the required '*back up*'.

Louise, a GP, advanced the allusion to war when making use of the term 'shell-shocked' to frame her personal experience of responding to domestic violence,

> And again, it was a nice family, y'know a lot of love family, a nice family, a nice address (.).ahh[3] and you have to be not too shell shocked by these things and. ahh just get on with it really and give them practical advice and psychological help.

The imagery invoked by the use of the term 'shell shocked' implies that responding to domestic violence is traumatic, akin to prolonged engagement in warfare. This imagery is significant when juxtaposed with the other descriptors in this text, '*nice*', '*love*', '*family*' which reflects the dominant stereotype that some families are constructed as being less likely to experience domestic abuse than others. It might be summised then that the 'shock' factor of responding to domestic violence is more intense for the health professional in relation to some families than others. Further, through this imagery, Louise appears to position herself, and others, as potential 'casualties' in the 'war' against domestic violence; ones who cannot withdraw but must '*get on with it*'.

However, such a positioning has implications for women, whereupon experiencing domestic violence they then access health care services (Figure 1). Within such constructions we suggest women risk being positioned in 'no-man's land', neither the '*front line*' nor the enemy. Moreover, this positioning appears precarious. Operating within a discourse of war, compliance with the health professional's direction may serve to position the woman as 'on our side', whereas failure to comply, for whatever reason may risk her being positioned as 'not with us, therefore "against us"'. This appears consistent with the research literature which suggests that being 'with us' equates with an expectation that women will follow the course of action prescribed by the health professional in order to overcome their 'illness' (Warshaw, 1989; Sugg & Innui 1991; Brown et al., 1993). However, the deployment of such discursive resources would appear to leave health professionals and women with a potential stand-off if women are unable to assist in the recovery process in the manner prescribed by the health professional (Williamson, 2000).

In such situations women become positioned as simply non-compliant if they are unable to follow the health professionals' directed course of action (Sassetti, 1993).

Directive practices: women's accounts

Women's talk about their experiences when accessing health care services provided further evidence for what we have termed 'directive practices'. Women indicated that they experienced these 'directive' practices as involving a reframing of their individual experience, from a context in which it had meaning for them, into a set of symptoms which the 'expert' health professional could treat. For example, this reframing is evident in Susan's account when accessing Accident and Emergency services following what she described as a particularly vicious attack by her husband. Importantly, Susan's injuries were sufficiently severe for the police to call an ambulance to take her to hospital. In this extract she is talking about the response of the doctor who treated her:

> ... even though y'know he asked me what had happened and I told him, but it seemed to, didn't bother him, he were right, he didn't have any (3) I were glad to get out ... he was just sort of, 'oh' and 'er', 'oh that's not much' and 'this isn't much' and 'oh that's not much' and 'this isn't much' and 'oh you've got a few abrasions', and he just wasn't interested. [Susan]

Her health issue had become framed as '*a few abrasions*' with no healthcare engagement regarding the cause or indeed a 'cure'. Susan tells of this interaction co-constructing a 'moral order' (see Wilkinson, 2004) that is minimising and sexist, deterring her from seeking help for aggressive male behaviour which is understood to be supported by other men – in this instance a doctor,

> So when I came away from that time (2) erm, I always thought that (3) men, other men, seem to quite agree with women being hit. Y' know, it didn't seem to bother them. [Susan]

This also reverberates with concerns in the literature suggesting that to gain medical assistance women must surrender themselves to a predetermined system. This system excludes and distorts the experiences of women (see Ussher, 1999). They become separated from their own 'story' of the circumstances which resulted in their injuries, and relocated within a discursive reality which enables health professionals to feel comfortable and in control (Warshaw, 1993; Anspach, 1988).

Eileen's very specific experience of directive practices highlights an issue we have already touched upon, namely health professionals' frustrations around women's non compliance with the treatments *they* prescribe (Brown et al., 1993; Ruddy & McDaniel, 1995). Indeed we have argued previously (Lavis et al., 2004) that there is an expectation inherent within the discourse of medicine that patients/women will follow the particular course of action health professionals prescribe in order to overcome their 'illness'. Eileen provides some context to this 'perceived' non compliance as she describes the response she received from her GP after having finally summoned up the courage to disclose the 30-plus years of abuse she had experienced.

> she just put me on, like (2) anti-depressants and things like that, which I, I don't like taking, 'cos I'm not a tablet (.) know what I mean? Like I'll read the instructions carefully, and it's, it frightens me again, because it tells you all these things and I won't do it. It brings me back to me, know what I mean? So I'm trying to do it on my own [Eileen]

The implication of this directive practice for Eileen is that she appears left in a 'stand off' where she is unable to comply with the recovery process in a way deemed appropriate by her GP. As a result, as she implies, this leaves her once again, alone, in her struggle against domestic violence and distanced from an anticipated source of support. Eileen's experience illustrates that there still remains a fundamental challenge within the health care service response to move away from 'expected' compliance. From these accounts it seems obvious that there is some way to go before women experiencing domestic violence can confidently lay claim to becoming key decision makers in the treatment process. Indeed, such accounts position health professionals as 'experts' whose determinations and courses of action are beyond challenge.

Constructions of 'participatory practices'

Moving beyond the long-standing traditional health care practices that position the health professional as 'expert' is clearly a challenge which extends beyond the response to domestic violence (DOH, 2001b). Nevertheless, Sassetti (1993) argued that health professionals should adopt a 'non-directive manner' when responding to women experiencing domestic violence. Adding to this viewpoint, concerns have been raised about the limited amount of input health professionals receive regarding domestic violence in their pre-registration and post-registration training (Davis, 1984; Sugg & Innui, 1992; Frost, 1997). Even so we would argue that an effective response needs to be more informed by practices that are located in alternate, non medical social constructions of women and their experiences.

The research interviews illustrated that such alternate strategies not only exist but were being successfully implemented by some health professionals – notably, those who had undertaken training. The impact of this training in enabling the development of 'participatory' rather than traditional 'directive' practices was highlighted by Helen, a health visitor,

> ...but, that's our background and you go in to fix things, and I think it's actually recognising that it's not your job to fix this, erm, but it's listening and guiding the woman though it, so that she takes responsibility and does it at her pace.

Caroline, a community nurse, had similarly, accessed training with a focus on raising awareness of domestic violence and developing basic skills and techniques to aid responding. The effect of this on changing her practices when responding is evident in her appraisal of her own post-training approach to working with women,

> ...ensure that the person knows that there is somebody there who is going to sit and listen, and not pass judgment, and not go and do something about it, but encourage you to look at, y'know 'well, what can I do?'

These participatory practices illustrate that individual health professionals are adopting practices which are bringing them in line with the requirements of the expert patient agenda, for example, recognising the importance of adopting a 'non directive' manner and attempting to work in partnership with women to assist them to take responsibility for their own care (DOH, 2001b). The benefits of these more participatory ways of working were indicated by women in the research as being both enabling and desirable. The following extract from an interview with Alima, a young, divorced, South Asian woman, suggests that participatory practices respect their wishes, offering women a say in what action might be taken following disclosure of domestic violence. The quote here illustrates the response, when Alima disclosed to her 'new' GP that she was experiencing domestic violence,

> She, re, she said 'I'm seriously concerned', erm, and y'know, 'What do you want? What would, do you want me to do about it, because I don't want to do something that you're, you're not happy with'. I said, 'Well, at this point, will, will you not do anything about it. I don't want you to do anything. I just wanted to know that if I ever need you that, you're here to support me', and she did, she's, she was brilliant, and she said 'I am'. [Alima]

We can see that within this health care interaction, Alima is afforded agency and an active role in determining not only what intervention takes place, but also its timing. Notably, in exploring women's talk about the practices of responding women found to be helpful and enabling, it became clear that some participatory practices were informed by discourses, which existed outside of the medical model. In some instances these practices appeared consistent with those which could be seen to reflect an advocacy or counselling context. For example, McLeod (1998, p. 10) explains that counselling, 'is a form of helping that is focused on the needs and goals of the person'. Presumably, to maintain this focus on the person there is a need to listen. Jo, a single mother in her early 30s, outlined her experience of participatory practices as those involving listening to the woman first:

> she (2) she listens and erm (3) she listens to what you've got to say and then, and, and, then she'll like carry on from it and then put her, her view from it. [Jo]

Other participatory practices involved a re-working of the medical interaction to provide the woman with sufficient information and context to actively participate in decision making about interventions. An illustration of this is the change that Susan noticed in her GP's response following an intervention from a domestic violence advocate:

> Like erm, she didn't sort of (.) just fill my prescription out, or my sick note, she's started taking time now and erm, (.) like when I went yesterday she asked me how I was sleeping and everything and I explained it all to her and then she said, she, she'd increase my tablets again to help me sleep on a night, 'cos I'm not sleeping again. But, she explained (.) what (.) erm, everything, what effect these tablets would have on me and if she took me off what effect, she exp (.) she went through everything really detailed with me and then asked me if I, I wanted her to up the tablets or not, rather than just going in saying 'oh right I'll just up your tablets.

What appears significant about these participatory practices are that they are less concerned with directing the actions of women, and more concerned with opening up possibilities for action to both the health professional and the woman. In line with some feminist approaches to counselling, new forms of social action are encouraged with the aim of empowering women and resisting oppression. Consequently, a more egalitarian position is taken up where the outcome is not one where the health professional has the power to direct the action of the woman/patient (Caplin, 1999). Women are enabled to occupy an agentive subject position, and the health professional occupies a position more consistent with knowledgeable advisor than directive 'expert'. It is clear from Susan's experience that such an approach holds the potential for women to make informed choices about interventions and their possible effects, adopting an 'expert patient' position where they are '... empowered with information and contribute ideas to help in their treatment and care' (DOH, 2001b: 9). Admittedly this falls short of a feminist agenda that would advocate consciousness raising and political action. Nonetheless, this is a huge step forward for women who have in the past experienced directive, or at the very least avoidant, practices when seeking support from health professionals.

Returning to Pandora's box: relational change, feminism and critical health psychology

In concluding this chapter we would want to concur with Sally Johnson who argued in Chapter 1, and others (Burman & Parker, 1993; Gergen & Zeilke, 2006; Gill, 1998), that the identification and illumination of discursive constructions and their power relations makes possible active resistance and alternate positive action and social change. Our analysis shows how the dominant medical discourse can shape and promote 'directive practices' within health care interactions. Such practices are constructed by women experiencing domestic violence as minimising and unhelpful, having the effect of distancing them from essential health care services. Arguably these practices, which serve to keep the lid of Pandora's box on domestic violence, are protective of health professionals who construct themselves as being 'at war' and in danger as they fight at the 'front line'. However, also revealed is social change and the development of women-centred 'participatory practices', involving a much closer working partnership *with* women. This partnership affords to health professionals the possibility of responding to domestic violence in ways which empower women, enabling women to take an active role in interventions which may be effective in supporting change. The research primarily illustrates the impact that localised integrated training programmes can have on enabling health professionals to gain the confidence and skills to re-position women as 'expert patients' and themselves as co-workers in the moral and political enterprise of health and well-being. We would like to think that 'participatory' practices embody the 'hope' which is contained within Pandora's box. Yet it is important to recognise that this change was brought about via local activism, people on the ground who invested time and energy in working together to 'dethrone' some of the underlying assumptions and practices embedded within normalised healthcare. Broader activism and change is now required to enable the development of integrated action-orientated services, underpinned by participatory practices of responding such as those identified here, across the wider NHS.

Key points

1. 'Directive' practices, shaped by the dominant medical discourse, appear unhelpful in assisting women experiencing domestic violence to access support from health care services.
2. 'Participatory' practices, influenced by discourses outside the sphere of medicine, afford women a more empowered and collaborative position within the healthcare interaction and a more agentic role in any subsequent interventions.
3. The adoption of a discursive approach, informed by Foucauldian and feminist theorising, can offer an effective means of gaining a critical insight into the discursive constructions and power relations which influence the health care response to issues whose cause is situated in the complex social world.
4. Adopting a discursive approach need not involve 'sidelining' the subjective experience of women, but is an effective means of identifying how people narrate the world and their experiences.

NOTES

1. All participants have been allocated pseudonyms to protect their identity.
2. Interviews were transcribed using Parker's (1992) conventions for denoting pauses and emphases in speech. Such conventions enable the researcher to undertake a more detailed discursive analysis. Thus pauses in speech are counted, with (.) signifying a pause of one second. Where the pause in speech is more prolonged a number is recorded inside the brackets to indicate the length of pause, e.g. (2) indicating a pause of 2 seconds.
3. The transcription notation.ahh is used to denote a sharp intake in breath.

REFERENCES

Anspach, R. R. (1988) 'The sociology of medical discourse: the language of case presentation', *Journal of Health and Social Behaviour*, 28, 215–31.

Armstrong, D. (1997) 'Foucault and the sociology of health and illness: a prismatic reading', in A. Peterson & R. Bunton (eds) *Foucault, Health and Medicine*, London: Routledge.

Brown, J. B., Lent, B. & Sas, G. (1993) 'Identifying and treating wife abuse', *Journal of Family Practice*, 36, 185–91.

Burman, E. and Parker, I. (1993) *Discourse Analytic Research: Repertoires and Readings of Texts in Action*, London: Routledge.

Caplin, J. (1999) *Feminist Counselling in Action*, 2nd edn, London: Sage.

Creswell, S. (1998) *Qualitative Enquiry and Research Design*, London: Sage.

Crossley, M. (2007) 'Narrative analysis', in E. Lyons & A. Coyle, (eds) *Analysing Qualitative Data in Psychology*, London: Sage.

Davis, L. V. (1984) 'Beliefs of service providers about abused women and abusing men', *Social Work*, May–June, 243–50.

Department of Health (2000a) *Domestic Violence: A Resource Manual for Health Care Professionals*, London: Department of Health Publications.

Department of Health (2000b) *Principles of Conduct*, London: Department of Health Publications.

Department of Health (2001a) *The Expert Patient: A New Approach to Chronic Disease Management for the 21st Century*, London: Department of Health Publications.

Department of Health (2001b) *Research Governance Framework for Health and Social Care*, London: Department of Health Publications.

Foucault, M. (1979) *Discipline and Punish: The Birth of the Prison*, New York, Random House. (First published in 1975).

Frost, M. (1997) 'Health visitor's perceptions of domestic violence', *Health Visitor*, 70, 258–59.

Gergen, K. & Zeilke, B. (2006) 'Theory in action', *Theory and Psychology*, 16, 299–309.

Gill, R. (1998) 'Dialogues and differences: writing, reflexivity and the crisis of representation', in K. Henwood, C. Griffin & A. Phoenix (eds) *Standpoints and Differences; Essays in the Practice of Feminist Psychology*, London: Sage.

Jeffrey, R. (1979) 'Normal rubbish: deviant patients in casualty departments', *Sociology of Health and Illness*, 1(1), 90–107.

King, N. & Horrocks, C. (2010) *Interviews in Qualitative Research*, London: Sage.

Landenberger, K. (1989) 'A process of entrapment in and recovery from an abusive relationship', *Issues of Mental Health Nursing*, 10, 209–27.

Lavis, V., Horrocks, C., Kelly, N. & Barker, V. (2004) 'Domestic violence and health care: opening Pandora's box, challenges and dilemmas', *Feminism and Psychology*, 15(4), 441–60.

Lees, S. (2000) 'Marital rape and marital murder', in J. Hanmer & C. Itzin, (eds) *Home Truths about Domestic Violence: Feminist Influences on Policy and Practice, a Reader*, London: Routledge.

Llewellyn, T., Roden, R. & O'Neill, V. (1995) 'Support for victims of assaults and domestic violence: are accident and emergency departments doing enough?' *Journal of Accident and Emergency Medicine*, 12, 32–33.

Lupton, D. (1997) 'Foucault and the medicalisation critique', in A. Peterson & R. Bunton (eds) *Foucault, Health and Medicine*, London: Routledge.

McCauley, J., Yurk, R. A., Jenckes, M. W. & Ford, D. E. (1998) 'Inside "Pandora's box": abused women's experience within clinicians and health services', *Journal of General Internal Medicine*, 13(8), 549–55.

McLeod, J. (1998) *An Introduction to Counselling*, 2nd edn Buckingham, Open University Press.

Mishler, E. (1984) *The Discourse of Medicine*, Norwood, NJ: Ablex.

Murray, M. & Poland, B. (2006) 'Health psychology and social action', *Journal of Health Psychology*, 11, 379–84.

Parker, I. (1992) *Discourse Dynamics: Critical Analysis for Social and Individual Psychology*, London: Routledge.

Reinharz, S. (1992) *Feminist Methods in Social Research*, Oxford: Oxford University Press.

Richardson, J. & Feder, G. (1996) 'Domestic violence: a hidden problem for general practice, *British Journal of General Practice*', 46, 239–42.

Ruddy, N. B. & McDaniel, S. H. (1995) 'Domestic violence in primary care: the psychologist's role', *Journal of Clinical Psychology in Medical Settings,* 2(1), 49–69.

Sassetti, M. (1993) 'Domestic violence', *Primary Care*, 20, 289–305.

Stake, R. (1998) 'Case studies', in N. Denzin & Y. Lincoln (eds) *Strategies of Qualitative Inquiry,* Thousand Oaks: Sage.

Sugg, N. K. & Innui, T. (1992) 'Primary Care physicians' responses to domestic violence: opening Pandoras's box', *Journal of the American Medical Association*, 267, 3157–60.

Ussher, J. M. (1999) 'Feminist Approaches to Qualitative Health Research', in M. Murray & K. Chamberlain (eds.) *Qualitative Health Psychology: Theories and Methods*, London: Sage.

Waitzkin, H. & Britt, T. (1989) 'A critical theory of medical discourse: how patients and health professionals deal with social problems', *International Journal of Health Services*, 19,4, 577–97.

Warshaw, C. (1989) 'Limitations of the medical model in the care of battered women', *Gender and Society*, 3(4), 506–17.

Warshaw, C. (1993) 'Domestic violence challenges to medical practice', *Journal of Women's Health,* 2(1), 73–80.

Warshaw, C. (1997) 'Intimate partner abuse: developing a framework for change in medical education', *Academic Medicine*, 72(1), 26–37.

Wilkinson, S. (2004) 'Feminist contributions to critical health psychology', in M. Murray (ed.) *Critical Health Psychology*, Basingstoke: Palgrave Macmillan.

Williamson, E. (2000) *Domestic Violence and Health*, Bristol: Policy Press.

Willig, C. (2001) *Introducing Qualitative Research in Psychology: Adventures in Theory and Method*, Buckingham: Open University Press.

CHAPTER 10

Feminist Health Psychology and Abortion: Towards a Politics of Transversal Relations of Commonality

CATRIONA MACLEOD

In 1992 Speckhard and Rue argued in the *Journal of Social Issues* for the recognition of a diagnostic category, post-abortion syndrome (PAS). This term was first used in 1981 by Vincent Rue in testimony to the American Congress, but was only formalised in a published paper a decade later. Speckhard and Rue (1992) posit that abortion is a psychosocial stressor that may cause mild distress through to severe trauma, creating the need for a continuum of categories, these being post-abortion distress, post-abortion syndrome and post-abortion psychosis. PAS, which is the main focus of their paper, and which has taken root in some professional language as well as lay anti-abortion discourse, is described as a type of post-traumatic stress disorder.

These moments (the testimony to the American Congress by Vincent Rue, the formal academic paper by Speckhard & Rue (1992)) epitomise the psychologisation of abortion that took root in the 1980s. Portrayals of the woman undergoing an abortion shifted during this time from somebody selfishly denying the foetus its right to life, or alternatively exercising her right to control her body and fertility, to somebody who unwittingly subjected herself to psychological harm through terminating her pregnancy (Lee, 2003). As such, the woman, who previously had been circumscribed by moral, health or gender narratives, started to be described in psychological terms. Her body, self, emotions and psyche were rendered visible within psychologised discourses (Rose, 1990), which mostly constructed her as the victim of inevitable depression and grief following a necessarily traumatic abortion event.

This process of psychologisation started in the United States, but has been taken up in a range of forms in other parts of the world, including the United Kingdom (Hopkins et al., 1996) and South Africa (Macleod, 2011). It has resulted in vigorous scientific debate regarding the psychological consequences of abortion (see, for example, the exchange between Reardon and Cougle (2002) and Schmiege and Russo (2005) in the *British Medical Journal* and the letters that followed each article), and has become part of the overt politics of abortion with anti-abortion activists using PAS to 'redefine the terms of the debate so that abortion is represented as contradicting women's interests' (Hopkins et al., 1996, p. 545).

The psychologisation of abortion has, however, mostly occurred within the context of relatively liberal abortion laws where abortions are performed relatively safely. While women in countries such as the United Kingdom and the United States have, for the most part, had access to safe legal abortion for decades, it is estimated that in 2003 about 20 million unsafe abortions took place, 98 per cent of which were performed in developing countries (World Health Organisation, 2007). Debate about the psychological consequences of, and hence a psychological discourse concerning, abortion is virtually non-existent in these contexts, chiefly because the most devastating effects of unsafe abortion are death or severe reproductive health outcomes (Warriner & Shah, 2006).

Other than the obvious differences concerning more or less restrictive abortion laws, how abortion is viewed differs significantly from country to country. It is an issue that speaks to, and draws on, localised understandings of the role of women, the role of the state, the sanctity of life, society's obligation to women and the right to privacy. The practice of abortion also differs vastly. For example, compare the situation in post-Soviet countries and Cuba with the situation in South Africa. In the former, the term 'abortion culture' has been coined to refer to 'the widespread and deep-seated view that abortion is a "normal" way of dealing with medical and socioeconomic hardships in personal and family life' (Karpov & Kaumläriäinen, 2005, p. 13). In the latter, abortion, despite being legal since 1996, continues to attract significant social stigma as a result of traditional moral values, so that fear of rejection by the community and partners limits women's use of the service (Department of Health, 2004).

In this chapter I pose the question of how feminist health psychologists should respond in light of (1) the psychologisation of abortion in particular contexts, (2) the uneven response of Psychology in relation to abortion globally and (3) the fact that abortion differs significantly both in legislation and as a social and cultural practice from country to country. I focus here on *feminist* health psychology as abortion has for some time now been a key feminist issue. Despite this, little has been written specifically about how health psychology may further the feminist agenda in terms of this aspect of reproductive health.

I argue, in the first instance, that the psychologisation of abortion in certain contexts dovetails, paradoxically, with the emphasis on 'choice' that underpins the mainstream Western feminist lobby for abortion. In order to avoid the pitfalls implicit in both the 'choice' rhetoric and PAS, feminist health psychology would be well served to turn to a framework of 'reproductive justice' rather than 'choice'. In the second instance, I discuss how feminist health psychologists could extend this framework by joining the public health debate concerning abortion in developing countries where the most unsafe abortions occur. Finally, I argue for a feminist politics of transversal relations of commonality in terms of reproductive justice and freedom, in order to accommodate the possibly antagonistic approaches that feminist health psychologists may take in different settings regarding psychology and abortion.

PAS and the rhetoric of 'choice': focussing on the individual woman and the abortion event

In this section I argue that in order for feminist health psychologists to arrive at a position on abortion, we need to grapple with the fundamental principles that have driven both mainstream Western feminist advocacy regarding abortion and the proposal of PAS. As indicated below, some of the underlying assumptions of each are remarkably similar, despite the fact that the anticipated outcomes are quite different (with mainstream feminist advocacy envisaging increased access to abortion (Ferree, 2003) and PAS advocates indicating that abortion should be restricted in order to avoid wide-scale psychological fall (Hopkins et al., 1996). I discuss below some of the chief tenets of mainstream feminist advocacy, criticisms thereof and its paradoxical linkages with PAS.

'Choice' and rights have been the cornerstone principles of mainstream Western feminist advocacy around the legalisation of and access to abortion. Fundamental to this advocacy is the argument that a woman should have the right to make decisions about her own body and that the choice concerning the outcome of a pregnancy should be the woman's alone. This position draws off liberal political theory, with women's competence to make abortion decisions being recognised and the state being forced to withdraw from any coercion in a significant area of women's lives (Ferree, 2003). For example, the American *Roe v. Wade* decision sent a clear material and rhetorical signal to women, girls, and the larger society: women's reproductive lives should be, and henceforth would be, governed by a regime of choice ... and not by fate, nature, accident, biology, or men' (West, 2009, p. 1401). In this way, American women's autonomy and life options were broadened, with liberal feminists arguing that in order to control their lives women had to be able to control their reproductivity. Without this, a woman would be denied equality with men: 'Without self-sovereignty over her body, all that remains of her life – her work, her sociability, her education, her mothering, and her impact on the world – is miniaturized. She lives a smaller life' (p. 1401).

Several critiques have been forthcoming concerning the notion of 'choice' as the mainstay of abortion advocacy. These have centred on,

(1) the assumption of active unfettered agency on the part of women seeking abortions which belies the power relations within which 'choices' are made (Petchesky, 1980);
(2) a lack of examination of 'the social context and conditions needed in order for someone to have and exercise rights' (Fried, 2006, p. 240) and of the social conditions which put pressure on women to abort 'incorrect' (for example, female) foetuses (Saharso, 2003);
(3) the suggestion that the appropriate response to unwanted, coerced or violent sex that may result in an unwanted pregnancy is to protect the decision to end the pregnancy rather than to address the gendered conditions that lead to unwanted sex (Smyth, 2002; West, 2009);
(4) the logical conclusion that the 'choice' *to parent* is as much an individual decision as the 'choice' not to parent, which means that individuals have to take full responsibility for their children and which legitimates inadequate social health and welfare programmes (West, 2009);
(5) the failure to 'address the existing social relations and sexual divisions around which responsibility for pregnancy and children are assigned' (Petchesky, 1980, p. 670);
(6) the masking of the fact that the fight for legal abortion has been associated in some quarters with eugenicist population policies which saw women's right to *have* children curtailed through, for example, being unknowingly sterilised or being injected with long-acting hormonal contraceptives without full informed consent (Fried, 2006).

What these critiques have in common is that they locate the woman within the context of her social, economic and health support milieu and her interpersonal and reproductive history.

As indicated by Ferree (2003) in her study of feminist advocacy for abortion, mainstream Western feminist advocates agree that the notion of 'choice' may be limited, but argue that it should remain the core of activism around abortion. The limitations of the 'choice' rhetoric to which they point are the fact that it hides the stigma associated with abortion and that women face several obstacles in terms of accessing abortion (Ferree, 2003). The latter critiques, however, focus on processes that are insufficiently supportive of women in *choosing abortion* rather than on processes that are insufficiently supportive of women in *avoiding unwanted pregnancies* or in having and providing for children. In other words, abortion is foregrounded, while the complexity of women's sexual, reproductive and mothering lives recedes into the background. West (2009) argues that this had to do, in the United States, with the politics surrounding the Equal Rights Amendment movement:

> Abortion rights were [for the first two-thirds of the past century] a branch on a tree, the trunk of which was the aspiration of equal citizenship and whatever social reimagining of basic structures of work and governance would be necessary to achieve it... [A]dvocacy for abortion was in effect severed from its trunk largely because of the politics surrounding the Equal Rights Amendments (ERA) movement and then transplanted into the quite different terrain of individual liberty. It then became its own 'tree,' rooted not so much in women's equality, but in marital, medical, and sexual privacy (p. 1423).

This unmooring of mainstream American abortion advocacy from its roots, the concentration on the individual and her choice rather than the social conditions under which women live, and the foregrounding of abortion as the key issue in reproductive freedom means that the fundamental terms of the debate used in 'choice' rhetoric are the same as those used in the proposal of PAS. As I have argued elsewhere (Macleod, 2009), the term 'post-abortion syndrome' is a reductionist concept that places emphasis on the abortion event itself and on the individual woman, in much the same way, ironically, as advocacy based on 'choice' does. In utilising a category termed post abortion syndrome psychologists ignore the fact that termination of pregnancy occurs in the context of, firstly a severely problematic and unwanted pregnancy, and secondly particular interpersonal, sociocultural and economic stressors. PAS places the abortion in the foreground, while neglecting the stress and possible trauma inherent in the discovery of an unwanted and severely problematic pregnancy; the fears around economic hardship; the difficult process of deciding how to resolve an unwanted pregnancy, especially in the absence of support; the expectation (whether real or imagined) of criticism, stigma and social isolation, not only because of the abortion but also because of the pregnancy; the potential lack of support and caring amongst health service providers; the lack of support structures for both child and mother carrying a pregnancy to term; and general contextual, sociocultural and socioeconomic issues.

An example of the kinds of contextual issues that need careful attention is the high rate of HIV experienced in South Africa. Many women have to take on additional care-taking roles as relatives fall ill or die and leave children who need to be taken care of (Hunter, 2010). Health resources are stretched and pregnant HIV+ women experience warranted concern about the possibility of mother-to-child transmission (Benatar, 2004). The multiple social and reproductive health impacts of HIV circumscribe women's responses to pregnancy and their decisions to continue or terminate a pregnancy.

Of course, the assumptions made about the individual woman in 'choice' rhetoric and in PAS differ substantially. Within the 'choice' rhetoric, women are depicted as rational and autonomous beings, able to exercise agency in decision making regarding the outcome of a pregnancy. Within the narrative of PAS women are positioned as victims in need of protection and care and as lacking sufficient rationality and autonomy to make an informed decision about terminating a pregnancy (Lee, 2003). Women, from this perspective, are duped into undergoing an abortion by overzealous pro-abortionists or by service providers who profit financially through performing abortions. This positioning has allowed for the development of an anti-choice woman-centred strategy that complements the focus on the foetus that has traditionally under-pinned anti-abortion activism (Cannold, 2002). As Ferree (2003) notes,

> [G]endered antiabortion mobilization ... takes up themes of women's exploitation and victimization and uses them, paradoxically enough, against feminism. ... They appeal to this constituency [marginalised women] by positing a 'postabortion syndrome' of guilt and remorse, which can make sense of some women's regrets over a decision that they felt was not a real choice in practice (p. 336).

Psychologists (e.g. Major et al., 2008; Schmiege & Russo, 2005; Stotland, 2001) who argue against PAS have had to engage in significant labour to dis-lodge the underlying assumptions of the abortion as the key event and the individual woman as the focus of attention. This has been achieved mostly through concentrating on methodological issues, in particular that studies in which PAS is found often do not take a number of confounding variables such as prior psychological functioning, partner support, material conditions, and social and cultural background in account, and frequently do not have valid control or comparison groups. The American Psychological Association (APA) task force on mental health and abortion (TFMHA) reports,

> A critical evaluation of the published literature revealed that the majority of studies suffered from methodological problems, often severe in nature. ... The TFMHA reviewed no evidence sufficient to support the claim that an observed association between abortion history and mental health was caused by the abortion per se, *as opposed to other factors*. (Major et al., 2008, pp. 3–4, emphasis added)

To conclude, choice rhetoric draws off liberal political theory to posit a wom-en's competence to make abortion decisions. PAS, on the other hand, high-lights the individual woman's psychological response to abortion. Despite having different aims, the major difficulty with both 'choice' rhetoric and PAS is that they foreground the abortion event and focus attention on the individual woman and her (in)capacity for agency. In the following section I explore the potential of a 'reproductive justice' approach.

The advantages of a 'reproductive justice' approach

A reproductive justice approach highlights the contextual nature of women's lives. Given overarching socioeconomic inequalities, racism and sexism that shape many women's lives, the reproductive justice approach focuses on achieving conditions that are necessary for comprehensive reproductive and sexual freedom (Fried, 2006). West (2009) explains that,

> Reproductive justice requires a state that provides a network of support for the processes of reproduction: protection against rape and access to affordable and effective birth control, healthcare, including but not limited to abortion services, prenatal care, support in childbirth and postpartum, support for breastfeeding mothers, early childcare for infants and toddlers, income support for parents who stay home to care for young babies, and high quality public education for school age children (p. 1425).

Such an approach incorporates, but does not centralise, a strong political case for legal abortion as being important to women's equal citizenship (West, 2009). It also regards 'reproductive freedom – indeed, the very nature of reproduction itself – [as] irreducibly social and individual at the same time; that is, it operates "at the core of social life" as well as within and upon women's individual bodies' (Petchesky, 1980, p. 663).

For the feminist health psychologist adopting such an approach, the social and interpersonal conditions under which unwanted pregnancies occur, as well as the experience and outcomes of the unwanted pregnancy, shift to the foreground, with abortion decisions and women's experiences of abortion forming part of this broad landscape of understanding. The rationale for this can be found in the fact, as reported by the TFMHA, that,

> women's psychological experience of abortion is not uniform, but rather varies as a function of characteristics and events that led up to the pregnancy: the circumstances of women's lives and relationships at the time that a decision to terminate the pregnancy was made; the reasons for, type, and timing of the abortion; events and conditions that occur in women's lives subsequent to an abortion; and the larger social-political context in which abortion takes place. Mental health and problem behaviors observed after abortion are often

a byproduct of conditions and characteristics that preceded or coexist with the unintended pregnancy and abortion (Major et al., 2008, p. 10).

Thus, for example, we can start to unravel the factors associated with unwanted pregnancies, such as poor reproductive health information and education, poor reproductive health services, women's vulnerablity to sexual exploitation, rape (Chhabra et al., 2009) and intimate partner violence (Stephenson et al., 2008), poor socioeconomic status, short previous pregnancy intervals and large current family size (Faghihzadeh et al., 2003), all of which are intricately linked with gendered relations in complex ways. We can begin to understand how 'unwanted pregnancies can be experienced as violations not only of women's bodies and autonomy but of their very identities' (Mullin, 2005, p. 71; see also the work of Lundquist, 2008). We can also locate abortion within its sociocultural discursive context, acknowledging that,

> social and cultural messages that stigmatize women who have abortions and convey the expectation that women who have abortions will feel bad may themselves engender negative psychological experiences. In contrast, social and cultural messages that normalize the abortion experience and convey expectations of resilience may have the opposite effect (Major et al., 2008, p. 12).

We can acknowledge that unwanted pregnancies are harmful not only because of women's experiences, but also for those born from unwanted pregnancies. This is clearly seen in what are referred to as the Prague studies in which children born in 1961–1963 to women twice denied abortion for the same pregnancy and pair-matched controls (matched for age, socioeconomic status and the partner's presence in the home) were assessed intermittently over 35 years, in which it is concluded that being born from an unwanted pregnancy is a risk factor for poor mental health in adulthood (David et al., 2003). A 'reproductive justice' approach which centralises advocacy for comprehensive reproductive and sexual freedom (with legal abortion being argued for within this framework) thus permits a broad platform for understanding and activism around sexual and reproductive health issues.

Extending feminist health psychology's voice, public health and unsafe abortion

In this section I argue that the above-mentioned reproductive justice approach within feminist health psychology needs to be extended to include, perhaps contradictorily, a discussion of the psychological consequences of unsafe abortion. Feminist health psychologists need to join the public health debate on abortion in contexts where it is severely restricted.

The public health costs of restrictive laws and poor access to abortion have been highlighted in recent advocacy efforts concerning abortion. It is estimated that the maternal mortality ratio (MMR) is 450 maternal deaths per 100,000 live births in developing countries – compared to 9 per 100,000 in developed countries – with unsafe abortion being one of the leading causes of maternal death (WHO et al., 2007). Where legislation allows abortion for a range of reasons, there is a decrease in both mortality and the health complications that arise from unsafe abortion. In addition, there are fiscal benefits, since the 'direct costs of treating abortion complications burden impoverished health care systems, and indirect costs also drain struggling economies' (Grimes et al., 2006, p. 1908). The success of the public health approach to advocacy is evidenced in countries such as South Africa (Klugman & Varkey, 2001), Nepal (Shakya et al., 2004) and Nigeria (Oye-Adeniran et al., 2004), all of which have seen a liberalisation of abortion laws.

What is striking about the public health approach to abortion is the absence of comment by psychologists. For example, in a Guttmacher Institute publication, which brought together 'internationally prominent researchers from a variety of disciplines to assess the global status of unsafe abortion and to identify a research and action agenda' (Warriner & Shah, 2006, p. viii), there is a distinct lack of discussion of psychological issues. Where mental health does feature, it is mentioned in relation to legislation which allows abortion on the grounds of threat to the mental health of the woman. This lack of comment by health psychologists in general is of concern. The absence of comment by feminist health psychologists is particularly troubling in light of the fact that evidence is available that links gender disadvantage, reproductive health and mental health issues (for example, Patel et al., 2006).

It must be conceded, however, that research on the consequences of unsafe abortion has been dominated by concerns with physical health complications. In a text on mental health issues in women's reproductive health, Astbury and Allanson (2009) note,

> The mental health consequences of unsafe abortion are not known, although qualitative data suggest that unsafe abortion can be traumatic before, during and after the abortion, and is likely to cause psychological harm. ... It is important to bear in mind that the lack of evidence and research on the mental health effects of conditions that predominantly affect women in low-income countries does not imply that there are no mental health consequences of these conditions ... The stress of facing an unintended pregnancy or unsafe abortion

might be expected to increase the risk of onset, or recurrence, of serious mental ill-health (pp. 54–55).

Although there is some evidence accruing concerning the psychological consequences of unsafe abortion (for example, Herrera & Zivy, 2002), clearly more needs to be done in terms of complementing evidence concerning the physical outcomes of unsafe abortion with evidence on the possible psychological and social fall-out. What is important in this kind of research is to note the methodological issues outlined in relation to studying the experiences of women under conditions where abortion is legal. Specifically, locating the abortion experience within the context of an unwanted pregnancy, which occurs within particular economic, social, cultural, familial, health and gender relations circumstances, needs careful attention.

A feminist politics of transversal relations of commonality

Given the uneven response of psychology to abortion as well as the legislative, social and cultural specificity of abortion, the question of whether feminist health psychologists can come to any agreement regarding their positions on psychology and abortion is pertinent. I argue, in this section, that a politics of transversal relations of commonality is indeed possible. Such an approach, which I have outlined in detail elsewhere (Macleod, 2006), has a number of features. Of importance here is that it, firstly, attunes its pronouncements on liberatory practices and discourses to social and historical conditions and, secondly, deploys multiple sources of resistance along chains of equivalence or transversal relations of commonality.

In the first of these requirements, determining the liberatory status of any discourse is not a matter of theoretical or political pronouncement. Rather these determinations are a matter of social and historical inquiry. Thus, in relation to the discussion above a discourse of 'women as victims of abortion' potentially has on the one hand liberatory effects in situations where abortion laws are restrictive and unsafe abortion is rife. Emphasising the medical and psychological consequences of unsafe abortion is essential in terms of feminist advocacy for women's reproductive justice and freedom in these contexts. On the other hand, a discourse of 'women as victims of abortion' in the context of legal and safe abortion has, as noted above, the reverse effect. Emphasising the contested (and mostly limited) medical and psychological consequences of legal and safe abortion in isolation from the various factors referred to earlier has the effect of restricting women's access to reproductive justice and freedom. It must be noted here, however, that the strategic use of a discourse of 'women as victims of abortion' is not simply opportunistic. Instead it is based on sound empirical evidence, as noted earlier in this chapter, that the medical and psychological consequences of abortion differ significantly under various conditions.

Within the approach I am advocating, the racial, geographical, economic and class-based differences between women, all of which have central implications in terms of their access to health resources and their experiences of reproductive justice, are recognised. This means, thus, that the grounds for feminist action for reproductive justice around abortion and psychology are adjusted to suit the specific historical, geographical and cultural location. There is a refusal of foreclosed identities (i.e. seeing women as a single oppressed class across time and space), and a moulding of advocacy efforts to the nuances of gendered power relations within a particular context.

Hand-in-hand with a cultural, social and historical specific approach and the refusal of foreclosed identities, however, goes a pursuit of transversal relations of commonality. Thus, although feminist health psychologists may use the language of psychological harm in the context of unsafe abortion and point to the dangers of this language in the context of safe, legal abortion, what underpins their pronouncements is a recognition of (1) the centrality of reproduction in women's lives, (2) the imperative of promoting reproductive health and access to healthcare, (3) the intersection of mental and reproductive health and (4) the pivotal role of gendered power relations in moulding women's lives. It is the recognition of these elements that provides the chain of equivalence, or the transversal relations of commonality, around which health psychology feminists can agree. Feminist health psychology practice, thus, becomes a matter of alliances around central chains of equivalence rather than one of unity around a universally shared interest (such as promoting 'choice'). Within this politics of difference, the aim is to establish multiple points of resistance to ensure reproductive justice that is attuned to the myriad relations of inequality and domination that occur in women's reproductive lives.

Key points

1. Abortion has been highly psychologised in the Western world, where the notion of Post-Abortion Syndrome (PAS) and the possible psychological consequences of abortion are debated in scientific and popular forums. In developing countries, where abortion is, for the most part, highly restricted and where there are high maternal mortality and morbidity rates, there is an absence of comment by psychologists or any engagement around the psychological consequences of unsafe and illegal abortion.

2. The psychologisation of abortion in developed contexts dovetails, para-doxically, with the emphasis on 'choice' that underpins the mainstream Western feminist lobby for abortion. Despite having different aims, 'choice' rhetoric and talk of PAS have similarities in that they both foreground the abortion event and focus attention on the individual woman and her (in) capacity for agency.
3. In order to avoid the pitfalls implicit in both the 'choice' rhetoric and PAS, feminist health psychology should turn to a framework of 'reproductive justice' in which achieving conditions that are necessary for comprehen-sive reproductive and sexual freedom is foregrounded.
4. Feminist health psychologists should extend this framework by joining the public health debate concerning abortion in developing countries where the most unsafe abortions occur.
5. Feminist health psychologists should engage in a politics of transversal relations of commonality in terms of reproductive justice and freedom, in order to accommodate the possibly antagonistic approaches that they may take in different settings regarding psychology and abortion.

Acknowledgements

Thank you to Tracy Morison who assisted with a literature search and editor-ial corrections; Tracy Morison, Clifford van Ommen and the editors of this book who commented on a draft of this chapter; and Rhodes University and the National Research Foundation of South Africa for funding my research on abortion.

REFERENCES

Astbury, J. & Allanson, S. (2009) 'Psychosocial aspects of fertility regulation', in World Health Organisation (ed.) *Mental Health Aspects of Women's Reproductive Health: A Global Review of Literature* Geneva: World Health Organisation.
Benatar, S. R. (2004) 'Health care reform and the crisis of HIV and AIDS in South Africa', *New England Journal of Medicine*, 351, 81–92.
Cannold, L. (2002) 'Understanding and responding to anti-choice women-centred strategies', *Reproductive Health Matters*, 10(19), 171–79.
Chhabra, S., Palaparthy, S. & Mishra, S. (2009) 'Social issues around advanced unwanted pregnancies in rural single women', *Journal of Obstetrics and Gynaecology*, 29(4), 333–36.
David, H. P., Dytrych, Z. & Matejcek, Z. (2003) 'Born unwanted: observations from the prague study', *American Psychologist*, 58, 224–29.
Department of Health (2004) *Saving Mothers: Third Report on Confidential Enquiry into Maternal Deaths in South Africa 2002–2004* Pretoria: Department of Health.

Faghihzadeh, S., Babaee Rochee, G., Lmyian, M., Mansourian, G. & Rezasoltani, P. (2003) 'Factors associated with unwanted pregnancy', *Journal of Sex and Marital Therapy*, 29(2), 157–64.

Ferree, M. M. (2003) 'Resonance and radicalism: feminist framing in the abortion debates of the united states and germany', *American Journal of Sociology*, 109 (2), 304–44.

Fried, M. (2006) 'The politics of abortion: a note', *Indian Journal of Gender Studies*, 13(2), 229–45.

Grimes, D. A., Benson, J., Singh, S., Romero, M., Ganatra B., Okonofua, F. E. & Shah, I. H. (2006) 'Unsafe abortion: the preventable pandemic', *Lancet*, 368(9550), 1908–19.

Herrera, A. A. & Zivy, R. M. (2002) 'Clandestine abortion in Mexico: a question of mental as well as physical health', *Reproductive Health Matters*, 10(19), 95–102.

Hopkins, N., Reicher, S. & Saleem, J. (1996) 'Constructing women's psychological health in anti-abortion rhetoric', *Sociological Review*, 44(3), 539–66.

Hunter, N. (2010) 'Measuring and valuing unpaid care work: assessing the gendered implications of South Africa's home-based care policy', unpublished PhD thesis, University of KwaZulu/Natal, Durban, South Africa.

Karpov, V. & Kaumläriäinen, K. (2005) 'Abortion culture in russia: its origins, scope, and challenge to social development', *Journal of Applied Sociology*, 22(2), 13–33.

Klugman, B. & Varkey, S. J. (2001) 'From policy development to policy implementation: the south african choice on termination of pregnancy act', in B. Klugman & D. Budlender (eds) *Advocating for Abortion Access: Eleven Country Studies* Johannesburg: Women's Health Project.

Lee, E. (2003) *Abortion, Motherhood, and Mental Health: Medicalizing Reproduction in the United States and Great Britain* Hawthorne: Aldine de Gruyter.

Lundquist, C. (2008) 'Being torn: toward a phenomenology of unwanted pregnancy', *Hypatia*, 23(3), 136–55.

Macleod, C. (2006) 'Radical plural feminisms and emancipatory practice in post-apartheid south africa', *Theory and Psychology*, 16, 367–89.

Macleod, C. (2009) 'Why we should avoid the term "post-abortion syndrome": commentary on Boulind and Edwards (2008)', *Journal of Psychology in Africa*, 19(3), 423–28.

Macleod, C. (2011) *'Adolescence', Pregnancy and Abortion: Constructing a Threat of Degeneration* London: Routledge.

Major, B., Appelbaum, M., Beckman, L., Dutton, M. A., Russo, N. F. & West, C. (2008) 'Report of the APA Task Force on Mental Health and Abortion', http://www.apa.org/pi/wpo/mental-health-abortion-report.pdf, date accessed 11 June 2009.

Mullin, A. (2005) *Reconceiving Pregnancy and Childcare: Ethics, Experience and Reproductive Labor* Cambridge: Cambridge University Press.

Oye-Adeniran, B. A., Long, C. M. & Adewole, I. F. (2004) 'Advocacy for reform of the abortion law in nigeria', *Reproductive Health Matters*, 12(24), 209–14.

Patel, V., Kirkwood, B., Pednekar, S., Pereira, B., Barros, P., Fernandes, J., Datta, Pai, J. R., Weiss, H. & Mabey, D. (2006) 'Gender disadvantage and reproductive health risk factors for common mental disorders in women: a community survey in India', *Archives of General Psychiatry*, 63, 404–13.

Petchesky, R. (1980) 'Reproductive freedom: beyond "a woman's right to choose"', *Signs*, 5(4), 661–85.

Reardon, D. & Cougle, J. R. (2002) 'Depression and unintended pregnancy in the national longitudinal survey of youth: a cohort study', *British Medical Journal*, 324, 151–52.

Rose, N. (1990) 'Psychology as a "social" science, in I. Parker & J. Shotter (eds) *Deconstructing Social Psychology* London: Routledge.

Saharso, S. (2003) 'Feminist ethics, autonomy and the politics of multiculturalism', *Feminist Theory*, 4(2), 100–215.

Schmiege. S. & Russo, N. F. (2005) 'Depression and unwanted first pregnancy: longitudinal cohort study', *British Medical Journal*, 331, 1303–8.

Shakya, B., Kishore, S., Bird, C. & Barak, J. (2004) 'Abortion law reform in nepal: women's right to life and health', *Reproductive Health Matters*, 24(12), 75–84.

Smyth, L. (2002) 'Feminism and abortion politics: choice, rights, and reproductive freedom', *Women's Studies International Forum*, 25(3), 335–45.

Speckhard, A. C. & Rue, V. M. (1992) 'Postabortion syndrome: an emerging public health concern', *Journal of Social Issues*, 48(3), 95–120.

Stephenson, R., Koenig, M. A., Acharya, R. & Roy, T. K. (2008) 'Domestic violence, contraceptive use and unwanted pregnancy in rural india', *Studies in Family Planning*, 39(3), 177–86.

Stotland, N. L. (2001) 'Psychiatric aspects of induced abortion', *Archives of Women's Mental Health*, 4, 27–31.

Warriner, I. K. & Shah, I. H. (2006) *Preventing Unsafe Abortion and Its Consequences: Priorities for Research and Action* (New York: Guttmacher Institute).

West, R. (2009) 'From choice to reproductive justice: de-constitutionalizing abortion rights', *Yale Law Journal*, 118(1392), 1395–1432.

World Health Organisation (2007) *Unsafe Abortion: Global and Regional Estimates of the Incidence of Unsafe Abortion and Associated Mortality in 2003*, 5th edn, Geneva: World Health Organisation.

WHO, UNICEF, UNFPA, & The World Bank (2007) *Maternal Mortality in 2005* Geneva: World Health Organisation.

PART IV

MAKING A CHANGE: HEALTH INEQUALITIES AND COMMUNITY WELL-BEING

CHAPTER 11

Discursive Psychology and Its Potential to Make a Difference

BREGJE DE KOK

Introduction

An increasing number of scholars identify themselves as using discursive psychology (Edwards & Potter 1992; Potter 2010a; Potter & Wetherell 1987), which is one form of discourse analysis.* In brief, discursive psychology examines how people use language to construct realities and how those constructions fulfill certain interactional and interpersonal functions, like disclaiming responsibility or justifying behaviours. Thus, discursive psychology treats descriptions as actively constituting, rather than passively reflecting, mind (e.g. attitudes, beliefs) and reality (e.g. events, behaviours). Discursive psychologists have examined health and illness-related topics such as constructions of illness beliefs and attributions and health professional–client interactions. These studies contribute to the field of critical health psychology because they share its critical stance towards positivistic, quantitative, cognitive and individualistic approaches in psychology (Murray & Campbell, 2003). For instance, critical health psychologists have criticized mainstream health psychology for defining health and illness as 'belonging' to the individual and for extracting suffering from the social context within which it develops (Murray & Campbell, 2003). Discursive psychology avoids this by examining how health and illness-related matters are jointly constructed and produced within particular social and interactional contexts, in response to interpersonal concerns (e.g. avoiding attribution of a problematic identity).

More latterly, critical health psychology's focus has shifted from critique to calls to action (Murray & Campbell 2003). Critical health psychologists have been urged to 'offer alternative practices that go beyond the status quo and its critique' (Prilleltensky, 2003, p. 2), to 'side with the oppressed and disenfranchised' and address inequalities and injustice (Murray & Campbell, 2003,

p. 234). In this chapter, I will explore how discursive psychology can meet this call to action. I will first provide a more detailed account of discursive psychology and its examination of health topics. I will then address some perceived dilemmas concerning discursive psychology's action-potential, before describing different ways in which it can inform the development of health interventions. I will subsequently discuss my own research on constructions of infertility in Malawi, a non-western, resource-poor context of suffering plagued by inequalities and injustice. Such non-western contexts have been largely neglected by discursive psychologists and extending the application of discursive psychology to such settings is desirable. I will conclude with suggesting how discursive psychology can meet the call to address health and well-being but also equality and social justice.

Discursive psychology and the study of health and illness

Discursive psychology[1] has been developed in British social psychology (Edwards & Potter 1992; Potter 2010a; Potter & Wetherell, 1987). Its intellectual roots are the sociology of scientific knowledge (Gilbert & Mulkay, 1984), ethnomethodology (Garfinkel, 1967) and conversation analysis (Sacks, 1992), of which it makes increasing use.[2] As mentioned, discursive psychology adopts an action-perspective on language, examining descriptions 'for the business they do' rather than the objects they describe (Potter, 2010b). A second feature is that it treats talk as situated. To begin with, talk is situated in its *proximate sequential environment* (Potter, 2010a). In conversations, speakers' turns provide the environment for upcoming ones, which orient to what has been said and done in prior turns. Thus, an invitation sets up a limited selection of appropriate next actions: accepting or rejecting the invitation. By taking up or declining an invitation, a recipient displays an understanding that this is precisely what has been issued. This understanding can be ratified or modified in subsequent turns. Hence, discursive psychologists acknowledge that people co-construct joint understandings in interaction, making talk and the actions it performs a concerted accomplishment rather than a product of isolated, single minds. Indeed, speakers orient to alternative interpretations and constructions and build theirs to counter or pre-empt them. In this way, talk is *rhetorically situated*. Furthermore, it is *institutionally situated*, and discursive psychology focuses increasingly on how talk accomplishes institutional tasks (e.g. advice giving in helplines) and institutional identities (e.g. biomedical expert) (Potter, 2010a).

Discursive psychologists have examined various health-related topics. A growing number of studies focus on professional–client interactions in for instance antenatal classes (Locke & Horton-Salway, 2010) or calls to helplines (Hepburn & Potter, 2007; 2010). These studies illuminate the discursive strategies used to engage in practices such as managing clients' crying (Hepburn & Potter, 2010) and giving, accepting or resisting advice (Hepburn & Potter, 2007; Locke & Horton-Salway, 2010). In addition, discursive psychologists have examined how those affected by health problems and practitioners actively construct illness states, attributions and knowledge in consultations and other settings. In so doing, lay people and practitioners alike manage identities and other interpersonal and inferential issues (Guise et al., 2010; Horton-Salway, 2001; 2008; Kok & Widdicombe, 2010), which they do as well in accounts of health-related behaviours and coping (de Kok & Widdicombe, 2008; de Kok, 2009; Wilkinson & Kitzinger, 2000).

Interpersonal concerns commonly managed in talk about health and illness include normative expectations concerning appropriate responses to health problems (de Kok & Widdicombe, 2008; Lamerichs & te Molder, 2003; Wilkinson & Kitzinger, 2000), accountability for health problems and ways of responding to them (Horton-Salway & Locke, 2010; de Kok & Widdicombe, 2008; de Kok, 2009) and related identity concerns such as portraying oneself as someone who is not responsible for one's ill health (Guise et al., 2007; Horton-Salway, 2008; Wilkinson & Kitzinger, 2000). Insights into how people employ discursive strategies to manage particular interpersonal concerns in talk about health and illness can be used to develop health (service) interventions. However, let me first address some existing reservations concerning discursive psychology's applied potential.

Meeting the call to action: perceived dilemmas

Some authors suggest that discursive psychology's focus on the local, interactional context leads to a problematic neglect of extra-discursive, material aspects of reality (e.g. poverty). This would limit discursive psychology's ability to address inequality and injustice (Murray & Campbell, 2003) and make it an inconsequential 'play of semantics, a decontextualized set of hermeneutic interpretations that can all too easily be dismissed' (Hook, 2001, p. 542). However, critical health psychology is a pluralistic field and can contribute to social justice in multiple ways. Generally, it should seek to illuminate social suffering within social, economical and political contexts (Murray & Campbell, 2003), but we can examine such contextual dimensions in various ways. The wider social, economical and political context is important to health and well-being, but so is the proximate context of social interactions (McVittie, 2006). Discursive psychology can provide important insights into how at a micro level, social interactions contribute to suffering and injustice and how for instance social inequalities and power differentials are interpreted, played out or resisted in everyday or institutional interactions (McVittie, 2006; McVittie & Goodall, 2009; Widdicombe, 1995).

Further, discursive psychology's relativist epistemology is sometimes thought to entail a dismissal of phenomena as unreal or inconsequential, subjective constructions, which would paralyse attempts to change 'reality'. However, relativism is easily misunderstood (Hepburn, 2000). Discursive psychology acknowledges that all descriptions of facts and reality are offered by interested actors and embedded in practices in which something is at stake (Hepburn, 2000). Consequently, any claim can be examined for how it is built and constructed so that it portrays phenomena as being of a particular kind, *regardless of what their 'real' or 'true' nature may be*. However, discursive psychologists live in the same material world as everybody else and do not intend to deny the reality of anything, if only because this is 'as realist a move as endorsing them' (Potter & Hepburn, 2008, p. 279). Being *epistemic* rather than ontological constructionists, discursive psychologists sidestep philosophical, ontological questions about whether things are real. Instead, they examine empirically whether and how certain phenomena are invoked and made relevant in talk, and for what purposes (Potter & Edwards, 2003).

Refusing to accept the existence of unmediated, uninterpreted facts (e.g. concerning illness or poverty) however, does not leave one without a moral compass. Like anyone, relativists hold beliefs about the world and its inequalities and can thus judge 'facts' as for instance unfair and promote political action (Hepburn, 2000). Such judgements and commitments do not require objective foundations but argumentation (op cit.), and discursive psychologists have no problem with that. Moreover, a relativist stance facilitates rather than obstructs promotion of change and resistance because it leads to a questioning of what is taken for granted: 'nothing ever has to be taken as merely, obviously, objectively, unconstructedly, true' (Edwards et al., 1995, p. 39).

Willig (2004) questions however whether applying discursive psychology to personal accounts of health and illness is ethically justifiable. Examining the use of discursive, rhetorical strategies in such accounts rather than treating them as self-expressions of experiences of illness and suffering would 'silence speakers' (Willig, 2004). Like any approach, discursive psychology attends to certain aspects and excludes others, including the phenomenology of experience. However, more than other analytic approaches, discursive psychology pays attention to the details of what people say and do with their talk and how people themselves portray and interpret their identities, actions and circumstances. Surely this is a way of giving voice to people rather than silencing them (Widdicombe, 1995). Arguably, discursive psychology has an ethical duty to be of use to the people whose constructions it examines, especially if they belong to vulnerable groups. It can live up to this ethical duty, because its examination of language's social effects exposes new aspects of suffering.

Hence, discursive psychology's relativism and its micro analysis of discursive strategies do not prevent it from contributing to bigger questions of social justice or development of interventions which seek to increase people's well-being. In the next section, I will review how discursive psychology can be made practically relevant.

Exploring discursive psychology's action potential

Discursive studies identify what health professionals and clients are doing in their communication (e.g. working up a particular identity) and can therefore illuminate why communication may or may not fulfil its goals (Willig, 2004). Feeding back analysis of interactions to professionals enables them to change unreflective work practices, leading to improved professional–client (Hepburn, 2006) and inter-professional interactions (Rance, 2005), and ultimately, better health services and health outcomes. Practitioners have found discussion of their interactions useful (Hepburn, 2006; Rance, 2005).

Furthermore, analysis of interactions between carers and sufferers of health problems and of the co-construction of support and coping suggests whether interactions and constructions are helpful and empowering or otherwise (Lamerichs & te Molder, 2003; Patterson & Potter, 2009; Wilkinson & Kitzinger, 2000). Such insights can inform development of support. More generally, knowledge of how illness talk is intertwined with management of identity, accountability for ill health and other interpersonal concerns enables the broadening of interventions to address these issues (Guise et al., 2010; Guise, Widdicombe & McKinlay, 2007).

Discursive psychology can also contribute to health promotion which seems to enable people to increase control over, and to improve, their health and well-being (WHO, 1986). Lamerichs et al. (2009) used discursive psychology in a participatory health promotion project. Dutch secondary school pupils recorded spontaneous interactions amongst peers. Together with the researchers, they analysed accounts concerned with health-themes such as exclusion and bullying. They focused on how adolescents use discursive strategies to legitimise (negative) assessments of their peers and how others' reactions to statements (e.g. laughter, silence) affect the trajectory of interactions. Having learnt how accounts perform actions which are not determined by individuals' intentions but emerge from the interaction and are co-constructed, adolescents developed interventions. These included a play showing how bullying depends on the course of interactions. This suggests that discursive psychology can be used to promote public awareness of discursive strategies' social effects and facilitate changing those which affect people's well-being.

Further, various authors have argued that accounts can constrain or facilitate behaviours outside verbal interactions (Foucault, 1973; Mills, 1940; Willig, 1999). Discursive psychology can therefore also be employed in attempts to change health related behaviours. To illustrate this, I will discuss my research on constructions of infertility in Malawi. This study, conducted in a setting with dire health and development statistics (UN, 2009), also suggests how discursive psychology can contribute to well-being *and* equality and social justice.

Extending discursive psychology's action potential: constructions of infertility in Malawi Infertility is a neglected, but common problem in sub-Saharan African countries. In Malawi, approximately 17% of couples of reproductive age suffers from secondary infertility, that is infertility after the birth of a first child (Ericksen & Brunette, 1996). Primary and secondary infertility have serious psychosocial consequences in resource-poor settings, including depression, social exclusion and marital stress (Ombelet et al., 2008). I used discursive psychology to examine how practitioners, men and women with a fertility problem and their relatives construct infertility's consequences and solutions in semi-structured interviews (de Kok, 2009). I treated these interviews as a site of social interaction (Wooffitt & Widdicombe, 2006), where participants manage interpersonal issues through their descriptions. I will discuss one data-extract, in which a respondent accounts for a common response to infertility (Ombelet et al., 2008): men taking another wife.

Extract 1 (Interview 48, brother of someone with a fertility problem)

48.	R.	So what I mean is in rural areas,
49.	I	Uhu
50.	R	they don't go to hospital,
51.	I	Uhu
52.	R	they always go for African doctors.
53.	I	Okay, yah=
54.	R	=And *if* African doctors *fail,* then it is up to the man, *if* he feels it is not his fault,
55.	I	Uhu
56.	R	then you look for an alternative
57.	I	Like, (1) what kind of alternative might he look for?
58.	R	(.5) You need children.(.5) In our context, in our eh cultural beliefs, if you marry have no
59.		children then you are unfortunate,
60.	I	Uhu
61.	R	Very unfortunate.
62.	I	Yah

(respondent lists two consequences)

73.	R	So, if I've a alternative, what alternative can you have, if you love your wife, you cannot
74.		divorce.
75.	I	Uhu
76.	R	Automatically you will marry another wife.
77.	I	Uhu
78.	R	So you automatically beco:me (.) a polygamist.
79.	I	Okay, yah.

The respondent explains that in rural areas people go to African doctors instead of to the hospital and that 'if African doctors *fail* then it is up to the man, if he feels it is not his fault, then you look for a alternative' (54–56). The respondent is then asked to specify the alternative (57), which he does several lines later: 'automatically you will marry another wife' (76).

I want to highlight three features of this extract (for similar extracts, see de Kok, 2009). First, the respondent starts his response to the interviewer's probe with constructing a need for children. He does this through an explicit reference ('you need children', 58), by making relevant that not bearing children when married has negative consequences ('then you are unfortunate, very unfortunate', 59–61; and by listing them, 61–62). Second, the need to bear children is constructed as cultural, rather than personal, by references to a shared, cultural context: 'in our context, in our eh cultural beliefs' (58). Third, the respondent refers to the 'alternative' only after the invocation of a cultural need for children and identifying an *un*viable alternative: 'if you love your wife you cannot divorce' (73–74). Hence, the respondent delays identification of marrying another wife as 'alternative' and appears to treat it as an accountable and sensitive matter, since delays are characteristic for interactionally sensitive responses (Pomerantz, 1986).

The respondent's account forestalls problematic inferences about the practice of polygamy and men who engage in it. First of all, constructing polygamy as based on a cultural need to bear children frames the practice as a reasonable, practical solution rather than a problematic consequence. The same goes for constructing polygamy as 'alternative' to consulting 'African doctors' because it allocates polygamy to the same category of health-seeking behaviours. Second, grounding polygamy in a cultural need portrays it as shared by members of the cultural tradition. Hence, this is a 'script formulation', which are descriptions which portray practices or events as widespread, recurrent and predictable (Edwards, 1994). The respondent uses other scripting devices, including the (implied) if-then construction (Edwards, 1995): 'if I've a alternative (...) if you love your wife [then] you cannot divorce' (67–68).

This makes not divorcing and its implication, polygamy, into a law-like and recurrent consequence of a childless marriage. One function which script formulations fulfil is normalizing practices (Edwards, 1994). Here, they make polygamy a routine response to infertility and 'the normal thing to do' for members of the cultural tradition. Third, script formulations manage actors' accountability (Edwards, 1994). Presenting an action as scripted makes it into something which anybody would do and does not require explanation in terms of the specific actor (op cit.). Similarly, McHoul (2004, p. 438) argues that references to culture can displace personal responsibility: 'imbrication in "a culture" can become a defence in its own right', by making someone a 'mere member of a larger constituency of wrong-doers'. Thus, presenting a response like polygamy as following a cultural script, minimises a man's personal accountability. This effect is achieved as well by the respondent's claim that 'automatically' you will marry another wife and become a polygamist (76, 78), which constructs this response as inevitable and independent of men's volition and agency. Note that the respondent constructs taking another wife as motivated by love: 'if you love your wife you cannot divorce' (73, 74). Consequently, he forestalls another potential negative inference, that men who take another wife in response to fertility problems are somehow harsh and selfish.

So, the interviewer's probe is followed by an account which constructs a cultural requirement to bear children, before the respondent provides further details about an 'alternative' response to infertility. This account and the business it performs may be triggered by the interviewer's probe, which treats the alternative as unknown and unexpected, suggesting it is not necessarily seen as normal or even appropriate (see de Kok, 2009). Constructing polygamy as a reasonable and widespread response, and playing down men's accountability for it, defuses ideas that the response is extraordinary or somehow reflect negatively upon those engaging in them.

Constructing a cultural requirement of procreation is particularly instrumental in normalizing practices when talking to a western interviewer, because it implies that the interviewer lacks the necessary cultural membership knowledge to assess the practices for their reasonableness or normality. However, in their accounts, interactants draw on culturally available resources, and we can assume that they are used and make sense beyond the interview setting (Guise et al., 2010), especially in this study: most participants had never been interviewed before. Moreover, various non-interview situations would raise similar interactional issues. Health professionals or church representatives may question men in African settings about taking another wife, or having affairs in response to infertility. In such encounters, similar accounts, referring to cultural needs may well be produced. Indeed, 'real life' situations in which cultural norms are invoked to justify sexual behaviours have been recorded. When South Africa's current president, Zuma, was tried for rape, he testified having had sex with the woman because she was sexually aroused and 'I knew *as we grew up in the Zulu culture*, that you didn't just leave a woman in that situation' (emphasis added, CNN Transcripts, 2006).

The analytic findings can be used as a starting point for the development of interventions. Constructing polygamy as reasonable, normal and 'automatic' or inevitable response for which individuals are not personally accountable and which is motivated by love, is likely to facilitate this practice. In other extracts, respondents account for and construct having affairs in response to infertility in a similar way (see de Kok, 2009). One should be cautious in assessing practices such as polygamy from a western outsider's perspective (cf. Arnfred, 2004). However, there are health consequences attached to them: having unprotected sex with additional partners puts people at risk of STDs including HIV. Additionally, polygamy, or affairs may lead to psychological stress, especially for the women who are 'replaced' due to fertility problems. They also risk losing their husband's social and economic support (Ombelet et al., 2008). Thus, the identified discursive practices arguably contribute to the reproduction of gender inequalities: they facilitate men's[3] engagement in behaviours which increase their wives' socio-economic vulnerability and put themselves and their wives at risk for attracting STDs including HIV (cf. Ombelet et al., 2008). This is in conflict with reproductive rights, according to which women, like men, have the right to have a safe sex life and to have control over matters related to their sexual and reproductive health (UN, 1994). Thus, the accounts examined appear disempowering for men (by minimizing their personal choice) and especially women, endangering their health, social security and fulfillment of human rights.

Willig (1999) suggests that discourse analysis can contribute to well-being and empowerment by critiquing and resisting language use which sustains undesirable practices, and exploring and legitimising alternative, more helpful accounting practices and constructions. Hence, we can seek ways to challenge Malawian communities' constructions of 'culture' as a force which makes people 'automatically' behave in certain ways, whilst acknowledging limitations in self-determination as well. Extracts and analysis could be used in (radio) plays or discussion groups which stimulate reflection and raise awareness of the disempowering effects of accounts. These could also facilitate the use of accounts which construct *not* engaging in extramarital affairs and polygamy as normal and reasonable and highlight people's agency and ability to make their own decisions. Such interventions constitute new ways of engaging in community empowerment and developing health-enhancing communities (Campbell & Murray, 2004). They chime with Freire's (1972) approach of critical consciousness raising, aimed at increasing communities'

understanding of how *social* conditions affect their well-being and their capacity to change these conditions.

Conclusion: advancing the applicability of discursive psychology

Using discursive psychology to analyse sufferers', carers' or practitioners'
accounts and interactions illuminates the use of generic discursive strategies
and their rhetorical functions. Discursive psychology also yields substantive
insights into interpersonal issues at stake for sufferers, carers or practitioners,
often related to normative expectations and the risk that others draw negative
inferences about oneself. Furthermore, it illuminates health-related behaviours
by identifying how various social actors interpret these behaviours, and to what
effect (for another opinion, see Willig, 2004). For instance, my own research
identifies how using the generic discursive device of 'script formulations' enables normalisation and minimisation of responsibility for taking another wife, or
having affairs (de Kok, 2009), in response to infertility. These accounts forestall
negative inferences about such practices or those performing them and facilitate
engagement in these arguably problematic responses. Insights into the meanings of health-related behaviours as made relevant by social actors themselves,
the interpersonal and inferential issues they manage in their interactions, and
the effects of discursive strategies they employ can be used to develop health
promotion interventions and support and improve professional–client or professional–professional communication. In these ways, discursive psychology has
implications for practice and can contribute to people's health and well-being.

   However, we can do more to achieve the shift from critique to action and
contribute to well-being as well as equality and social justice. We require more
'actionable understandings' into the reproduction of inequality and injustice (Murray & Campbell, 2004). While intervening in the socio-economic
mechanisms cementing injustice appears outwith the psychologist's remit,
psychologists can address the human processes and 'individual–society dia-
lectic' which underpin social inequalities and damage health and well-being
(Murray & Campbell, 2003). Wider social issues (e.g. poverty, inequality)
get translated into people's daily lives through community-level processes
(Campbell & Murray, 2004). Discursive psychology can yield valuable insights
into such processes by illuminating empowering or disempowering, culturally shared discursive practices and by demonstrating how inequalities are
reproduced in social interactions. Discursive psychology treats gender-based
inequalities, cultural norms and psychological concepts such as illness cognitions or coping styles as at least partly interactionally produced, in response to
the interpersonal business at stake. It refrains from treating them as internal,

fixed and individualistic attributes or determined by the cultural context (de Kok & Widdicombe, in press). This makes discursive psychology a liberating and empowering approach (cf. Potter, 2010b), particularly suitable for the promotion of social change.

Furthermore, understandings of discursive strategies and their interpersonal effects should be connected more to concrete attempts to address well-being, equality and social justice (cf. Murray & Campbell, 2003). Interventions can focus on discussing discursive strategies and their effects in order to empower community members to challenge constructions and practices which directly affect their lives and well-being (McVittie, 2006).

Finally, addressing social justice and inequality requires siding with the 'oppressed and disenfranchised' (Murray & Campbell, 2003). It is desirable that more discursive psychologists focus on non-western, resource-poor settings, which are plagued by a high burden of disease and economic and social (e.g. gender) inequalities. Applying discursive psychology to translated and interpreted materials collected in settings 'foreign' to the analyst is challenging, but feasible.

There is however a risk that a 'rush' to change the world and be political makes analysts lose sight of important details of the way people use talk to make sense of their actions, worlds and identities (Widdicombe, 1995). Hence, we need to do analysis first, politics second (Kitzinger, 2008) and link analysis of discursive strategies and the actions they accomplish to wider social justice and equality concerns *after* the analysis is done. In this way, discursive psychology allows for a truly bottom-up approach, led by participants' concerns and orientations rather than the analyst's. Surely this is crucial for critical health psychologists who are concerned with reducing inequalities and social injustice by giving voice to, and empowering, people.

Key points

1. Discursive Psychology's micro analytic approach does not prevent the approach dealing with bigger questions of social inequality and injustice; after all injustice and inequality enters people's lives through community-level processes and concrete social interaction.
2. Critical health psychologists seek to illuminate social suffering in context; discursive psychology can elucidate how inequalities are reproduced or resisted in the context of social interactions.
3. Discursive psychology offers actionable understandings regarding meanings of health-related behaviours as made relevant by social actors themselves, and the interpersonal effects of descriptions and discursive strategies.

4. There is scope for making more use of discursive psychology's insights for the development of health promotion interventions which are in line with principles of community empowerment and critical consciousness raising in resource-rich *and* resource-poor settings.

5. In order to give voice and empower people, we should as much as possible focus on, and examine, research participants' concerns and orientations linking these to social justice and equality.

NOTES

* I would like to thank Dr. Sue Widdicombe for her advice and feedback on this chapter.

1. This description is necessarily partial and constructive. For fuller descriptions see, for example, Potter (2010a) and Potter & Hepburn (2008).

2. Discursive psychology has also increasingly adopted conversation analysis' focus on the analysis of *naturally occurring* 'talk' rather than interviews or focus groups. See, for example, Speer (2002) for a critical discussion of this development.

3. In some other data extracts, respondents indicate that a woman could try to become pregnant from somebody else but respondents do not normalise and minimise responsibility for this practice in the same way.

REFERENCES

Arnfred, S. (ed.) (2004) *Re-Thinking Sexuality in Africa*, Uppsala, Sweden, The Nordic Africa Institute.

de Kok, B. C. de & Widdicombe, S. (in press). 'Interpersonal issues in expressing lay knowledge: a discursive psychology approach', *Journal of Health Psychology*.

de Kok, B. C. de & Widdicombe, S. (2008) '"I really tried": management of normative issues in accounts of responses to infertility', *Social Science and Medicine*, 67(7), 1083–93.

de Kok, B. C. de. (2009) '"Automatically you become a polygamist": "culture" and "norms" as resources for normalization and managing accountability in talk about responses to infertility', *Health: An Interdisciplinary Journal for the Social Study of Health, Illness and Medicine*, 13(2), 197–217.

Edwards, D. (1994) 'Script formulations: an analysis of event descriptions in conversation', *Journal of Language and Social Psychology*, 13(3), 211–47.

Edwards, D. (1995) 'Two to tango: script formulations, dispositions, and rhetorical symmetry in relationship troubles talk', *Research on Language and Social Interaction*, 28(4), 319–50.

Edwards, D., Ashmore, M. & Potter, J. (1995) 'Death and furniture – the rhetoric, politics and theology of bottom line arguments against relativism', *History of the Human Sciences*, 8(2), 25–49.

Edwards, D. & Potter, J. (1992) *Discursive Psychology* London: Sage.

Ericksen, K. & Brunette, T. (1996) 'Patterns and predictors of infertility among African women: a cross-national survey of twenty-seven nations', *Social Science and Medicine*, 42(2), 209–20.

Foucault, M. (1973) *The Birth of the Clinic: An Archaeology of Medical Perception* London: Routledge.

Freire, P. (1972) *Pedagogy of the Oppressed* Harmondsworth: Penguin.

Garfinkel, H. (1967) *Studies in Ethnomethodology* Cambridge: Polity Press.

Gilbert, N. & Mulkay, M. (1984) *Opening Pandora's Box: A Sociological Analysis of Scientists Discourse* Cambridge: Cambridge University Press.

Guise, J., McKinlay, A. & Widdicombe, S. (2010) 'The impact of early stroke on identity: A discourse analytic study', *Health*, 14(1), 75–90.

Guise, J., Widdicombe, S. & McKinlay, A. (2007) '"What is it like to have ME?": the discursive construction of ME in computer-mediated communication and face-to-face interaction', *Health: An Interdisciplinary Journal for the Social Study of Health, Illness and Medicine*, 1(1), 87–108.

Hepburn, A. (2006) 'Getting closer at a distance: theory and the contingencies of Practice', *Theory and Psychology*, 16(3), 327–42.

Hepburn, A. (2000) 'On the alleged incompatibility between relativism and feminist psychology', *Feminism and Psychology*, 10(1), 91–106.

Hepburn, A. & Potter, J. (2007) 'Crying receipts: time, empathy, and institutional practice', *Research on Language and Social Interaction*, 40(1), 89–116.

Hepburn, A. & Potter, J. (forthcoming) 'Designing the recipient: managing advice resistance in institutional settings', *Social Psychology Quarterly*.

Hook, D. (2001) 'Discourse, knowledge, materiality, history: Foucault and discourse analysis', *Theory and Psychology*, 11(4), 521–47.

Horton-Salway, M. (2001) 'Narrative identities and the management of personal accountability in talk about ME: a discursive psychology approach to illness narrative', *Journal of Health Psychology*, 6(2), 247–59.

Horton-Salway, M. (2008) 'The Local Production of Knowledge: Disease Labels, Identities and Category Entitlements', *Health: An Interdisciplinary Journal for the Social Study of Health, Illness and Medicine*, 8(3), 351–72.

Horton-Salway, M. & Locke, A. (2010) '"But you might be damaging your baby", Constructing choice and risk in labour and childbirth', *Feminism and Psychology*, in press.

Kitzinger, C. (2008) 'Developing feminist conversation analysis: a response to work', *Human Studies*, 31, 179–208.

Lamerichs, J., Koelen, M., & te Molder, H. (2009) 'Turning adolescents into analysts of their own discourse: raising reflexive awareness of everyday talk in order to develop peer-based health activities', *Qualitative Health Research*, 19, 1162–75.

Lamerichs, J. & te Molder, H. (2003) 'Computer-mediated communication: from a cognitive to a discursive model', *New Media Society*, 5(4), 451–73.

Locke, A. & Horton-Salway, M. (2010) '"Golden age" versus "bad old days": A discursive examination of advice-giving in antenatal classes', *Journal of Health Psychology*, in press.

McHoul, A. (2004) 'Specific gravity: a brief outline of an alternative specification of culture', *Continuum: Journal of Media and Cultural Studies*, 18(3), 427–46.

McVittie, C. (2006) 'Critical health psychology, pluralism and dilemmas: the importance of being critical', *Journal of Health Psychology*, 11(3), 373–77.

McVittie, C. & Goodall, K. (2009) 'Harry, Paul and the Filipino maid: racial and sexual abuse in local contexts', *Journal of Health Psychology*, 14(5), 651–54.

Mills, C. W. (1940) 'Situated action and the vocabulary of motives', *American Sociological Review*, 5, 904–13.

Murray, M. & Campbell, C. (2004) 'Community health psychology: promoting analysis and action for social change', *Journal of Health Psychology*, 9(2), 187–95.

Murray, M. & Campbell, C. (2003) 'Living in a material world: reflecting on some assumptions of health psychology', *Journal of Health Psychology*, 8(2), 231–36.

Ombelet, W., Cooke, I., Dyer, S., Serour, G., & Devroey, P. (2008) 'Infertility and the provision of infertility medical services in developing countries', *Human Reproduction Update*, 14(6), 605–21.

Patterson, A. & Potter, J. (2009) 'Caring: Building a 'psychological disposition' in pre-closing sequences in phone calls with a young adult with a learning disability', *British Journal of Social Psychology, 48*, 447-65.

Pomerantz, A. (1986) 'Agreeing and disagreeing with assessments: some features of preferred/ dispreferred turn-shapes', in J. M. Atkinson & J. Heritage (eds) *Structures of Social Action: Studies in Conversation Analysis* Cambridge: Cambridge University Press.

Potter, J. (2010a) 'Discourse analysis and discursive psychology', in H. Cooper et al. (eds) *Handbook of Research Methods in Psychology* Washington: American Psychological Association.

Potter, J. (2010b) 'Contemporary discursive psychology: issues, prospects, and Corcoran's awkward ontology', *British Journal of Social Psychology* 49(4), 657–78.

Potter, J. & Hepburn, A. (2008) 'Discursive constructionism', in J. A. Holstein & J. F. Gubrium (eds) *Handbook of Constructionist Research*, New York: Guildford, pp. 275–93.

Potter, J. & Edwards, D. (2003) 'Rethinking Cognition: On Coulter on Discourse and Mind', *Human Studies*, 26, 165–81.

Potter, J. & Wetherell, M. (1987) *Discourse and Social Psychology: beyond Attitudes and Behavior* London: Sage.

Prilleltensky, I. (2003). Understanding and overcoming oppression: towards psychopolitical validity. *American Journal of Community Psychology*, 31, 195–202.

Rance, S. (2005) 'Abortion discourse in Bolivian hospital contexts', *Sociology of Health and Illness*, 27(188), 214.

Sacks, H. (1992) *Lectures on Conversation* Oxford: Basil Blackwell.

Speer, S. (2002) '"Natural" and "contrived" data: a sustainable distinction?' *Discourse Studies*, 4(4), 511–25.

United Nations (2009) Human Development report 2009, Geneva: UN [online] available from http://hdrstats.un.org/en/countries/country_fact_sheets/cty_fs_MWI.html

United Nations (1994) Report of the International Conference on Population and Development, Geneva: UNFPA.

Widdicombe, S. (1995) 'Identity, politics and talk: A case for the mundane and the everyday', in S. Wilkinson & C. Kitzinger (eds) *Feminism and Discourse: Psychological Perspectives* London: Sage.

Wilkinson, S. & Kitzinger, C. (2000) 'Thinking differently about thinking positive: a discursive approach to cancer patients' talk', *Social Science and Medicine*, 50, 797–81.

Willig, C. (1999) *Applied Discourse Analysis: Social and Psychological Interventions* Buckingham, Open University Press.

Willig, C. (2004) 'Discourse analysis and health psychology', in M. Murray (ed.) *Critical Health Psychology* Basingstoke: Palgrave Macmillan.

Wooffitt, R. & Widdicombe, S. (2006) 'Interaction in interviews', in Drew, P. (ed.) *Talk and Interaction in Social Research Methods* London: Sage.

CHAPTER 12

'I Forget My Problems – The Problems Are in the Soil': Encountering Nature in Allotment Gardening

NIGEL KING

Introduction

Since the late twentieth century questions about how we as human beings relate to the natural world have moved from the fringes to the centre of political discourse. Increasingly these debates are influencing health and well-being policy agendas and informing interventions and practices that directly influence people's lives. In this chapter I will present an overview of the orthodox psychological literature on human responses to nature, and its translation into "green exercise" interventions aimed at improving individual mental and/or physical health. I will then describe recent research at the University of Huddersfield that took a qualitative approach to examining experiences of allotment gardening and their perceived consequences for health and well-being. In conclusion I will consider the future for critical health psychology research in this area, and how it should relate to the mainstream.

Psychological responses to nature

The effects of contact with nature: the literature

Research into the links between health/well-being and human engagement with the natural world is a multi-disciplinary endeavour and has from the start had a strong applied emphasis, with practitioners in areas such as therapeutic horticulture, landscape management and urban planning (amongst others) providing a major impetus for academic developments. There is also a clear political dimension to this work, with its connections to the wider environmentalist movement and campaigns to improve the quality of urban life (especially in settings with high deprivation and especially for children) and to protect the natural environment. Academics – including psychologists – have been very willing to use their research to argue for changes in policy and practice at local, national and global levels.

The role of psychology in this field has principally been to attempt to provide explanations of how and why contact with nature should have a beneficial effect on individual human beings. Many of these are grounded in evolutionary accounts. Put simply, the argument runs that because we as a species evolved in the natural world; we have an innate affinity with it. In contrast, man-made urban environments are a very recent phenomenon in the history of our species, therefore we are not 'pre-programmed' to find them psychologically restorative. A highly influential formulation of this evolutionary perspective is the 'biophilia hypothesis' put forward by biologist Edward Wilson and social ecologist Stephen Kellert (Kellert and Wilson, 1993).

When we turn to the mechanisms by which the beneficial effects of natural environments are claimed to operate, the main debate has been between explanations in terms of attentional demands and those in terms of stress reduction. The former position is exemplified by Kaplan's 'Attention Restoration Theory' (ART) (Kaplan and Kaplan, 1989; Kaplan, 1995). According to this, attention can be separated into two components: involuntary, where attention is captured by inherently fascinating stimuli, and voluntary, where attention is directed at a stimulus through a conscious control process. Voluntary attention is potentially fatiguing because it requires cognitive effort. Nature is psychologically beneficial because it contains many intriguing stimuli which "modestly" attract involuntary attention or 'fascination' as Kaplan prefers to call it. In contrast, urban environments contain many stimuli that capture attention 'dramatically' and require directed, voluntary attention to deal with them – for instance, stimuli associated with road traffic (Berman, Jonides and Kaplan, 2008).

"Fascination" is an essential component of the restorative effect of nature, according to Kaplan, but it is not in itself sufficient. Three other components are also required:

1. Being away: a break from familiar settings can help the individual to free him or herself from fatiguing mental activity involving directed attention.
2. Environmental extent: to be restorative, the natural environment must be sufficient in scope to engage the viewer's mind. It must be '…rich enough

and coherent enough so that it constitutes a whole other world' (Kaplan, 1995, p. 178).
3. Compatibility: the natural environmental setting must fit with the purposes and inclinations of the person experiencing it.

Ulrich et al. (1991) criticise the primary focus on the nature of attention in Kaplan's theory. Instead he advocates a 'psycho-evolutionary' theory, which explains the restorative effects of nature in terms of general stress reduction, including physiological and psychological (especially emotional) components. Ulrich proposes that in early human history the ability to experience a restorative response to unthreatening environments was advantageous and therefore would be selected for in human evolution. As a result, modern humans have a predisposition to respond positively to natural environments and find them relaxing and restorative. Note that he is not claiming that such a preference is invariant and automatic amongst all people, nor that people can never find urban environments restorative. Rather the positive response to nature is learnt very easily through biologically prepared learning (Ulrich, 1993). The same process, it is argued, leads to common negative responses to certain 'natural' stimuli, such as snakes and spiders (Seligman, 1971; Öhman and Mineka, 2001).

Neither Kaplan nor Ulrich deny that to some extent preferences for, and reactions to, nature can be learned; after all, even within particular social settings there is clearly variation between people in how they respond to particular natural and urban environments. Equally, there have been historical shifts in how the natural world is seen, for instance with the advent of the Romantic movement in late eighteenth century Europe (Worster, 1994). However, both see learning as secondary to intrinsic cognitive or psycho-physiological processes. They point to substantial similarities in what people find attractive and/or restorative in their environment across cultures with very different patterns of urbanisation and aesthetic tradition.

'Green Exercise': nature as a prescription for health

The term 'green exercise' is used to refer to activities through which participants may simultaneously gain the benefits of physical exercise and contact with nature. Over the past decade or so it has featured with increasing prominence in policy documents relating to health and well-being, with many examples of schemes based on the concept described in the academic and practitioner literatures (Pretty et al., 2005). Recommendations for green exercise commonly cite in support the kind of research described above, with its claims of an innate basis to the psychological benefits of nature, as well as epidemiological studies that suggest a relationship between general health/ well-being and access to green spaces. For instance, Mitchell and Popham (2008) showed that health inequalities were reduced in areas with high access to green spaces, compared to those with more limited access.

Initiatives to promote green exercise are generally targeted at specific client groups such as older people (Milligan, Gatrell and Bingley, 2004), people with mental health problems (Fieldhouse, 2003) or learning disabilties (Smith and Aldous, 1994), young offenders (McGuin and Relf, 2001) or children (Blair, 2009). Regarding the content of green exercise initiatives, many fit within the 'therapeutic horticulture' tradition – a movement that long pre-dates the recent interest in the health-giving qualities of nature (Parr, 2007). Other types of organised activity include walking groups (Natural England, 2011) and nature conservation projects (Birch, 2005).

The psychology of gardening

For people in much of the western world perhaps the most common activity that involves them directly in the natural world is gardening. Certainly in the United Kingdom gardening is a hugely popular leisure activity, supporting a multi-million pound industry supplying plants, seeds, tools and other equipment, as well as books, magazines and television shows on the topic. It is therefore striking how little psychological research has focused on issues relating to gardening. It is referred to in some of the literature on the impact of nature, though rarely in much detail. Work addressing it directly is most frequently found in the area of therapeutic horticulture, generally examining the impact of specific programmes on client groups such as those with mental health or substance abuse problems, or with learning disabilities (Sempik, Aldridge and Becker, 2005). A separate stream of research focuses on attempts to engage children with nature through school-based horticultural activities (e.g. Pecaski McLennan, 2010).

Particularly scarce is research investigating the health and well-being consequences of 'ordinary' gardening, whether it be in domestic gardens or on allotments. A rare example is Gross and Lane's (2007) grounded theory study of experiences and perceptions of gardening amongst a sample of 18 domestic gardeners. Their analysis demonstrated the importance of the notion of the garden as a 'retreat' from the varied pressures of everyday life, and also showed how the meaning of gardening changed for people over the course of their lifespan. From a very different theoretical and methodological tradition, Van den Berg and Custers (2010) have recently published the first experimental evidence for the ability of gardening to significantly reduce the symptoms of acute stress. While not directly concerned with health and well-being issues, Clayton's (2007) survey of US garden centre visitors showed that appreciation of nature was a major motivator for engagement in gardening, and social concerns and uses were also important.

Psychological responses to nature: a critical view

From a critical perspective, I would argue that the literature on psychological responses to nature has some significant merits. It addresses some interesting questions about the ways that people's environments shape their lives. It engages with other disciplines, including the arts and humanities, more broadly than much of the mainstream health psychology literature. Perhaps most importantly it recognises the political nature of research on this topic, and the need for researchers to be actively involved in changing policy and practice from local to global levels. In his Prelude to Kellert and Wilson's (1993) edited collection 'The Biophilia Hypotheses', McVay states,

> It seems essential that the habits of mind and heart that evoked the notion of biophilia be assumed more broadly by universities, laboratories, think tanks, and government agencies that share responsibility for guiding our prospects (p.17).

Nevertheless, some aspects of this literature remain problematic. The emphasis on a general innate affinity with nature, operating through cognitive and/or biophysiological processes, can lead to the nature–human relationship being presented in rather a stimulus–response manner. This neglects the active meaning-making involved in how people respond to natural environments, including what they count as constituting 'nature', and reflects the predominance of laboratory-based experimental methods. Studies have typically involved the presentation of images of urban and natural environment to participants and the measurement of psychological and physiological responses to them. Such methods cannot address how nature figures in people's everyday lived experience, or enable us to consider how the conditions of people's lives shape such experience.

Public health research such as Mitchell and Popham's study can reveal the links between social and economic variables and access to nature at a population level, which is undoubtedly important in terms of influencing policy. However, as Brown and Bell (2007) point out, the 'medicalisation of nature' that has accompanied the development of green exercise policies has limitations, especially in terms of what kind of outcomes are sought and what counts as evidence for such outcomes. In particular, it may lead to an emphasis on what is readily measurable – such as discrete areas of health improvement – rather than a more holistic understanding of how involvement with nature relates to a person's sense of well-being as they themselves define it.

LIVERPOOL JOHN MOORES UNIVERSITY
LEARNING SERVICES

The empirical research described in the remainder of this chapter aimed to add to the very limited literature on the how gardening outside of an explicitly therapeutic context impacts on health and well-being. Like Gross and Lane (2007), its approach is qualitative as its focus is on understanding the place of gardening (in this case specifically allotment gardening) in the wider context of people's lives.

Health, well-being and the lived experience of allotment gardening

Background to the University of Huddersfield studies

The research I am describing here is drawn from two studies of health and well-being in relation to allotment gardening in urban settings. Both studies were part of a programme of evaluation work related to healthy living initiatives in deprived areas of the adjacent northern English former industrial towns of Huddersfield and Halifax. Here I will provide some brief background to the allotment system as it exists in England, before describing the settings for the research projects.

Allotment sites are areas of land divided into plots that are rented out to local people for cultivation. They are typically in urban areas, and most are owned by local authorities, though some are privately owned. Allotment use peaked in the mid-twentieth century, when allotments were an integral part of urban working class culture, not only providing families with fresh food but also serving as a focal point for social activities. In 1950 there were 1,100,000 allotment plots in existence. However, soon after this there was a swift decline, attributable to the increasing availability of cheap processed food and a general increase in affluence as post-war austerity turned to economic growth. By 1964, fewer than 80,000 plots remained (Ducker, 1999). The past decade or so has seen a reversal of the pattern of declining interest in allotment gardening that typified the later twentieth century. The benefits of 'allotmenteering' (personal and societal) have been trumpeted in the media, and many sites now have lengthy waiting lists for those wishing to take up a plot (Vidal, 2008). Commentators generally agree that the new allotmenteers tend to be from a different socio-economic background than the traditional profile: younger, more middle-class and with a higher proportion of women. Concerns about food quality and ecological issues are more likely to motivate people to take on an allotment than economic necessity (Poole, 2006).

A key difference between domestic and allotment gardening is that on taking up a plot, the gardener becomes part of an allotment community on their site. Typically each site has a committee, who liaise with the local authority, enforce site regulations, resolve disputes between plot-holders and may organ-ise communal purchase of seeds and tools and site-based events (if members so wish). Many allotment societies are affiliated to local, regional and national allotment gardening organisations.

The two studies I am drawing on for this chapter focus on allotment sites that were supported in various ways by 'Healthy Living Partnerships' (HLPs). This was a government-funded initiative to concentrate resources aimed at improving health and well-being in areas of high deprivation, sup-porting projects and activities identified through local consultation. The HLPs my team and I worked with were Paddock Pathways to Health (PPH) in Huddersfield (King, Mirza and Bates, 2007), and West Central Halifax Healthy Living Partnership (WCHHLP) (King and Rodriguez, 2007). In Paddock, PPH invested in the renovation and development of three long-standing sites, which to varying degrees had suffered from years of neglect and vandalism. In West Central Halifax, the HLP supported a smaller site which at the start of the project was mostly derelict save for a couple of indi-vidual plots. The new plots they developed were mostly gardened collectively by groups of inexperienced allotmenteers, with the allotment worker directly involved in their horticultural activities.

Capturing the allotmenteering experience: our approach

The overall approach we took in the two allotment studies can be described (following Hammersley, 1992) as 'subtle realist'. This position holds that the data produced in social research are never free from the particular perspective of the researcher(s) who collected it, since researchers cannot stand outside the social world to observe it. However, unlike radical relativist approaches such as social constructionism, it retains a belief in phenomena that are inde-pendent of the researcher and knowable through the research process. A sub-tle realist approach can thus make claims as to the validity of a represen-tation arising from research, while recognising that other perspectives on the phenomenon are possible. As Murphy et al. (1998) put it, the aim is to 'search for knowledge about which we can be reasonably confident' (p. 69). This is an appropriate position for applied qualitative research that seeks to evaluate health and well-being initiatives, and potentially influence practice and/or policy.

Design and participants

Both studies principally used individual interviews to collect data. The Paddock sample (n = 20) was recruited through allotment site secretaries, who distributed invitations to participate and information sheets to allotmenteers. We sought to gain a variety in terms of age, gender and experience in allotment gardening. In Paddock, three interviews were held with pairs of allotmenteers who worked plots together, at the request of the participants. In Halifax, users of the allotment site were approached by the allotment development worker. Of nine who initially agreed to participate, we were able to carry out interviews with six within the time frame of the project: three individually plus three members of the Asian women's group were interviewed together in Punjabi; the interviewer translated the recording into English.

All interviews were audio-recorded and transcribed verbatim with the exception of Bonny in Paddock who chose not to be recorded. (Note that all

Table 1: Participant details

Pseudonym	Age	Gender	Approx years as allotmenteer	Area
Adele	59	Female	1	Paddock
Anna	34	Female	1	Paddock
Beryl	60	Female	1.5	Paddock
Bonnie	46	Female	3	Paddock
Bryn	58	Male	24	Paddock
David	31	Male	1	Paddock
Delia	67	Female	4	Paddock
Francis	35	Male	5	Paddock
Gloria	68	Female	15	Paddock
Hannah	60	Female	13	Paddock
Harvey	57	Male	3	Paddock
Ian	74	Male	5	Paddock
James	65	Male	6	Paddock
Jill	64	Female	6	Paddock
Kath	77	Female	5	Paddock
Louisa	79	Female	10	Paddock
Mavis	82	Female	approx. 50	Paddock
Nina	59	Female	13	Paddock
Ron	63	Male	6	Paddock
Thomas	73	Male	approx 35	Paddock
Tim	38	Male	1	Halifax
Reggie	59	Male	2	Halifax
Dan	89	Male	'many, many years' (15 at this site)	Halifax
Parinder	48	Female	< 1	Halifax
Tahfeem	54	Female	< 1	Halifax
Neelum	30	Female	1	Halifax

Note: Anna and David (married couple), Ian and Kath (married couple) and Hannah and Nina (friends) gardened together and were interviewed in pairs. Parinder, Tahfeem and Neelum also worked together and were interviewed in a group.

names have been changed to protect identities.) In her case detailed notes were taken by hand during and immediately after the interview. Table 1 provides summary details of all the allotmenteers interviewed at each site.

Analysis

The transcript data from both studies were analysed separately, using a version of the 'matrix' style of thematic analysis (Nadin and Cassell, 2004). This is a relatively top–down approach, in which main thematic categories are specified early in the process, usually reflecting key issues identified a priori theoretical and/or practical concerns of the research. In our studies, they were defined largely in relation to evaluation criteria identified in discussion with the HLPs. Within the thematic categories, we identified subsidiary themes in a more bottom–up fashion, of the kind used in approaches such as template analysis (King, 2011). For the purposes of this chapter, I further developed the themes relating to issues of health and well-being, incorporating data from both studies into the analysis. In presenting the findings, I will focus on the main theme *perceived benefits of allotment gardening*, which incorporates *the produce itself*, *physical health and well-being* and *psychological/social health and well-being*. I will also consider the theme *being outside*, which cuts across all the areas of perceived benefit (in template analysis these are referred to as 'integrative themes' (King, 2011)).

The impact of allotmenteering: participants' views

The produce itself

The produce itself was of course of major importance to participants. There was a widespread view that food grown on the allotments was superior to that available in shops, in terms of taste and for some participants also in ecological status – such as being organic, or not having been transported from abroad. Allotment-grown produce is contrasted (explicitly or implicitly) with the unnaturalness of supermarket produce which is characterised as artificial and unseasonal:

> Some of my vegetables, they wouldn't win any beauty competitions but it doesn't matter, and they are not all uniform, they are not all the same, but they do taste better. Everybody says the same – they do. (Adele, Paddock)
>
> I think for me the thing is ecological…so instead of getting something that has been flown in from wherever, you are getting things that are more

home-grown because you understand, well, that's the season in this country. (Anna, Paddock)

None of the participants portrays allotment gardening as an economic necessity. While some describe it as a cheap hobby, and argue that at least for some of the pricier products it can save you money, others argue that mass-produced food is so cheap you are unlikely to make any significant savings by growing your own. Bryn, who has gardened at one of the Paddock sites for 24 years, notes the historical change in motivations for growing your own food, from financial to quality concerns:

> I would say that most people were growing food for the table. They were work-ing class guys, probably not very well off, so the reasons were cheaper food. I don't think the health food aspects that we might think about today came into their thinking. (Bryn, Paddock)

Physical health and well-being

While many of the allotmenteers we interviewed saw their home-grown food as 'healthy', rather fewer explicitly related allotment gardening to the over-all healthiness of their diet. Rather participants tended to frame the phys-ical health benefits in terms of the effects of regular exercise, which include for some not only the gardening itself but also walking to and from the site several times a week. Nobody cites exercise as a major reason for taking up allotment gardening, though it is portrayed as a valuable incidental gain of the activity. James (Paddock) contrasts this positively with activities where exercise itself is the main goal:

> This exercise [gardening], I mean the point is, it's natural. I mean I have to say I totally despise the notion of going to the gym because I think you can self exercise in a normal human life – it's not something you do for its own sake, it's a means to an end isn't it?

It is notable that James uses a contrast between the 'natural' and the artificial here, just as many participants did in relation to the quality of the food they produced on their plots. In addition to citing such general health benefits relat-ing to (natural) exercise, some allotmenteers described more specific health improvements. These included the alleviation of conditions such as asthma, heart disease, gastric problems and arthritis, and contributing to successful smoking cessation. Such effects were sometimes attributed to exercise and/or diet, but also to less tangible things such as the sense of purpose provided by allotmenteering and simply 'being outdoors' – points I will return to below.

Social/psychological health and well-being

Consistently the most extensive area of discussion regarding the perceived benefits of allotment gardening was the social/psychological. In analysing participants' accounts of such benefits we divided this theme into four sub-themes: *sense of recuperation, sense of purpose, sense of achievement* and *sense of community*.

1. Sense of recuperation

Almost all the participants spoke about the restorative and/or therapeutic qualities of allotment gardening. Gloria talked about the allotment as 'my country address – it's the only bit of Paddock I like!' Several participants discussed how their allotment helped them to cope with specific crises in their lives, such as illness (their own or a family member's), work stress and bereavement:

> My mother was rushed to hospital and she was there for 4 or 5 weeks and then she died, so I would go to the hospital and then from the hospital I would go to the allotment and I found it very very soothing you know, as I say, therapeutic in that respect. (Beryl, Paddock)

> I do suffer from depression so being on the allotment, I forget my problems – you know, the problems are in the soil sort of thing. (Nina, Paddock)

Often interviewees spoke in more general terms about the recuperative effects of visiting their allotment, which they attributed to direct contact with nature, and sometimes also to the opportunities for social interaction that allotmenteering afforded them. The quotes from Delia in Paddock and Parinder in Halifax illustrate these two attributions:

> I think you benefit by being outside … and it's so quiet there, you are digging and the robins are there or the blackbirds come and feed the family while you are digging and it is very pleasant; the fox walks through now and again. (Delia, Paddock)

> We [the Asian women's group] go to see each other and for them few hours I don't have any worries and I don't think about other problems. We grow vegetables but that is secondary; erm, we don't need vegetables or the food really, it is good for our health and relieves stress. (Parinder, Halifax)

2. Sense of purpose

Allotment gardening provided participants with a sense of purpose – a meaningful activity on which to spend their time. This was especially true for those who were retired, such as Louisa and for the South Asian women in Halifax, who felt they lacked other opportunities for absorbing and enjoyable ways of spending their time:

> It was just to get out of the house, somewhere to go, something to do because as I said I was sitting here nearly on my own all day and didn't know what to do with myself. (Louisa)

> We are here for a few hours and it passes the time, we enjoy it here. We also grow flowers and for a few hours our minds are occupied with gardening. (Tahfeem, Halifax)

Even where declining health limited the amount of physical work some participants could engage in, keeping an involvement with their plot provided some participants with an important focus in their lives. This was most evident in the case of Thomas:

> I mean it keeps your mind active and that's the main thing like I think now, when I am stuck in a lot, it keeps your mind going thinking about it [i.e. working on the plot], whether you can do it or not, thinking about it. (Thomas, Paddock)

3. Sense of achievement

An important psychological benefit described by participants was their sense of achievement in harvesting and eating (or sharing with others) plants they had grown:

> Well it was lovely, it was lovely to actually see them growing and to be able to pick them ... I think the first thing that I actually cut and brought home and ate was broccoli and that broccoli really meant something you know, I had actually grown it and it was a very nice feeling. (Beryl, Paddock)

It was striking that very often in talking about their feelings of achievement, participants focused as much on the process of growing as on the produce gathered at the end of it. There is a sense that their pleasure was linked to working successfully with nature, and at nature's tempo. Ron points out that part and parcel of this is recognising that natural processes are not under your control. Learning to accept this, he suggests, is an important life lesson. It is interesting that he reflects on this point shortly after discussing working on the plot with his wife, who had died a couple of years earlier.

> You have no control over the weather, you have no control over lots of things, and things sometimes come out good that you didn't expect and sometimes better than the ones you have made a lot of effort with ... you learn about things,

you learn about life, you have no control over life whatsoever. You may think you have, but you really haven't (laughs). Ron (Paddock)

4. Sense of community

The notion of the allotment site as a community was widely shared by participants. At the most basic level this means simply seeing other people and having the opportunity for a chat. Mavis, who has had a plot on one of the Paddock sites for almost 50 years, says '.. . the men like to have a Sunday morning gossip, you know, a bit of digging and a lot of gossip.' Dan in Halifax tried to go down to the site at times he knew other people would be there: '... I can look around and know that I have got company.' Simple social interaction was a key aspect of allotmenteering for some participants, such as Thomas whose social world was restricted by ill-health:

> I can't get to many places I mean as I say…so it's the one place where I see somebody different and that's the big thing for me and that's why I want to keep mine as long as I can, even if I can't do much. It's because if it's a nice day and I can see them from here if there is somebody down there and you know I can go and see somebody. (Thomas, Paddock)

However, sense of community means more than just a chance to talk to others with a common interest. A key aspect repeatedly mentioned in interviews was a norm of reciprocity amongst allotmenteers on a site. Plot holders were expected to share plants, produce and knowledge with each other:

> I think there is a kind of community thing that if somebody comes on you will say 'hello' and give them your name and if you have got plants then you offer them at least. I inherited things like blackcurrant, redcurrant bushes, gooseberry bushes so if you are moving them and there is a spare one, you tend to offer it to people. (Harvey, Paddock)

Some participants were keen to increase the amount of communal activity on their site. Francis, for instance, had organised events such as barbecues, and on one site an art exhibition had been held. There was evidently variation in the extent to which allotmenteers were interested in getting involved in such activities, and several (mostly those in full-time employment) stressed the importance of working on their plots away from the demands of other people. This was not, however, seen as incompatible with enjoying a sense of community on the site:

> I do enjoy the seclusion of it actually a lot of the time, you know, and usually there are so few down at any one time – weekends there is likely to be floods

of people sitting out, I imagine they will practically all be down at weekends, but I don't have to restrict myself to weekends you see... but I mean I do see people. I have a few jars with Ron every couple of weeks or so I mean he was up on Saturday night and we had a few over the bowling club. (James, Paddock)

Being outdoors

Participants consistently cite 'being outdoors' as a key aspect of allotment gardening; indeed it is often one of the first things they refer to when asked about the health and well-being benefits of their hobby. Sometimes it is not elaborated any further than this, but frequently, they provide suggestions as to what exactly *is* beneficial about spending time outside. These accounts tend to focus on contact with the natural world, contrasts with everyday working life and/or escape from the physical and psychological constraints of the home.

1. Contact with the natural world

In our interviews, the notion that allotmenteering as an 'outdoor' activity involves contact with nature takes two main forms. Firstly, in some cases participants describe themselves as privileged witnesses to a natural world that is unfolding around them. Here the allotmenteer's access to this world is portrayed as restorative through quiet contemplation, often with an emphasis on the sensory element of the experience. Delia's comment quoted above under *sense of recuperation* illustrates this, as do the following examples:

> Anna: We go up there and feel a lot better – the sunshine and just being outside.
> David: Just getting outside is always good, isn't it?
> Anna: So I don't know whether it's actually physically doing the gardening work or whether it's just being outside in fresh air, hearing the birds tweeting...
> (Anna and David, Paddock)
> I like to stand at the gate because they [birds] can't see me... and I like to watch them all come and they are all waiting in the trees until I disappear. (Gloria, Paddock)

Elsewhere the benefits of contact with the natural world are framed in terms of working *with* nature. Gardening involves attunement to the cycle of the seasons, and to the pace of growth of different plants. The skilled gardener can facilitate these processes but cannot control them, as recognised in Ron's comments about acceptance quoted earlier, and shown also in many rueful comments about the depredations caused by slugs and birds, despite the allotmenteers' best efforts.

2. Contrast with working life

Those participants who were in work valued the outdoor nature of allotmenteering because of its contrast with their indoor (and in some cases sedentary) jobs. Harvey (Paddock) says, 'I think when you have got a job that is not very physical I enjoy getting my fingers dirty.' Quite often participants highlight the fact that particular workplace stressors are absent from the allotment site environment. Ron talks about the contrast between the mental effort required in his former job (he was recently retired) and the physical work of gardening, and also refers to a sense of escape from work-related conflict when on the allotment site:

> When I was working, it was fighting with management quite a lot; then it was nice to go down there [the allotment] and sort of switch off your mind, you know [laughs]. I mean, you can go down there and you don't think of anything, and you can go half an hour and come back quite refreshed. Yes, it was good because it was a complete break from what I did at work. (Ron, Paddock)

3. Escaping the constraints of home

The quote from Ron depicts the allotment as a place of escape. A similar portrayal can be found from those interviewees who described themselves as potentially 'trapped' in their homes. This could be because of the limitations of ill-health as in the case of Thomas (quoted earlier), the dangers of slipping in to a purposeless retirement, or for the Asian women in Halifax, a life dominated by domestic responsibilities:

> We'd just vegetate. Honestly we would, we would be nothing, we wouldn't be getting out, we'd just be sitting in all the time and as you're getting older you see you can't be bothered. Whereas we know we've got something there that needs to be done and we go and do it. (Hannah, Paddock – speaking for herself and Nina)

> It's different here (in England) than it is in Pakistan. Over there it's open spaces and lots of land but here it's just the four walls and there is nowhere to go. (Parinder, Halifax)

Relating our findings to the mainstream literature

In many respects the findings described above are congruent with the mainstream literatures on human responses to nature and the consequences of
'green' exercise. The descriptions of the recuperative effects of allotment
gardening, and the benefits of 'being outdoors' would be predicted by both
Kaplan and Ulrich (albeit with differing theoretical explanations), especially
the prominence of sensory aspects of participants' experiences. Equally, the
strong sense of escape from the pressures of daily life, at work or home, fits
with Kaplan's claim that 'being away' contributes to the restorative effect
of nature. Kaplan's notion that for involvement with nature to be beneficial
it has to occur in a manner that is compatible with the person's purposes
and inclinations is also supported here. Interest in gardening as an activity –
rather than as a means to the ends of improved health or fitness – is central to
why our participants took up allotmenteering.

As well as backing up the existing literature, I would argue that our qualitative, subtle realist approach adds to it in important ways. Firstly, it provides
insights into the meaning of involvement with nature in the context of allotment gardening. 'Naturalness' was without doubt a very relevant concept to
our participants. It was applied not just to horticultural activity and contact
with plants and animals on the sites, but also as a contrast to other aspects
of life: the stresses of work, the constraints of the home, the danger of 'vege-
tating' in front of the television, the artificiality of exercise at the gym. The
produce of allotment gardening was itself seen as more 'natural' than the fruit
and vegetables one could buy in the supermarket. The temporal dimension
of involvement with nature also emerged as a key element for allotmenteers,
as their gardening required them to work with the seasonal growing cycles of
their plants.

Secondly, our research showed that ordinary allotment gardening, outside of an explicitly therapeutic context, could have a wide range of health
and wellbeing benefits for participants. The sense of being part of an allotment community was valued by all our participants, and for some was a vital
source of social interaction – an important distinction from domestic gardening. These findings, building as they do on previous research, argue for the
consideration of allotments in policy initiatives to improve health and well-
being in urban areas. In an economic climate where local authorities may be
tempted to raise money through the sale of allotment sites, it is crucial that
their value is recognised and at the very least existing sites are protected – and
where possible land for new sites made available. More targeted initiatives
should prioritise measures to enable people to continue gardening in the face
of chronic ill-health and age-related infirmity; such simple things as ensuring
paths are well-surfaced, providing seats and basic toilet facilities can make

a real difference for those who rely on their allotment to remain active and socially engaged.

Conclusion

In this chapter I have sought to show that human involvement with 'nature' is a topic that encompasses much to interest critical and qualitative health psychology. It has an overtly political dimension to it, both at the macro level of environmental campaigns to combat global warming and protect biodiversity, and at the micro level illustrated by my specific topic of allotment gardening, which links to local campaigns to protect and extend urban green space. A critical approach helps to bring attention to the context in which the natural world is encountered, in terms of such things as personal and family histories, and socio-economic status. This perspective is at best under played and at worst ignored in the cognitive and evolutionary explanations that dominate mainstream psychological research.

In arguing for the pertinence of this topic to critical health psychology, I recognise that the definition of what counts as 'critical' is itself a matter of dispute within the discipline (see, for example, Crossley, 2008; Hepworth, 2006). One key debate is with regard to whether we should be principally focused on a critique of mainstream health psychology, or should see the translation of research into action to improve society as our over-riding goal. As suggested by Johnson and contributors to this book, I would not see the two positions as mutually exclusive, and certainly agree that we need research that is dedicated to a radical critique of taken-for-granted assumptions in health psychology. However, I do feel that if we never go further than that, there is a danger of becoming an inward-looking intellectual clique, with little to say to the world outside. I do believe we should use whatever skills and resources we have as academic researchers to do work that can further politically and socially progressive causes. I would argue that allotment gardening is such a cause: while individual allotmenteers may differ in the extent to which they recognise a political dimension to their activity, as a whole the allotment movement has strong synergies with wider environmental campaigns. Above all, it challenges the dominant influence of multi-national producers and the big supermarkets on the growing and retailing of food, which has been increasingly criticised for its impact on farmers and local communities (Friends of the Earth, 2005; Guthrie et al., 2006; Weis, 2007). I am therefore willing to work with government-funded agencies in such research, recognising that compromises may need to be made – particularly in how findings are reported to funders – in order to have a chance to influence practice and policy.

The necessarily limited selection of findings from our studies, presented above, suggests several fruitful directions for future research. I was struck by how strongly temporal issues emerged in participants' accounts – especially as we did not explicitly seek these in our questioning. They included the allusions to working at nature's pace which I have discussed here, but also many interviewees spoke at some length about the place of allotmenteering in their own life stories. For some this was to emphasise continuity in personal and family history through involvement with gardening. For others, taking up allotment gardening marked an important life transition such as retirement. These findings indicate that a narrative approach to experiences of allotment gardening could prove a valuable addition to the literature.

Another strong feature of participants' accounts was the notion of the allotment site as a community, with both formal and informal rules and expectations. This also linked to a theme I have not had the space to consider in the present chapter – the construct of 'being a proper gardener' – that appeared in many interviews. It included ideas about dedication and even sacrifice in order to maintain the allotmenteer's plot, but also the notion that one is aware of and acts open the obligations one has as part of the site community. These issues could be very effectively explored in an ethnographic study, in which researchers would be able to participate in the life of the allotment and build relationships with plot-holders over an extended period of time. Finally, the increasing popularity of mixed-method studies amongst large-scale funders of health research (Adamson, 2005) provides opportunities for critical and qualitative health psychologists to play a part in major projects that have a real potential to influence policy and practice. One potentially rewarding focus would be to examine longitudinally the experiences of new allotmenteers and assess how their hobby influences their health and well-being in the social, economic and biographical context of their lives.

Key points

1. Mainstream psychological research emphasises a general innate affinity with nature, explained through cognitive and/or psychophysiological processes. This serves as an important basis for the increased recognition of the importance of 'green exercise' in public health policy. However, it neglects the active meaning-making involved in how people respond to natural environments, including what they count as constituting 'nature'. It also fails to address how the conditions of people's lives shape their experiences of nature.

2. Gardening is one of the most popular ways in which people gain regular contact with 'nature', yet psychological research relating to it is minimal. Allotments in particular constitute a physical and social setting for gardening that offers much of interest to research from a critical health psychological perspective.

3. A team from the Centre for Applied Psychological Research, University of Huddersfield, carried out studies of the lived experience of allotment gardening on four urban sites in West Yorkshire, UK. Twenty-nine 'allotmenteers' took part in semi-structured interviews, which were analysed thematically.

4. Participants perceived the products they grew themselves as intrinsically healthy, and for some there was a recognition of the ecological benefits of the activity. They recognised the value of regular exercise, but most focused much more on the psychosocial benefits of 'allotmenteering'. These included: a sense of recuperation; a sense of purpose; a sense of achievement and a sense of community.

5. On the basis of this work, I argue that critical health psychology should be concerned with making a difference in the 'real' world. To achieve this, it will need to acknowledge what is valuable in mainstream research, and show what it adds to that body of knowledge. This is not incommensurable with a commitment to critically scrutinising the assumptions and practices of conventional psychology.

REFERENCES

Adamson, J. (2005) 'Combined qualitative and quantitative designs'. In A. Bowling and S. Ebrahim (eds) *Handbook of Research Methods in Health: Investigation, Measurement and Analysis*. Buckingham: Open University Press.

Berman, M., Jonides, J. and Kaplan, S. (2008) 'The cognitive benefits of interacting with nature'. *Psychological Science*, 19(12): 1207–12.

Birch, M. (2005) 'Cultivating wildness: three conservation volunteers' experiences of participation in the Green Gym Scheme'. *British Journal of Occupational Therapy*, 68(6): 244–52.

Blair, D. (2009) 'The child in the garden: an evaluative review of the benefits of school gardening'. *Journal of Environmental Education* 40(2): 15–38.

Brown, T. and Bell, M. (2007) 'Off the couch and on the move: global public health and the medicalisation of nature'. *Social Science and Medicine*, 64: 1343–54.

Crossley, M. (2008) 'Critical health psychology: developing and refining the approach', *Social and Personality Psychology Compass*, 2, 21–33.

Ducker, K. (1999) 'Allotment gardening and the East End'. *Rising East*, 4(3): 65–85.

Fieldhouse, J. (2003) 'The impact of an allotment group on mental health clients' health, well-being and social networking'. *British Journal of Occupational Therapy*, 66(7): 286–96.

Friends of the Earth (2005) *Good Neighbours? Community Impacts of Supermarkets*. London: FoE.

Gross, H. and Lane, N. (2007) 'Landscapes of the lifespan: exploring accounts of own gardens and gardening'. *Journal of Environmental Psychology*, 27(3): 225–41.

Guthrie, J., Guthrie, A. and Lawson, R. (2006) 'Farmers' markets: the small business counter-revolution in food production and retailing'. *British Food Journal*, 108(7): 560–73.

Hammersley, M. (1992) 'Ethnography and realism'. In M. Hammersley (ed.) *What's Wrong With Ethnography?* London: Routledge.

Hepworth, J. (2006) 'Strengthening critical health psychology: a critical action orientation'. *Journal of Health Psychology*, 11, 401–408.

Kaplan, S. (1995) 'The restorative benefits of nature: toward an integrative framework'. *Journal of Environmental Psychology*, 15: 169–82.

Kaplan, R. and Kaplan, S. (1989) *The Experience of Nature: A Psychological Perspective*. New York: Cambridge University Press.

Kellert, S. R. and Wilson, E. O. (eds) (1993) *The Biophilia Hypothesis*. Washington, DC: Island Press.

King, N. (2011) 'Doing template analysis'. In G. Symon and C. Cassell (eds) *The Practice of Qualitative Organizational Research: Core Methods and Current Challenges*, London: Sage.

King, N., Mirza, M. and Bates, E. (2007) *Paddock Pathways to Health, Allotment Project: Qualitative Evaluation Report*. CAPR, University of Huddersfield.

King, N. and Rodriguez, A. (2007) West Central Halifax Allotment Project: *Qualitative Evaluation Report*. CAPR, University of Huddersfield.

Milligan, C., Gatrell, A. and Bingley, A. (2004) '"Cultivating health": therapeutic landscapes and older people in Northern England'. *Social Science and Medicine*, 58: 1781–93.

Mitchell, R. and Popham, F. (2008) 'Effect of exposure to natural environment on health inequalities: an observational population study'. *Lancet*, 372: 655–1660.

Nadin, S. and Cassell, C. (2004) 'Using data matrices'. In C Cassell and G Symon (eds). *Essential Guide to Qualitative Methods in Organizational Research*. London: Sage.

Natural England (2011) Walking for Health Newsletter – 2010 Review. Natural England. Available online at http://www.wfh.naturalengland.org.uk/sites/default/files/WfH%20volunteers%20newsletter%20Feb%202011.pdf

Öhman, A. and Mineka, S. (2001) 'Fears, phobias and preparedness: toward an evolved module of fear and fear learning'. *Psychological Review*, 108(3): 483–522.

Parr, H. (2007) 'Mental health, nature work, and social inclusion'. *Environment and Planning D: Society and Space*, 25(3): 537–61.

Pecaski McLennan, D. (2010) '"Ready, Set, Grow!" Nurturing young children through gardening'. *Early Childhood Education Journal*, 37(5): 329–33.

Pretty, J., Griffin, M., Peacock, J., Hine, R., Sellens, M. and South, N. (2005) 'A countryside for health and well-being: the physical and mental health benefits of green exercise'. *Countryside Recreation*, 13(1): 2–7.

Poole, S. (2006) *The Allotment Chronicles: A Social History of Allotment Gardening*. Kettering: Silver Link Publishing.

Seligman, M. (1971) 'Phobias and preparedness'. *Behavior Therapy*, 2: 307–21.

Sempik, J., Aldridge, J. and Becker, S. (2005) *Health, Well-being and Social Inclusion: Therapeutic Horticulture in the UK*. Bristol: The Policy Press.

Smith, V. D. and Aldous, D. E. (1994) 'Effect of therapeutic horticulture on the self concept of the mildly intellectually disabled student'. In Francis, M., Lindsey, P. and Rice, J. S. (eds) *The Healing Dimensions of People-Plant Relations*, UC Davis, CA: Centre for Design Research, pp. 215–21.

Ulrich, R. (1993) 'Biophilia, Biophobia, and natural landscapes'. In S. Kellert and E. Wilson (eds) *The Biophilia Hypothesis*. Washington, DC: Island Press.

Ulrich, R., Simons, R., Losito, B., Fiorito, E., Miles, M. and Zelson, M. (1991) Stress recovery during exposure to natural and urban environments'. *Journal of Environmental Psychology*, 11: 201–30.

Vidal, J. (2008) 'Coming up roses? Not any more as UK gardeners turn to vegetables', 22 March, *Guardian*. http://www.guardian.co.uk/environment/2008/mar/22/food.gardens, accessed online 2 August 2011.

Weis, A. (2007) *The Global Food Economy: The Battle for the Future of Farming*. London: Zed Books.

Worster, D. (1994) *Nature's Economy: A History of Ecological Ideas,*. 2nd edn, Cambridge: Cambridge University Press.

CHAPTER 13

Being Creative around Health: Participative Methodologies in Critical Community Psychology

REBECCA LAWTHOM, CAROLYN KAGAN, MICHAEL RICHARDS, JUDITH SIXSMITH AND RYAN WOOLRYCH

Introduction

Community social psychology is a developing area within the UK and other global North contexts (Kagan et al., forthcoming). Taking a values-based approach which prioritises stewardship, social justice and collaboration, community social psychology problematises individual approaches to health and well-being, instead advocating a focus on social and community processes. As such, community social psychologists are interested in promoting not just the betterment of individual health and well-being, but social change towards a more fulfilling and just society **through** working with individuals and groups, within their social contexts (ecological, systemic and environmental). Participative techniques are key to working and collaborating '**with**' people to create positive options for change in their own lives rather than imposing potential solutions on them. One important area for community psychology is that of health, particularly public health. Indeed, there are strong links between assumptions, values and approaches between critical health psychology and community psychology.

In this chapter, we explore links between community psychological approaches and understandings of health, notably embracing a public health and wellness approach. Drawing on a body of work around arts and health, this chapter has a number of aims. First, we unpack notions of health, mental health and well-being using a community psychology lens. Concepts of wellness and prevention are central here in understanding the ways in which normative definitions of health prescribe an overly medicalised and individualised model. Second, we draw upon an array of creative and participatory approaches to working with people. These methodologies include working collaboratively with innovative techniques including cooking, art, photography and music (in addition to other qualitative methods). Third, we demonstrate ways in which community psychology interfaces with health through a number of health-related projects. These encompass a refugee project involving inter-generational understanding between Somali young men and elders, a health project with disadvantaged young men and regeneration work undertaken with local residents. As authors, we work collaboratively and creatively around projects and writing, but the case study authors are identified at the outset of each case study. Finally, we critically explore the potential benefit of these innovative and creative projects for engaging people in research and developing understandings of critical and community health.

Notions of health

Across the Western world the treatment of ill health is based almost entirely on the biomedical model (Hughner & Kleine, 2008). The biomedical model tends to focus on curing illness rather than promoting health and often looks for single factors as causes of disease as opposed to a range of contributory factors (Banyard,1996). Often poor health is defined simply in terms of the bodily decline of an individual person.

Community social psychology (CSP) engages rather differently with health, constructing health and well-being as more than an individualised issue. Community social psychologists see illness and, crucially, the prevention of ill health as residing in wider social contexts i.e. settings beyond the individual such as groups, communities and societies. This systemic understanding denotes health and well-being as issues which can be explained and addressed only through a wider lens – emphasising social causes of distress, illness and community misery. Issues such as inequality, poverty, unemployment, exploitation, colonisation, racism, disablism, heterosexism and other manifestations of social injustice are seen as central to understanding how difficult it is to achieve wellness (note here the turn to wellness rather than illness). Adopting a social justice approach, CSP engages with settings and people to transform rather than simply ameliorate problems (Prilleltensky, 2005). Also, CPS principles frame people and problems rather differently. In traditional medicalised settings individuals are entreated to seek professional medical help, whilst in the CSP paradigm self and mutual help are espoused. Rather than seeing help/

treatment as occurring to passive individuals in formalised settings, CPS char-acterises people as participants, collaborators and 'experts' whose knowledge can help. Whilst traditional approaches seek to 'psychologise' and diagnose pathology, a community approach is concerned with building on identified strengths of individuals and groups. Finally, the illness model is critiqued in favour of the promotion of wellness, where the focus is as much on prevention as it is on treatment or cure. This radical orientation utilises an explicit value base rather than being, as in the traditionalist view, value free.

Given this rather distinct approach to health/wellness and well-being, it is important to describe how community social psychologists work. In the next section, we explore how participatory creative methods are employed in a range of community psychological health projects.

Creativity: a panacea?

A large body of work (spanning academic and practitioner circles) links cre-ative engagement in art practices with enhanced health and well-being (e.g. Kilroy et al., 2007; Sixsmith & Kagan, 2005). Art practices here are loosely defined as activities ranging from singing, making art products, photography, creative writing or utilising creative methods which are transformed into dissemination products (for example films, magazines). These methods are utilised not in a therapeutic sense but as a way of engaging people as collabo-rators in, and agents of, promotion of their own health and well-being. The process of engagement in creative work enables participants, art practitioners and researchers to reflect rather differently on the process.

This change is mirrored more widely in the social sciences, where a creative turn is apparent, which builds on the earlier turn to language (Parker, 1989). In addition to traditional qualitative methods of obtaining verbal accounts, a range of creative methods have been developed. Space precludes coverage of the wider field, but projects we have been involved with include collabora-tive film making (Kagan & Michallef, 2009; Woolrych & Sixsmith, 2008), participatory photo-taking (Kellock et al., 2011), singing, talking heads, storyboards (Sixsmith & Pratesi, 2010) and experience sampling methods (Kellock et al., forthcoming; Mountian et al., forthcoming). These projects explore health-related issues such as flow, well-being, inter-generational understanding and urban regeneration, providing examples where cre-ative practices are employed collaboratively. Diverse stakeholders in these projects represent members of the public (such as community residents and migrants), interested researchers and professional artists. Whilst collabor-ation and participation are often guiding principles of the work, tensions can arise around outputs and interpretation of meanings (see Mountain et al., forthcoming). The project outputs arising from this kind of research include traditional academic outputs as well as artistic products such as exhibitions, films, magazines etc. Not only do creative approaches demand radically different ways of working with people but the outputs, the 'texts' can have multiple meanings. Whilst these creative methods and outputs appear to be more accessible to participants in research enterprises, they are not without challenge. In the case studies below, we present a short summary of each project and the links to public health, demonstrating the participative creative practice employed and teasing out the challenges and merits of this approach.

Young men's health calendar: Michael Richards

One of the major issues for young men in the UK today is their reluctance to acknowledge health problems and to find solutions to resolve them (Lloyd & Forrest, 2001). In collaboration with a young men's project in a disadvantaged area in Manchester, a men's group was formed to create a men's health calendar for 2010 (Richards, 2009). The project was funded through a small public health grant and funders wanted an accessible output. The aim of this project was to identify the most pertinent areas of male health and devise a semi-structured programme of activities to which young men (aged 18–25) were invited to participate. This project set out to create a non-clinical place for young men to say what they really think, believe and feel about their health. The project was set in Wythenshawe, one of the largest social housing areas in Europe. It is an area of little ethnic diversity and contains some of the most deprived areas in Manchester, which, itself, remains one of the most deprived districts in England (Talukder & Frost, 2008). Educational achievement is low and work prospects are limited: white working class young men are the most consistent low educational achievers compared to young women generally and other ethnic groups (Cassen & Kingdon, 2007).

At the first workshop, relevant themes which were important to young men's health were identified. The group agreed that these themes represented male health needs: healthy relationships, safer sex, drinking less alcohol, exercise, seeking help accessing services, talking more, eating healthy, smoking less, positive hobbies, taking less risks and developing a positive self image. Of note here is the collaborative approach which unearthed a positive health/wellness model rather than a highly medicalised understanding of health. The next sessions were focused on the specific health themes. The two male facilitators (MR and a youth worker) started to talk more explicitly about male health and men's attitudes and ways to find solutions to these problems. The facilitators were young men encouraging collaboration from peers.

All members of the group took part in discussions and debates about 'what a healthy relationship is?' and produced posters depicting the importance of safe sex.

For the 'exercise' theme, the focus was on difficulties young men have accessing services that might be able to help with their health. Instead of just talking about the health issue, a leisure centre was visited, showing how they could access health services. The group played basketball and dodge ball, and although most of the group do not engage in physical activity in their day-to-day lives much, they all enjoyed running about and laughing. Furthermore, one of the most engaging sessions we created was on the theme of 'talking'. I felt that they all knew each other more now, so we could be more open about our beliefs. We sat in a circle whilst I (MR) read out statements such as 'who has mental health issues?' We had to stand up if that applied to us. We would then, if we felt comfortable enough, talk about the issue. Following this activity, we did a continuum on our views of different issues such as 'females are more intelligent than males.' We had to stand at one if they agreed or ten if they disagreed. The point of both exercises was simply to get the young men talking within a different space. The blunt statements were simply a tool to develop relationships and critical consciousnesses. The Freirian (see, for example, Freire, (1972)) notion of conscientisation is of use here – as young men articulated together and shared experiences with each other and the facilitators, there was space for critical reflection and developing relationships. Health was sometimes an explicit focus, as we considered 'diet'– what healthy and unhealthy food is. We completed a typical weekly diet and looked at how different a footballer's diet is to our diet. We had discussions around this and it was suggested that we should do some cookery sessions, which we did in subsequent sessions involving going to the shops and budgeting our food, picking healthy food and cooking simple meals. Here a direct health issue (tackled through self reflection and collaboration) led to education around shopping, budgeting and cooking – activities not normally prioritised in their gendered environments.

We had a lively debate on 'smoking and cannabis'. The group was divided into two and debated the use of cannabis. Whilst literacy was often an issue for these young men, verbal articulation could be framed as evidence of education. The environment created other opportunities as some members demonstrated improved confidence and personal development. One member, who seemed at times immature, amazed his peers when he got on the piano and started to play 'Eleanor Rigby' (a famous Beatles song). It was a hidden talent, which he said not many people knew about. After spending a number of weeks on identified sessions, the focus turned to the production of the 'calendar'. The photographer visited and helped to structure the themes identified into pictures and words for the calendar. As a result of this visit, the group decided to take a trip to central Manchester to take pictures that represented the different health themes. We all enjoyed the trip and had a 'good laugh' (one of the comments by one of the participants). It strengthened the dynamics of the group and enabled travel (albeit locally). The day began by attending an art gallery (an alien space for the group), which was not well received by everyone, but others did enjoy it. Most of the young men rarely go beyond the vicinity of Wythenshawe, so it was unusual for the group to overcome their anxieties and income difficulties.

Overall, the group created a positive informal learning environment in which they developed skills including photography, cooking, debate and critical thinking. The methods used included group work, one-to-ones and worksheets, which were used to stimulate debate and discussion. The spaces for dialogue created and combined the expertise of youth workers and community psychologists, with the tacit knowledge brought by the young men. A CSP approach argues learning is best achieved through dialogue between people. Through sharing feelings, thoughts and behaviours, the group become aware of the possibilities for positive change (Freire & Faundez, 1989). Whilst the young men did not see the utility of the calendar for them, the images they co-created allowed different representations to occur which may have wider implications for the audience of the calendar. The output and the making of the calendar worked here as a tool for collaboration and change. The young men, through both standard and creative participative methods could conceptualise, enact and reflect upon health rather differently. Talking alone with young men, would not have inspired change, but building skill capacity and knowledge around healthy lifestyles at least offers the possibility of sustained change.

Intergenerational issues between Yemeni men living in the UK (Carolyn Kagan)

We (a team of academics, professionals and community members) worked in partnership with a locally based community psychology project in a large Northern City in the UK. This was part of a much wider project involving collaboration between four universities. The project was concerned with intergenerational conflict amongst Somali and Yemeni men in families and in the community: it was developed and led by staff from Building Bridges (Fatimilehin & Dye, 2003). In line with CSP principles, the nature of the problem had developed from working collaboratively within the community; indeed the intergenerational conflict was identified as impacting upon the health and well-being of the community. The ethos of the project was one of building on cultural knowledge, skills and understanding – it was an assets-based, not problem-oriented approach (Foot & Hopkins, 2010). An assets-based approach appreciates and mobilises the individual and community talent, skills and assets (in contrast to deficits and needs). As such it reflected a contemporary understanding of some of the ways of working to reduce enduring health inequalities (Marmot et al., 2009).

As part of a complex project, the young Yemeni men thought they would like to make a film about what it is like being young and Yemeni in the UK, and the extent to which older men understood pressures they experienced and vice versa. We linked the group with a community film maker, who had little knowledge or experience of the Yemeni community. Together with a group of young men aged 12–18 they explored ideas for a film, wrote the script and learnt skills of film making in order to make and produce the film. They decided on a film made up of sketches involving a number of different film genres, including talking heads (older and younger men, edited and inter cut to present a coherent intergenerational 'dialogue'), role-played scenarios (which themselves involved straight role playing and role reversals wherein the youngest lads took the parts of the oldest men in the scenarios) and black and white public information format. As one of the participants described it,

> We got together with the film director to talk about the issues and then made the film. I know some teenagers with problems with families, and when their fathers see the film they may learn about their children and different ways of communicating (Kagan, 2008, p. 35).

Thus in the process of making the film, the young men had to think about their own and other's experiences, and how best to communicate these. They learnt how to plan and conduct interviews which they then carried out with men of their father's generation. They learnt about script writing and filming, about editing and making the film and about acting. Most importantly they worked together, cooperatively as a group. Through the different activities involved in taking part in and making the film, the young men gained insight and understanding not only into themselves and their generation, but also their fathers' generation. They had to find out information, link with other organisations and groups to get this information and work with the film makers to produce the film. The whole process enabled them to discover and learn about their past, about their collective cultural identities, and to clarify what was important to them in life and how this was similar or different from the values of their fathers. Elsewhere, it has been suggested that through this process the young men drew on and built social capital (bonding and bridging capital) and enhanced their well-being – both eudemonic (being challenged and stretched, continually developing) and hedonic (enjoyment) well-being (Kagan et al., 2008). At the end of the process they had a really good film – something they could be proud of. One of the advantages of a film is that it can be shown to others and thus its impact extends beyond those who directly participated in its making. It provides a legacy which is more accessible than a project report and can communicate more widely. When the film was shown at a large dissemination event, attended by families, wider members of the community, as well as service and project workers, the wider impact of the film was evident:

> Making this film was good – we had a lot of fun. I see it now and think – 'did we do that'. I think it's great. The points we make are important too. I think our fathers can see this too…we have begun to understand them more, now. Just watching (younger boy) loading the shelves of the shop made me realise what it must be like for our fathers to work so hard – and not doing what they were trained to do. How hard! (Young participant in making the film, Dissemination Event)

The film became part of an educational pack that members of the community developed after our project had finished and so its impact continues. It is clear that the project was a positive experience and contributed to intergenerational understanding, social capital and well-being. Through the activity of the film making the young men gained powerful insights. However, it is worth for a moment considering a further issue. Fifteen months after the film had been completed another dissemination event, similarly broad in its reach was held in the city. An observation made at that event raises an important ethical issue:

> I sat next to a group of Yemeni boys. I recognised one of them as one of the younger boys in the film and I asked 'Have you seen the film before?' He said he hadn't seen it since it was finished. He was at school when it was shown initially. In one of the sketches he was dressed in traditional men's clothing and was acting the part of an older man who was having difficulty with his son who was reluctant to help in the shop. As this sketch appeared in the film the young man next to me put his hands over his eyes. He sat for a while like this and then ran out of the room before the film had ended. His friend told me later he hated what he saw and thought he looked really silly. He thought the film was stupid. (Researcher field diary)

Whilst all the young men had been active participants initially, clearly as time had gone on, at least one of them no longer liked to view himself as 'object' in the film. This raises the question of the shelf life of the film and the duration of consent and agreement to participate, particularly when working with teenagers.

This project did – certainly in its initial stages – strengthen well-being of the immediate participants and played an important role in revealing and understanding intergenerational tensions in a particular community. Evidence gathered indicated that stronger bonds formed had also enabled the wider community to share understanding and link outside the community for help. The film dissemination (whilst not without problems) had allowed and continues to present audiences with alternative framings of intergenerational understanding. Beyond preventative and direct health gains, such projects also strengthen community cohesion and have a further indirect impact on quality of life and well-being. As Pain (2005, p. 5) suggests,

> Intergenerational relations are a part of our social identity. They have material effects on the experiences and quality of life of older and young people in particular settings, and important implications for community cohesion.

Well-being and regeneration (Judith Sixsmith and Ryan Woolrych)

There has been a paucity of research situating the notion of well-being within the context of local residents living within an area of regeneration. The discourse of regeneration as renewal and transformation is often a top–down interpretation from developers or regeneration professionals. Work which directly accesses resident voices is limited and has resulted in little understanding of the impact of physical transformation and change on how local residents operationalise their well-being. A research project was undertaken in East Manchester, an area of the North-West of England currently undergoing significant physical transformation as part of an ongoing programme of urban regeneration. The ongoing regeneration has brought about the creation of modern education facilities, sports stadia, leisure opportunities, public libraries, community centres and integrated health centres with the 2002 Commonwealth Games acting as the primary catalyst for the area. New East Manchester (NEM) recognises that the long-term sustainability of the area is dependent on creating a legacy of opportunity, access and provision facilitated by strong and sustainable communities. This project built on findings from an earlier research project (Woolrych et al., 2007). The primary aims and objectives of the project were,

- to define how concepts of health and well-being are conceptualised and articulated by the resident and professional community within an area undergoing regeneration;

- to determine how regenerated facilities may act as community 'hubs' and explore community involvement within them;
- to investigate the processes of social change within community settings, and how certain facilities can increase well-being for some local people while operating differently for other residents; and
- to reveal how processes of participation and engagement can improve the health and well-being of local residents.

A participatory action research approach was adopted, where all project participants were encouraged to share control and influence decision making throughout the duration of the research. This involved the co-production of knowledge between the research team and local residents, whereby processes of empowerment were prioritised and enabled the production of video diaries and photography. In addition, residents were trained and supported to undertake interviews with other members of the community, utilising a co-researcher model. This method was supplemented by a researcher (Woolrych) engaging in semi-structured interviews (with regeneration professionals, service providers and local residents) and participant observations (undertaken at various sites across East Manchester). Residents were then actively involved in the analysis of the visual data, being engaged in reflective discussion with the research team to provide additional narrative around important emergent themes. Local residents, regeneration professionals, service providers and academics were then involved in an action research event, where knowledge café workshops enabled active dialogue to develop between and across the groups.

Reflecting on the research process alongside the participants helped highlight the benefits, challenges and limitations associated with undertaking a participatory approach. There were practical challenges for both the researcher and the participant when collecting and interpreting the visual imagery within a participatory framework. Firstly, the collection and analysis of visual data within the context of participatory research requires significant unplanned effort from the researcher. The idea of accessible cameras being utilised as a democratic tool did not always materialise as co-researchers needed skill and confidence building. This included one-to-one or group training with the participants before data collection, ongoing daily support for the participants during the project and the time to co-analyse the video or photographic imagery collected. Secondly, participatory research can be discomforting for the co-researcher who is engaging in potentially risky and hazardous activity, collecting visual imagery in and around communities which they may already perceive to be dangerous or unsafe environments. In communities where unemployment, crime and other risky behaviours are part of daily life, the making of films (ethically, politically and personally) needs careful consideration in all stages. Lastly, there are challenges to the researcher in terms of their positionality during the collection, analysis and dissemination of the research product. The researcher can find themselves in an unenviable position, committed to prioritising the experiences of local residents whilst also ensuring that they work within the aims and objectives of the research. Here, the researcher must be prepared for unexpected findings, which may cause them to continually re-evaluate their expectations from the research. This is more complex when undertaking a funded research project, with fixed research boundaries and partner expectations.

Despite the problems and challenges, visual participatory methods can also bring about significant benefits, representing a powerful tool for engaging and involving participants in the research process. Visual methods represented a creative and enjoyable way for participants to engage in the research process:

> I've always hated to do research. I've always thought it's not really interested me. But after this it's, you know, it can be quite enjoyable, especially if you're...I think it always matters if you're interested in something. If you're interested in something you'll read around it, you'll read about it, you'll learn everything there is about it.

Visual methods also enabled participants to 'concretise' their experiences, which can be empowering and enable a greater sense of confidence. Here, providing participants with a tangible research product enabled a sense of achievement and also provided the means for further self-reflection:

> Well it's made me more confident that I have developed something to show people...it is something that I own and can use to demonstrate the things that we are going through on the estate...I watch it now and use it to think about how things have changed.

Engaging in collecting and analysing visual data also provided some participants with a sense of purpose. Here, there was an identifiable process and personal journey for the participants, providing stimulation and engagement along the way:

> The project from start to finish was something that gave me something to do. I am more or less restricted to my house these days. This occupied my mind...It got me thinking.

Traditional forms of research often necessitate the research establishing the agenda, facilitating the research and extracting information from the participant as a research subject, reinforcing the 'gap' between the researcher and the researched (England, 1994; Mohammad, 2001; Rose, 1997). By placing the participant as creators of their own knowledge, it challenges these power relations and dynamics of accounting, where research participants are in a position to exercise control over the presentation of themselves through the research:

> ... it [visual methods] adds another dimension to things that we have been involved in. I think when you video it's more engaging because it's not boring. Especially when you, when you show it to people as well. But, you know, with having the video coverage and a lot of visual information, it makes it a bit more involving for people, especially residents as well. For us residents we don't like to be talked at a lot, you know, or given pieces of paper to read. It was nice that we could finally produce something and show it to people.

Participatory visual methods thus represent a tool for empowering local residents to feel a sense of ownership of the research product rather than traditional research methods which can reinforce power imbalances between the researcher and the participants. However, whilst such methods are potentially transformative in opening up new forms of visual narrative, they require the researcher to critically consider and re-evaluate their position in the research. Residents and regeneration professionals were able to use the film to open up dialogue and reflect upon how residents experienced regeneration within their communities. Here, visual participatory methods offer the opportunity to demonstrate the impact of regeneration upon well-being. Films showed how transforming spaces and allowing commercial development has negatively impacted upon social ties and sense of community. For true insight, reflection and change, there needs to be more critical consideration of the application and development of the method. Only then can visual research provide an opportunity to challenge the hierarchical power relationships between the researcher and participant and to facilitate a more equitable relationship with the participants.

Developing critical community understandings of health

The three projects outlined above pivot on a hugely different conceptualisation of health, ranging from bodies and healthy eating, through individual well-being and encompassing community cohesion and intergenerational understanding. Seeing health as truly social and relational engenders different approaches both to the problem and the process. Community psychology,

- recognises that peer support can be mutually beneficial and an effective means to change;

- attempts to devolve professional power in the interests of sharing control and decision-making;
- develops people's strengths rather than focusing on diagnoses and problems;
- promotes prevention, support and coping; and
- engages in personal and social action designed to address pathology in services.

(adapted from Bostock & Diamond, 2004)

Rejecting individualism and psychologism, the creative methods utilised here are participatory and non-clinical. Whilst professionals are often involved, all stakeholders are seen as collaborators who bring knowledge to the table. If knowledge is seen as something which is constructed jointly, the possibility occurs of learning being transferred and sustainable. The projects above may well have enhanced particular creative skills but in shifting representations, attitudes and beliefs of entitlement to and responsibility for health, social change is also possible. Creative methods can widen notions of health and well-being – in the young Men's health project, the negotiated content of the workshops encouraged young men to engage in critical dialogue around health, whilst the regeneration project enabled local residents to talk back to developers and regeneration professionals.

The methods are not entirely unproblematic as the meanings of creative products and participative processes can shift dynamics between people. Space here precludes a discussion of the issues but see Lawthom et al. (2007) for a perspective here.

In increasingly neoliberal times, health and the management of health is more and more seen as an individualised responsibility. Situating the causes of illness as proximal individual problems, ignores the distal inequalities which impact upon health outcomes. Utilising collaborative methods, and repositioning concepts of health, politicises health, locating it within a social justice model. Burton et al. (2008) comment on the role of community psychologists here.

We believe psychologists are well placed to comment on the impacts on health and well being of the current policy mix and we will contribute to the development of a positive alternative people-oriented policy framework, contributing experience, skills, knowledge and evidence to the efforts of groups campaigning for an effective, adequate public policy framework that places people ahead of profit, recognises the value of publicly owned resources and services and that fearlessly tackles vested interest for a better society'. (p. 16)

Seeing health as mediated through layers of inequality entails precisely this kind of political awareness. Albee, a critical community psychologist, is remembered by Fryer (2006) as being concerned to,

> depower those who benefit from such injustice, especially those seeking to explain away unjust societal arrangements by use of victim-blaming, status-quo preserving, highly profitable, psychiatric, medical, and pharmaceutical models (p. 192).

Health and well-being are clearly political concepts which require much consideration. The projects outlined show the opportunities and tensions of using creative methods within a community social psychology paradigm. Critical awareness of individualised ill health as solely a medical problem is gaining some recognition. The North West Director of Public Health summed it up thus:

> For too long we have concentrated on the deficits and problems within communities and it is time for a different approach. Assessing and building the strengths of individuals and the assets of a community open the door to new ways of thinking about and improving health and of responding to ill-health. It has the potential to change the way practitioners engage with individuals and the way planners design places and services. It is an opportunity for real dialogue between local people and practitioners on the basis of each having something to offer. It can mobilise social capacity and action and more meaningful and appropriate services. (Foot & Hopkins, 2010, Introduction).

The time is right for a community social psychology approach which truly embraces this philosophy and engages in action.

Key points

1. A community social psychology lens sees illness and, crucially, the prevention of ill health as residing in wider social contexts i.e. settings beyond the individual such as groups, communities and societies.
2. Creative methods can be used, not in a therapeutic sense but as a way of engaging people as collaborators in, and agents of, promotion of their own health and well-being.
3. Creative outputs can take many forms: exhibitions, films, magazines, DVDs etc. which can engage participants and policymakers differently. These kinds of 'texts' offer different readings and require careful thought.

4. Community social psychologists work in collaboration, however, participative approaches can be problematic. Tensions can arise around creative
   outputs and interpretation of meanings.
5. A CSP approach utilising creative approaches can offer an asset-based
   view of community health.

REFERENCES

Banyard, P. (1996) *Applying Psychology to Health* London: Hodder & Stoughton.

Bostock J. & Diamond, B. (2004) 'The value of Community Psychology: being critical in the NHS', Paper presented to Community Psychology UK Conference, Exeter, Accessed from www.compsy.org.uk

Burton, M., Kagan, C. & Duckett, P. (2008) 'Making the psychological political – challenges for community psychology', Paper presented at *International Conference of Community Psychology*, accessed from www.compsy.org.uk

Cassen, R. & Kingdon, G. (2007) *Tackling Low Educational Achievement* York: Joseph Rowntree Foundation.

England, K. V. L. (1994) 'Getting personal: reflexivity, positionality, and feminist research', *Professional Geographer* 46, 80–89.

Fatimilehin, I. A. & Dye, L. (2003) 'Building bridges and community empowerment', *Clinical Psychology*, Issue 24, 51–55.

Foot, J. with Hopkins, T. (2010) *A Glass Half-Full: How An Asset Approach Can Improve Community Health and Well-Being*, London, I&DeA, Healthy Communities Programme, www.idea.gov.uk

Freire, P. (1972) *Pedagogy of the Oppressed* Harmondsworth: Penguin.

Freire, P. & Faundez, A. (1989) *Learning to Question: A Pedagogy of Liberation*, Geneva, World Council Churches.

Fryer, D. (2006), George Wilson Albee (1921–2006), 'Radical Community Psychologist: a critical obituary', Reprinted with permission in: *Journal of Critical Psychology, Counselling and Psychotherapy*, 6(4), 191–94.

Fryer, D., Duckett, P. & Pratt, R. (2004)'Critical community psychology: what, why and how?' *Clinical Psychology*, 38, 39–43.

Hughner, R. S. & Kleine, S. S. (2008) 'Variations in lay health theories: implications for consumer health care decision making', *Qualitative Health Research*, 18(12), 1687–703.

Kagan, C. (2008) *Active and Positive Fatherhood: HEI-Community Engagement Project Evaluation* Manchester: RIHSC.

Kagan, C. & Micaleff, A. M. (2008) *Active and Positive Parenting: Composite Evaluation Report* Manchester: RIHSC.

Kagan, C., Burton, M., Duckett, P., Lawthom, R. & Siddiquee, A. (forthcoming) *Critical Community Psychology: Critical Action and Social Change* London: Wiley.

Kagan, C., Micallef, A. M., Siddiquee, A., Fatimelehin, I., Hassan, A., de Santis, C., Ali, R., Zack Williams, T. & Bunn, G. (2008) 'Intergenerational work, social capital and wellbeing', *Paper presented to Global Community Psychology Conference,* Lisbon, June 2008.

Kellock, A., Lawthom, R., Sixsmith, J., Duggan, K., Mountian, I., Haworth, J. T., Kagan, C., Brown, D. P., Griffiths, J., Hawkins, J., Worley, C., Purcell, C. & Siddiquee, A. (2011) 'Using technology and the experience sampling method to understand real life', in

S. N. Hesse-Biber (ed.) *The Handbook of Emergent Technologies in Social Research* Oxford: Oxford University Press.

Kilroy, A., Garner, C., Parkinson, C., Kagan, C. M. & Senior, P. D. (2007). *Towards Transformation: Exploring the Impact of Culture, Creativity and the Arts on Health and Wellbeing*, for The Critical Friends event, Manchester, Arts for Health.

Lawthom, R., Sixsmith, J. & Kagan, C. (2007) 'Interrogating power: the case of arts and mental health in community projects', *Journal of Community and Applied Social Psychology*, 17(4), Date: July/August 2007, 268-79.

Lloyd, T. & Forrest, S. (2001) '"Boys" and young men's health; literature and practice review', an interim report, Working with Men for the Health Development Agency: London.

Marmot, M., Allen, J., Goldblatt, P., Boyce, T., McNeish, D., Grady, M. & Geddes, I. (2009) *Fair Society, Healthy Lives, The Marmot review: Strategic Review of Health Inequalities in England post 2010*, Final Report and Executive Summary, www.ucl.ac.uk/marmotreview.

Mohammad, R. (2001) '"Insiders" and/or "outsiders": positionality, theory and praxis', in M. Limb & C. Dwyer (eds) *Qualitative Methodologies for Geographers: Issues and Debates* London: Arnold, pp. 101–20.

Mountian, I., Lawthom, R., Kellock, A., Duggan, K., Sixsmith, J., Kagan, C., Hawkins, J., Haworth, J., Siddiquee, A., Worley, C., Brown, D., Griffiths, J. & Purcell, C. (forthcoming), 'On Utilising a Visual Methodology: Shared Reflections and Tensions', in P. Reavey (ed.) *Visual Methods in Psychology Using and Interpreting Images in Qualitative Research* Routledge: London.

Pain, R. (2005) *Intergenerational Relations And Practice In The Development Of Sustainable Communities*, Durham: ICRRDS.

Parker, I. (1989) *The Crisis in Modern Social Psychology, and How to End It* London and New York: Routledge.

Prilleltensky, I. (2005) 'Promoting well-being: time for a paradigm shift in health and human services', *Scandinavian Journal of Public Health*, 33, 53–60.

Richards, M. L. (2009) *Working with Young Men around Health: A Collaborative Approach*, unpublished MSc Dissertation, Manchester Metropolitan University.

Rose, G. (1997) 'Situating knowledge: positionality, reflexivities and other tactics', *Progress in Human Geography*, 21(3), 305–20.

Sixsmith, J. & Kagan, C. (2005) 'Arts for Mental Health', Final Report, Manchester: Manchester Metropolitan University.

Talukder, R., Frost, R. & L. (2008) *Manchester City Council: Index of Multiple deprivation 2007*, Manchester: Manchester City Council, Economic development Unit, http://www.manchester.gov.uk/downloads/F1_IMD2007.pdf retrieved 3.3.09.

Woolrych, R. & Sixsmith, J. (2008) *Understanding Health and Well-Being in the Context of Urban Regeneration: Manchester Case Study*, Final Report, Manchester Metropolitan University.

Woolrych, R. D., Sixsmith, J. & Kagan, C. M. (2007) *The Impact of Regeneration on the Well-Being of Local Residents: The Case of East Manchester for New East Manchester* Manchester: Metropolitan University.

Glossary

Agency:	The capacity of an agent (person) to act in and on the world.
Agreeableness:	One of the traits in the Big Five model of personality – the extent to which someone has a tendency to be compassionate and cooperative towards others.
Androcentric:	Focussed on or dominated by men's or masculine interests.
'Choice' rhetoric:	The feminist argument that a woman should have the right to make decisions about her own body and that the choice concerning the outcome of a pregnancy should be the woman's alone.
Confounding variables:	In quantitative research, variables that are not central to the main research questions or hypotheses and that the researcher fails to control, or eliminate, thereby bringing the validity of the research into question.
Conscientiousness:	One of the traits in the Big Five model of personality – the extent to which someone has a tendency to be is organised, careful, self-disciplined and responsible.
Conscientisation:	Process of increasing personal awareness of social contradictions and the need for social change.
Critical realism:	An ontological position (a view of reality) which suggests that whilst *some* of the data received by our senses provide an accurate representation of objects in the external world, *some* of them do not. Moreover, the meanings a person ascribes to such information may differ, depending on their individual sense making and experience.
Dialogism:	Emphasises the linguistic, communicative and cognitive construction involved in our understanding and recognition of the world. Meaning is dialogically constituted, made in dialogue (cognition and communication), with reference to the world and against the background of the world.
Discourse:	In the poststructuralist sense of the word discourse means a socially produced system of statements or network of meanings that construct subjects, objects and events in particular ways.
Discourse analysis:	A complex and general term that pertains to a number of approaches to analysing written, spoken or any symbolic language use.
Discursive resources:	The range of discourses that an individual is able to draw upon in making sense of themselves/the world is referred to as the set of discursive resources that is available to them.
Disempowerment:	To deprive a person of power, authority or status.

Ecological model:	A model devised by Bronfenbrenner to depict the relationship between the individual and social systems. The model consists of three levels of analysis: the micro includes the most immediate i.e. family, friends, neighbourhood; the meso defined as relationships between different micro systems; and the macro defined as community, societal and cultural structures.
Epistemology:	A branch of philosophy concerned with the nature of what constitutes knowledge.
Femininity:	The quality that society(ies) see to be womanly or associated with the female sex.
Feminist/feminism:	A person, body, organisation or structure that supports equal rights for women and challenges wider injustice and social inequalities.
Gender mainstreaming:	A strategy for making women's as well as men's concerns and experiences an integral dimension of policies and programmes in all political, economic and societal spheres so that women and men benefit equally hence avoiding the perpetuation of gender inequality.
Governmentality:	A term coined by Michel Foucault from the words govern and mentality that is frequently defined as the rules or principles used in government or governing.
Grounded theory:	A research methodology that emphasises the generation of theory from data in the process of conducting research.
Hegemonic femininity:	The dominant culturally normative ideal for feminine behavoiur.
Hegemonic masculinity:	The dominant culturally normative ideal for masculine behavoiur.
Hyper-femininity:	The exaggeration of qualities that society(ies) see to be womanly or associated with the female sex.
Ideologies:	A system of ideas and ideals.
Individualisation:	Discriminating the individual from her/his social, political and historical grouping.
Intra-psychic:	Something that exists or takes place in the mind.
Intersectionality:	Analytic approaches which considering the meaning and consequences of occupying a range of different social categories simultaneously.
Liberation psychology:	A form of community psychology that emphasises the connections between social and personal liberation and political transformation.
Masculinity:	The quality of that society(ies) sees to be manly or associated with the male sex.
Matrix analysis:	A form of thematic analysis that emphasises the importance of a clear visual display when analysing qualitative data and disseminating findings. Data are summarised on a grid or table ('matrix') to facilitate comparisons between cases, thematic categories and so on. Different forms of matrix may be used at different stages of analysis – for example, data displayed at the level of individual participants may be condensed to enable analysis at the level of groups or organisations.

Neoliberalism:	An internationally prevalent (and arguably increasingly dominant) ideology that constructs a wide range of social and cultural practices as being matters of individual choice, autonomy and personal responsibility. It has been argued that this ideology shifts attention away from governments, corporations and other institutions as the source of societal problems (or as the ones responsible for bringing about societal change) and focuses this instead on the individual.
Neuroticism:	One of the traits in the Big Five model of personality – the extent to which someone has a tendency to experience anger, anxiety, or depression.
Normative:	Of or pertaining to an assumed standard that society(ies) has regarding the acceptability of any given practice.
Objectified:	Degraded to the status of an object.
Ontology:	The philosophical study of what constitutes existence; reality of being.
Openness:	One of the traits in the Big Five model of personality – the extent to which someone has a tendency to be open to experience, creative, flexible, curious and adventurous.
Pair-matched controls:	In studies in which a comparison between groups is made, each subject is matched with a comparable subject in terms of relevant measurable parameters; matching reduces the chances of confounding variables interfering with the results.
Paradigm:	Shared understanding about what the problems, structures, values and assumptions are in any given area/discipline or community.
Participatory action research:	A form of action research that involves participants actively throughout the process.
Passivity:	A state of inactivity, enabling what happens or what others do, without active response or resistance.
Performative:	An interdisciplinary term often used to denote the way language and other forms of non-verbal expression are used to do something rather than being seen as simply reflecting reality.
Phenomenological approach:	The theory that practices are determined by the way the person perceives reality (or truth) rather than by any objective external reality (or truth).
Positioning/Positioning theory:	An approach often associated with discourse analysis which explores how the characteristics individuals assume or are ascribed influence the interpretation of their behaviour. Individuals might position themselves, someone else or others might position them in particular ways.
Post-abortion syndrome (PAS):	A diagnosis first formalised by Speckhard and Rue (1992), in which they argue that PAS is a variant of post-traumatic stress disorder, which includes exposure to or participation in an abortion experience, uncontrolled negative experiencing of the abortion 'death' event, unsuccessful attempts to avoid or deny abortion recollections and emotional pain and experiencing associated symptoms not present before the abortion.

Post structuralism/Post structuralist:	A complex and general term that is used to describe any approach arguing that discourse (written, spoken or any symbolic language) has no absolute meaning and so is open to a range of interpretations.
Psychologisation:	Processes whereby emphasis is laid on psychological explanations for particular behaviours, health issues or social phenomena.
Psychometric measures:	Any standardised procedure for measuring something that is seen to take place or exist in the mind.
Public health approach:	An approach to health that is concerned with the health of the community as a whole and that involves (1) assessing and monitoring the health of populations, (2) identifying health problems and priorities, (3) the formulation of policies and interventions to ameliorate identified health problems and priorities, (4) advocating for all sectors of society to have access to appropriate and cost-effective health care, (5) ensuring that health-care includes health promotion, the prevention of health problems, (6) an evaluation of the effectiveness of health care interventions and systems.
Scholar–activist:	A person who is engaged in challenging social injustice through various forms of scholarly work and activism.
Social justice:	A complex concept that can be defined in many ways but is often associated with the fair and equitable allocation in society of burdens, resources and powers.
Subjectivities:	The multiple, sometimes fluid, identities that a person draws on to make sense of who they are and how they act.
Template analysis:	A form of thematic analysis which seeks to balance flexibility and structure in the process of analysing textual data. It typically involves construction of an initial version of a coding template on the basis of a sub-set of the data, which is then applied to further data, modified as necessary and reapplied. It allows the tentative use of some a priori themes, drawing on theoretical or practical commitments of a particular analysis. Unlike some forms of thematic analysis, it does not specify the number of levels of themes that can be created nor what particular levels represent – rather it encourages a flexible approach where the richest areas of the data may be coded in much greater depth than other areas.
Victim-blaming:	A focus on the individual as the cause of unhealthy practices while neglecting the broader social context.

Index